NOTES ON THE TEXT

French titles of Descartes' works have been retained throughout the text. Unless otherwise noted, translations from French, German, Spanish, and Italian texts are my own. My translation of the *Discours* uses the generally excellent version by Donald A. Cress, *Discourse on Method and Meditations on First Philosophy* (Indianapolis: Hackett, 1980), as a basis of reference and comparison from which it sometimes differs. Similarly, my translation of the *Géométrie* is based on the standard bilingual edition translated by David Eugene Smith and Marcia L. Latham, *The Geometry of René Descartes* (Chicago: Open Court, 1925), with modifications aimed at maintaining original vocabulary.

The use of masculine pronouns in the text usually indicates the autobiographical subject, "Descartes." When, less frequently, they indicate a general subject inferred from Descartes' writings, they should be construed in conformity with the French subject marker, "on."

LINES OF THOUGHT

LINES OF THOUGHT

Discourse,

Architectonics,

and the

Origin of

Modern

Philosophy

Claudia Brodsky Lacour

Duke University Press   Durham and London 1996

© 1996 Duke University Press
All rights reserved
Printed in the United States of America on acid-free paper ∞
Typeset in Adobe Garamond by Tseng Information Systems, Inc.
Library of Congress Cataloging-in-Publication Data
appear on the last printed page of this book.

For Camille

CONTENTS

ACKNOWLEDGMENTS

I would like to thank the Howard Foundation for their support during the conception of this work, and the Committee on Research in the Humanities and Social Sciences of Princeton University for permitting me to engage in extended summer research at the Bibliothèque Nationale in Paris. Thanks also go to Ken Wissoker and Pam Morrison of Duke University Press for their prompt and careful attention to the manuscript.

Preface: What Is Modern?

In the end this book defines modernity as the drawing of a line. It began as a study of Descartes accessory to an ongoing project on the relationship between writing and architectonics in philosophical and literary texts, starting with the theoretical role of architectural form in Kant and Hegel, and then extending chronologically from Racine, Goethe, Hölderlin, and Baudelaire to Proust, Benjamin, and Broch. What linked these texts across different disciplines, genres, styles, and periods was a relationship with building that could not be adequately described as figural. The subjects of architecture and architectural form did not arise in them as a metaphor for the formations of *poiêsis,* whether in the guise of a particular construction, a house, or a temple, or of a complete refiguring of the face of the earth or sky. Nor did they signify an originary form of writing or "archetext," a prefigural ground upon which philosophical conceptualizations rest.

The persistence of architectural metaphors in philosophy and literature is indeed significant, both for what they enable organizationally, in the cause of description as well as abstraction, and for what they reveal, viewed from a critical remove, about the desires and limitations of discursive work. But attempts to underscore the presence of metaphoric *identifications* of writing with architectonics tend to repeat the gesture they indicate, further concealing the vital difference upon which those metaphors depend. Recent discussions of the presence of architectural figures and objects in discourse have focused primarily on what the architectonic, in its individual linguistic appearances, *represents:* realism in the novel, the systematic structure of ideology, the ambition of the philosopher, and the origin — both as foundation and as problem — of philosophy.[1] While Jacques

1. See Philippe Hamon, *Expositions: Littérature et architecture au XIXème siècle* (Paris: José Corti, 1989); Denis Hollier, *La prise de la Concorde: Essais sur Georges Ba-*

Derrida has cautioned against discursive implementations of architecture as a "metaphor for a kind of thinking" and attempted to distinguish the architectonic specifically from the mimetic or symbolic—"to raise the question of architecture as a possibility of thought, which cannot be reduced to the status of a representation of thought"[2]—the representational

---

taille (Paris: Gallimard, 1972) (*Against Architecture,* translated by Betsy Wing, with an introduction by the author [Cambridge, Mass.: MIT Press, 1989]); and Daniel Payot, *Le philosophe et l'architecte: Sur quelques déterminations philosophiques de l'idée d'architecture* (Paris: Aubier, 1982). Beginning, at least explicitly, with Bernard Tschumi's invitation to Derrida to collaborate on a textual project to be incorporated within Tschumi's winning design for the *grand projet* at Le Parc de la Villette, a series of critical works appearing in close succession have attempted to indicate a (more or a less metaphoric) link between deconstruction and architecture. See Christopher Norris and Andrew Benjamin, *What Is Deconstruction?* (London: Academy Editions, 1988); Andrew Benjamin, "Deconstruction, Architecture, and Philosophy, in *Deconstruction: Omnibus Volume,* ed. Andreas Papadakis, Catherine Cooke, and Andrew Benjamin (London: Academy Editions, 1989, pp. 80–84; and, most recently, Mark Wigley, *The Architecture of Deconstruction* (Cambridge, Mass.: MIT Press, 1993). My own interest in the link between architectural form and philosophy was first sparked by Kant, whose description of his *Critique* in architectonic terms and description of the practical "use" of architecture in *The Third Critique,* linking architecture to the freedom from representational limits of *The Second Critique,* are the subject of my "Architecture and Architectonics: 'The Art of Reason in Kant's *Critique*," *Canon,* vol. 3 of *The Princeton Journal: Thematic Studies in Architecture,* ed. Taisto H. Mäkelä (New York: Princeton Architectural Press, 1988), pp. 103–17.

2. Jacques Derrida, "Architettura ove il desiderio può abitare," *Domus* 671 (1986): 17. In writings since La Villette that have dealt explicitly with the relationship between architecture and philosophy, Derrida indicates that the "architectural metaphor" which may appear present in "deconstruction," like those which reappear throughout the philosophical tradition and his own writings, has always been questioned by the work of deconstruction itself: "Contrary to appearances, 'deconstruction' is not an architectural metaphor. The word ought and will have to name a thought of architecture, a thought at work. In the first place it is not a metaphor. One no longer trusts the concept of metaphor. Next a deconstruction should first deconstruct, as its name indicates, construction itself, the structural or constructivist motif, its schemas, its intuitions and concepts, its rhetoric. But deconstruct also the strictly architectural construction, the philosophical construction of the concept of architecture, that concept whose model rules the idea of the system in philosophy as well as the theory, practice and teaching of architecture" ("Cinquante-deux aphorismes pour un avant-propos," in *Psyché* [Paris: Galilée, 1987], p. 517); "Deconstruction is perhaps a way of questioning this architectural model itself—the architectural model which is a general question, even within philosophy, the metaphor of foundations, of superstructures,

or analogical model still holds sway over considerations of architectonics and writing, especially when there is mention, customarily swift and self-evident, of the presence of "architectural metaphors" in Descartes.[3]

What became apparent to me in the post-Cartesian writings I worked on was that the language of architectonics employed within them was *not* symbolic in the conventional sense. It was pragmatic and functional, even when it took the form of an object; it was active, even when it was explicitly abstract, a means of doing rather than a determined category, schema, or concept. At the same time, it was never merely a convenient way—in the manner first suggested with deceptive modesty by Plato's Socrates—of representing a metaphysical idea that would otherwise remain unintelligible, even such an inevitably contextual, politically and socially palpable idea as "justice":

> I said then as I thought, The inquiry we are undertaking is no easy one but calls for keen vision, as it seems to me. So since we are not clever persons, I think we should employ the method of search that we should use if we, with not very keen vision, were bidden to read small letters from a distance, and then someone had observed that these same letters exist elsewhere larger and on a larger surface. We should have accounted it a godsend, I fancy, to be allowed to read those letters first, and then examine the smaller, if they are the same.
>
> Quite so, said Adimantus, but what analogy to this do you detect in the inquiry about justice?
>
> I will tell you, I said. There is a justice of one man, we say, and, I suppose, also of an entire city?
>
> Assuredly, said he.
>
> Is not the city larger than the man?
>
> It is larger, he said.

---

what Kant calls 'architectonic' etc., as well as the concept of the *arche*. . . . So Deconstruction means also the putting into question of architecture in philosophy and perhaps architecture itself" ("Jacques Derrida in Discussion with Christopher Norris," in *Architectural Design* 59 (1989): 8. See also Derrida, "Point de folie—Maintenant l'architecture," and Derrida, "Pourquoi Peter Eisenman écrit de si bons livres," in *Psyché* (Paris: Galilée, 1987), pp. 477–508.

3. See, for example, Andrew Benjamin's categorization and interpretation of "the justly famous architectural metaphor" in Part Two of the *Discours de la méthode*, in "Deconstruction, Architecture and Philosophy," *Deconstruction: Omnibus Volume*, p. 80. Other references to this "metaphor" are given in chapter 3.

Then, perhaps, there would be more justice in the larger object, and more easy to apprehend. If it please you, then, let us first look for its quality in states, and then only examine it also in the individual, looking for the likeness of the greater in the form of the less.

I think that is a good suggestion, he said.[4]

As the extensive development of the *Republic* makes clear, the conceit of imagining a planned city, on the order of letters written large, as the site of an idea less "easy to apprehend" in the "small letters" of the individual, turns from a handy visual aid and detour into the central activity of the dialogue. Once the discursive move to a "larger surface" has been proposed and taken up, Socrates' interlocutors, like Plato's readers, turn their attention from the undefined idea that occasioned it, the notion of "justice" now buried beneath the elaborate description of a state with no demonstrable foundation. If the ensuing discursive formulation of the well-ordered republic is "symbolic," it is so only in the highly unconventional sense of "symbolic action" formulated by Kenneth Burke, the saying of something by which the act of representation overshadows the "thing" said.[5]

Nowhere is this pragmatic aspect of architectonics more central to the act of discourse than in the second beginning of philosophy, the "I" which speaks for itself, rather than as a ventriloquized dialogist. In Descartes, the "method of search" suggested by Plato's Socrates—the step back from discursive language, from the representation of meaning, to the representation of words as letters, and of letters as lines—is the detour that founds modernity.

Like Daniel Payot, I had been struck by the linguistic images of architecture and architect which appear throughout Descartes' writings.[6] But the more I read in Descartes' early, foundational writings, the more it became evident that architecture functions as anything but an expressive motif in the origin of method and modern philosophy. Architectonic form is instead another kind of writing which discursive writing, including the

---

4. *The Republic* II: 368c–369a, in *The Complete Dialogues of Plato*, ed. Edith Hamilton and Huntington Cairns (Princeton: Princeton University Press, 1973), p. 615.
5. See especially Burke, *The Philosophy of Literary Form: Studies in Symbolic Action*, rev. ed. (New York: Vintage, 1957 [1941]), and *Language as Symbolic Action: Essays on Life, Literature, and Method* (Berkeley: University of California Press, 1966).
6. Cf. Payot, *Le philosophie*, pp. 111–20.

writing of metaphor, requires. It is a method that cannot be presented "outside" a discursive context; it is the writing of the *cogito* in the context of a representational autobiography, the link between the "I" of Cartesian philosophy and the simple "extension" of his *Géométrie*.

Like the *Géométrie*, the *Discours de la méthode* produces *discursively* the possibility of drawing a line—call it "I"—based on no previously available figure or form. It does this by way of discourse, but not on the basis of metaphor. It draws a line through representation by reinventing discourse as notation. This explicit reliance on discourse also differentiates the origin of the modern in Descartes from the contemporary development in the seventeenth century of that conceptual and aesthetic tendency recently redefined as "baroque."[7] If, as Gilles Deleuze has described, the continuous, organic unfolding of forms already contained and determined by preexisting forms best characterizes the baroque "vitalism" of Descartes' philosophical rival, Leibniz, it is, by contrast, artificial, architectonic form, first drawn by way of discourse, that epitomizes Descartes' creation of the modern.[8] Emphasizing the "inseparability" of body and soul in Leibniz's philosophy—a conjunction he embodies in his own text in a sketch of a "two-story" house symbolizing the monad—Deleuze employs Leibniz to argue against the tendency in philosophy he has consistently combated in his writings with Guattari, the tradition of analytic division and categorization initiated by Cartesian "ontology": "In the Baroque the coupling of material-force is what replaces matter and form (the primal forces being those of the soul)."[9]

The form taken by this non-Cartesian coupling of matter and force is, according to Deleuze, "the fold." While obviously a plastic concept, the

7. Gilles Deleuze, *Le pli: Leibniz et le baroque* (Paris: Minuit, 1988) [*The Fold: Leibniz and the Baroque,* trans. Tom Conley (Minneapolis: University of Minnesota Press, 1993), cited as *The Fold* in this volume].

8. Ibid., p. 11. The modern impulse precisely to make the world from scratch is investigated in Marshall Berman's now classic, dialectical analysis, *All That Is Solid Melts into Air: The Experience of Modernity* (London: Penguin, 1988).

9. *The Fold*, p. 35. "C'est le couple matériau-force qui, dans le Baroque, remplace la matiére et la forme (les force primitives étant celles de l'âme)" (Deleuze, *Le pli,* p. 50). The architectural imagery of Deleuze's study is chiefly limited to its introduction, including the drawing of "la Maison baroque (allégorie)" (p. 7), although the hierarchical figure of the "two stories" ("deux étages") of soul and body interconnected by a "fold" occurs throughout his description of Leibniz's "elastic" vitalism; see Deleuze, pp. 7, 17–18, 28, 162.

fold is not architectonic. Rather than constructing from a free, or nonsymbolic, imagination (an antimimetic mental power that Descartes, Claude Perrault, and Arnauld and Nicole name by the distinctive seventeenth-century usage of the term "fantaisie"), every fold reworks existent material in an ongoing equilibrium of making and unmaking. Wherever there is folding, Deleuze explains, there must also be unfolding, much like the maintenance and manipulation of matter in "origami."[10] Furthermore, these "infinite" permutations of matter have nothing to do with mental operations; most *unlike* origami, they are already "preformed" and "pre-determined" at every stage by the self-determining progress of life forms: "Not only is there preformation of bodies, but also a pre-existence of souls in fertile seeds."[11]

Deleuze's description of the fold as the basic element of the baroque, and of the Leibnizian monad as the unit in which folding occurs, clearly recalls his earlier notion of a mobile "rhizome" composed "only of lines," of infinite "plateaux."[12] (Indeed, in view of the combination of "animism and materialism" attributed to Leibniz in *Le pli,* Deleuze's "nomad" rhizome appears to signify nothing so much as a latter-day anagram—re-constitution or "fold"—of the Leibnizian monad.[13]) Whether or not their

---

10. The image of "origami" (*Le pli,* p. 9), along with those of "Russian dolls" and fractal geometry (ibid., pp. 13, 23, 23n), all serve Deleuze as metaphors for the infinitesimal procedures in which, as discussed later, Descartes saw neither mathematical nor philosophical interest.

11. *The Fold,* p. 11. "Il n'y a pas seulement préformation des corps, mais préexistence des âmes dans les semences" (Deleuze, *Le pli,* p. 16). On the infinite function of folding and unfolding, see Deleuze, p. 5, 8, 10, 16, 48, 164, 178ff.

12. Gilles Deleuze and Félix Guattari, *Mille plateaux,* vol. 2 of *Capitalisme et schizophrénie* (Paris: Minuit, 1980), p. 14: "Il n'y a pas de points ou de positions dans un rhizome, comme on en trouve dans une structure, un arbre, une racine. Il n'y a que des lignes" (There are no points or positions in a rhizome, as one finds in a structure, a tree, or a root. There are only lines); see "Introduction: rhizome," pp. 9–37ff. Deleuze in fact calls the "floor" or "fold" of the "baroque house" a "plateau" (*Le pli,* p. 17). On monads, see ibid., p. 93: "Telles sont les monades, ou les Moi chez Leibniz, automates dont chacun tire de son fond le monde entier, et traite le rapport à l'éxterieur ou le rapport aux autres comme un déroulement de son propre ressort, de sa propre spontanéité réglée d'avance" (Such are the monads, or Leibniz's selves, automata, each of which draws from its depths the entire world and handles its relations with the outside or with others as an uncoiling of the mechanism of its own spring, of its own prearranged spontaneity) [*The Fold,* p. 68].

13. Deleuze, *Le pli,* p. 163; Deleuze and Guattari, *Mille plateaux,* p. 526ff.

illustration in infinitely repetitive fractal patterns, or Deleuze's figure of the two-story baroque house, accords with art historical descriptions, beginning with Wölfflin's, of the "atectonic," "painterly" effect of "open," baroque form,[14] the givenness of Deleuze's baroque folds, their inevitable development or entelechy, is directly opposed to the act of canceling, *rather than* repeating or representing, that defines the construction of the modern and Descartes' philosophy.

Finally, while Deleuze opposes Leibniz to Descartes by way of a binary series of concepts — inflection vs. essence, fluidity vs. substance, mannerism vs. classicism, inclusion vs. attribution, elasticity vs. separability, and continuity vs. unit, among others[15] —, the fundamental difference between the baroque as he defines it, and the modern as it is defined in this study, is perhaps most easily recognized by way of the overlapping but ultimately incompatible notions of line and fold. Seen in two-dimensional profile, the fold Deleuze describes is indeed a line. But this line represents and results from the reproduction of nature: its demarcation of the matter it shapes is determined by the inherent, "auto-plastic" forces that shape the entire contents of the animate world, its living "organisms" as well as its "natural geography."[16] Descartes' architectonic line, however, is a specifically one-dimensional construct without plastic reality. It does not illustrate the forms of nature, but, like Socrates seeking to read the inscrutable "letters" of the soul, it translates thought onto an empty surface. It reiterates nothing and represents no preexisting process, but commits an unprecedented form to being. Rather than develop inevitably from a given material core, *it is drawn*. And in order for the hand to draw a line produced only in the mind, the mind and hand *must first invent notation* — discourse with no worldly analogue, instead of another permutation in a predetermined (natural and intellectual) world. The difference between

14. On the fractal model of infinite series, see Deleuze, *Le pli*, pp. 23–24, 35. See Heinrich Wölfflin, *Renaissance und Barock: Eine Untersuchung über Wesen und Entstehung des Barockstils in Italien* (Munich: T. Ackermann, 1888), pp. 16–17, 20–21, 40–41ff; Wölfflin, *Kunstgeschichtliche Grundbegriffe: Das Problem der Stilentwicklung in der neueren Kunst* (Munich: Bruckmann, 1943, pp. 10, 75, 128ff. Cf. my discussion of Wölfflin's definition of the baroque in Brodsky, " 'The Impression of Movement': Jean Racine, Architecte," *Yale French Studies* 76 (1989): 162–81.

15. Deleuze, *Le pli*, pp. 5, 8–10, 20–22, 27–28, 31, 71, 76–77. We will return to the opposition between Leibnizian and Cartesian mathematics in greater detail later.

16. Ibid., pp. 93, 9–10.

Deleuze's fold and the line that Descartes "thinks" and draws would be for Descartes the difference between new philosophy and the old.

For, if architectonics provides Descartes with the image of the new philosophy he seeks to found—the replacement of scholastic forms, received ideas, and sensory images by "method"—this method is also literally the drawing of a line, and cancellation of discursive figures of thought, that characterize modernity. The discursive beginning of modern philosophy, the founding of the subject of thinking, occurs not as a linguistic picture or image but as line, an iconoclastic line, a "line of thought."[17] Dependent for its own manifestation on the discursive means with which it is never identical, the thinking of thought as line—medium and manifestation of science as well as art—dispels every regressive and recurrent myth of cognition as the effect of resemblance, whether the coin of imitation be categorized as copy, type, or archetype, just as it demonstrates the impurity of nonimitative, "pure" thought.

The linearity—as opposed to pictoriality—of other modernisms may now be apparent to us, the modernism of painting, sculpture, dance, and architecture itself. But in Descartes, the modern, the drawing of a line from an "imagination" free of imaged forms, must take place by way of discourse, writing which conceals its own status as line in its intelligibility as representation. In Descartes the invention of the modern subject requires text, a linguistic context: lines of thought require a *discours de la méthode*.

17. I use the commonplace phrase "line of thought," which, like "line of argument" and "the party line," is a cliché of speech in English because, although it has no equivalent in spoken French, its most powerful conceptual and textual source is Descartes' correlation of "line" and "thought" in the *Géométrie* and *Discours de la méthode*. Drawing upon the arguments and methods elaborated and enacted in those works, the following analysis extends that correlation to Descartes' "foundation" of modern philosophy in the *cogito* (see, in particular, chapters 3, 5, 6, and 7).

ONE.   DESCARTES' "DESIGN"

You would have to lend me your attention, and let me talk a while with Poliandre, so that, first, I can overturn all knowledge that has been acquired up to the present. For since it is not sufficient to satisfy him, such knowledge can only be poor, and I hold it for some badly built house whose foundations are not sure. I know of no better way to remedy it than to raze it to the ground and build a new one from it, for I don't want to be one of those minor artisans who only employ themselves in adjusting old works because they feel incapable of undertaking new ones. But, Poliandre, while we work at this demolition, we can, by the same means, dig the foundations that must serve our design, and prepare the best and most solid materials that are necessary to fill them.

—*Descartes*, RECHERCHE DE LA VÉRITÉ

1 *Traité* or *Discours de la méthode*

From the beginning, Descartes' *Discours de la méthode* presented a strange conjunction. To the perplexity of his friends and correspondents, Descartes kept a suite of projects in various stages of development from the public eye: the extensive methodological tract, *Regulae ad directionem ingenii* (Rules for the Direction of the Spirit),[1] remained unfinished, reportedly finished treatises remained unpublished, and still others appeared to have been conceptually stillborn. Yet the long-awaited *Discours* found even its most eager readers unprepared. As the text was being readied for printing, Descartes defended to Mersenne the uncustomary title he had chosen for his first major published work. He responded, first, with cheerful equanimity to Mersenne's rather grim proposition to the effect that the world would benefit by his death: "Je n'ai su m'empêcher de rire, en lisant l'endroit où vous dites que j'oblige le monde à me tuer, afin qu'on puisse voir plus tôt mes écrits" (I couldn't help but laugh in reading where you state that I oblige the world to kill me so that one can see my writings earlier). This more consequential version of our onomastic "publish or perish"—perish, my friend, so that you may be published—only produced another serene evasion from the secretive Descartes.[2] Descartes did, how-

---

1. First published in Amsterdam, 1701.

2. Letter to Pierre Mersenne, 27 February 1637, in Descartes, *Correspondance*, 8 vols., ed. Charles Adam and Gérard Milhaud (Paris: Félix Alcan, 1936–63), 1:328 (hereafter referred to as *AM*). Descartes continues: "À quoi je n'ai autre chose à répondre, sinon qu'ils [mes écrits] sont déjà en lieu et en état que ceux qui m'auraient tué, ne les pourraient jamais avoir, et que, si je ne meurs fort à loisir et fort satisfait des hommes qui vivent, ils ne se verront assurément de plus de cent ans après ma mort" (To this I have nothing else to say except that they [my writings] are already in such a place and condition that those who would have killed me could never have them, and that, if I do

ever, take direct exception to Mersenne's next observation, his criticism of Descartes' use of the word *discours:*

> Mais je n'ai su bien entendre ce que vous objectez touchant le titre; car je ne mets pas *Traité de la méthode,* mais *Discours de la méthode,* ce qui est le même que *Préface* ou *Avis touchant la méthode,* pour montrer que je n'ai pas dessein de l'enseigner, mais seulement d'en parler. Car, comme on peut voir de ce que j'en dis, elle consiste plus en pratique qu'en théorie; et je nomme les Traités suivants des *Essais de cette méthode,* parce que je prétends que les choses qu'ils contiennent n'ont pu être trouvées sans elle, et qu'on peut connaître par eux ce qu'elle vaut: comme aussi j'ai inséré quelque chose de Métaphysique, de Physique et de Médecine dans le premier *Discours,* pour montrer qu'elle s'étend à toutes sortes de matières.[3]

> But I could not understand your objection regarding the title; for I am putting not *Treatise on Method,* but *Discourse on Method,* which is the same as *Preface* or *View concerning Method,* to show that it was not my design (*dessein*) to teach it but only to talk about it (*d'en parler*). For, as one can see from what I say of it, it consists more of practice than of theory; and I name the treatises that follow "Experiments of this Method," because I claim that the things they contain could not have been found without it, and that one can know its worth through them: so, also, I put something of metaphysics, physics, and medicine in the first *Discourse,* to show that it extends to all kinds of subject matter.

---

not die at my own leisure and happy with the men who live, they will surely not see them for more than a hundred years after my death) (ibid., 328).

3. *AM,* 1:328–29. In an earlier letter to Mersenne (March 1636) Descartes described the work he planned as consisting of "four treatises" bearing the "general" title *Le Projet d'une Science universelle, qui puisse élever notre nature à son plus haut degré de perfection. Plus, la Dioptrique, les Météores, et la Géométrie, où les plus curieuses matières que l'auteur ait pu choisir, pour rendre preuve de la Science universelle qu'il propose, sont expliquées en telle sorte, que ceux mêmes qui n'ont point étudié les peuvent entendre* (The Project of a universal Science, which can elevate our nature to its highest degree of perfection. In addition, the Optics, Meteorology, and Geometry, in which the most curious subject matters that the author could choose to render proof of the universal science which he proposes are explained in such a way as to make them understandable even to those who have not studied) (ibid., p. 301).

Unlike *Le monde, ou le traité de la lumière*, *L'homme et un traité de la formation du foetus* (also called the *Traité de l'homme*[4]), and the *Traité de la mécanique*,[5] all published posthumously,[6] or the unpublished *Traité sur la divinité* and *Traité de métaphysique* (which Descartes probably destroyed),[7] the *Discours* does not explicate physical phenomena or metaphysical ideas; its given subject is rather a general mode of procedure, a "method." This "method" could not be the subject of a treatise because it makes the writing of treatises possible, defining the order and manner in which the scientific treatment of "all kinds of subject matters" must be carried out.[8] Not an object of theoretical analysis but a matter of "practice," "method," according to Descartes, is more properly "talked about" than taught. For just this reason Mersenne faced bureaucratic obstacles in procuring the copyright privilege for the *Discours* in France: the department in charge of inspecting scientific treatises could not review the work, Mersenne reports, "because it consists of discourse" ("à cause que cela consiste en discours"), and would fall under the category of "works of eloquence, in verse and in prose" ("les pièces d'éloquence, tant en vers qu'en prose") over which other inspectors had mandate.[9]

4. This appellation is adopted by Alquié in Descartes, *Oeuvres philosophiques*, ed. Ferdinand Alquié, 3 vols. (Paris: Garnier, 1963), 1:377 [hereafter referred to as *OP*]. On the publication history of the treatises, see 1:307–8.

5. Originally included in a letter to Huygens (5 October 1637) and published as "Explication des machines et engins," it was renamed "Traité . . ." in the standard edition, Descartes, *Oeuvres*, ed. Charles Adams and Paul Tannery, 12 vols. (Paris: Léopold Cerf, 1897–1913) [hereafter referred to as *AT*].

6. Paris, 1664, 1664, and 1668, respectively.

7. Based on references in the *Correspondence*, both these writings have been dated 1629; see Edwin M. Curley, "Cohérence ou incohérence du *Discours*," in *Le discours et sa méthode*, ed. Nicolas Grimaldi and Jean-Luc Marion (Paris: Presses Universitaires de France, 1987), p. 43n, and Sylvie Romanowski, *L'illusion chez Descartes* (Paris: Klincksieck, 1974), p. 114.

8. Cf. Hugo Friedrich, *Descartes und der französische Geist* (Leipzig: Felix Meiner, 1937), pp. 9, 15: "What interested Descartes—and this is the most universal meaning of the *Discours*—was not the content of new knowledge in the natural sciences, but, in a more fundamental way, the possibility of knowledge"; "the famous four rules . . . are not new contents of knowledge, but principles which should lead to the acquisition of knowledge."

9. Mersenne to Descartes, 15 February 1837, *AM* 1:323. On Mersenne's difficulties, see Pierre Costabel, "Les *Essais de la Méthode* et la réforme mathématique," in Grimaldi and Marion, *Le discours et sa méthode*, p. 215.

If Descartes remained steadfast in the face of the royal compartmentalization of genres, refusing to call the *Discours* a treatise (and publishing the *Discours* in Leiden), he also rejected the alternative notion of naming his work instead for the *Essais* described as putting the method into practice. In a letter contemporary with his response to Mersenne, he writes to Huygens:

> vous jugiez le mot de *Discours* superflu en mon titre, et c'est l'un des sujets de remerciement que j'ai à vous faire. Mais je m'excuse sur ce que *je n'ai pas eu dessein d'expliquer toute la Méthode, mais seulement d'en dire quelque chose,* et je n'aime pas à promettre plus que j'en donne. C'est pourquoi j'ai mis *Discours de la Méthode,* au lieu que j'ai mis simplement *La Dioptrique* et *Les Météores,* parce que j'ai tâché d'y comprendre tout ce qui faisait à mon sujet."[10]

> you find the word *Discourse* superfluous in my title, and this is one of the things I wanted to thank you for. But I excuse myself in that *I did not have the design to explain the whole Method, but only to say something about it* and I don't like to promise more than I give. This is why I put *Discourse on Method,* instead of simply *Optics* and *Meteorology,* because I tried to include in it everything that pertained to my subject.

On the one hand, then, Descartes conceived of his *Discours* as a practical demonstration rather than a didactic treatise, while on the other he considered the practical *Essais* an inadequate stand-in for his "design." For although it was not Descartes' "design"—plan or intention—to "explain the whole Method," he did want to "say something about it."[11] In accordance with that "design," as it is described in both letters, *discours* could neither be replaced and excluded by the formal, scientific sense of *traité* nor be subsumed under the names of particularly focused experiments.

Descartes' decision not to name his work a "treatise" has remained noteworthy to this day.[12] Far less frequently noted, however, is the fact that

---

10. Letter to Huygens, 25 February 1637, *AM,* 1:327 (my emphasis).
11. On the vanity of such a design, given the power of discourse to work independently of authorial intentions, see Romanowski, *L'illusion,* pp. 136–37: "But 'only' to talk about it is precisely the inaccessible and impossible enterprise, for the discursive word is the least innocent act possible, once it is set in motion. . . . The victorious discourse is always self-referential, and the *Discours de la méthode* does not escape this fact."
12. "Discours" is the first item of commentary in Étienne Gilson's authoritative anno-

the *Discours* is also not a "discours" *sur* "la méthode," a discursive work "on" or "concerning" the subject of method in conformity with an essayistic formula now most familiar to us from Rousseau, and whose precedents in the seventeenth century include works by Pascal, Corneille, and Bossuet.[13] The general shift from "de" to "sur" in the entitling of "discours" may in fact have arisen partly in response to Descartes' lexical choice; there are some examples of Descartes' usage before the *Discours*, but almost

---

tated edition of the *Discours de la méthode* (Paris: Vrin, 1925), p. 79 [cited hereafter as Gilson, *Discours*]. Friedrich distinguishes *discours* from its customary German translation, *Abhandlung*, as well as from the scientific *traité*, noting that "Descartes chose the least conspicuous and least binding expression available in the linguistic usage of his time to designate his work" *Descartes und der französische Geist*, p. 12). In *Descartes* (Oxford: Basil Blackwell, 1986), John Cottingham explains Descartes' choice of "the label 'discourse' rather than 'treatise'" as primarily stylistic: "Even a cursory inspection of the work reveals that the *Discourse* is an intensely individual work which is indeed quite unlike a conventional scholarly or philosophical treatise" (p. 13); cf. the equation of the *Discours* with literary fiction in Jonathan Rée's *Philosophical Tales* (London: Methuen, 1987), p. 10: the *Discours* is not a "methodical treatise . . . ; on the contrary, it is a conspicuously narrated story. . . . The line between truth and fiction in autobiography is sometimes impossible to draw." Jean-Luc Marion argues that Descartes' use of *discours* instead of *traité* "implies already that the method is *not* to be found explicitly thematised as such. The paradox begins very early" ("Ouverture," in *Problématique et réception du Discours de la Méthode et des Essais*, ed. Henry Méchoulan [Paris: Vrin, 1988], p. 13 [emphasis in text]). Daniel Garber similarly notes that, according to Descartes' letter to Mersenne, the *Discours*, unlike a treatise, "does not contain a true exposition of the method" ("Descartes et la méthode en 1637," in Grimaldi and Marion, *Le discours et sa méthode*, p. 73), while Berel Lang explains the "choice of 'Discourse' rather than 'Treatise'" as the reflection of a method in "use": "the *Discourse* both recounts Descartes' discovery of a method and affords a view of that method at work" ("Descartes between Method and Style," chap. 3 of *The Anatomy of Philosophical Style: Literary Philosophy and the Philosophy of Literature* [Oxford: Basil Blackwell, 1990], pp. 45–46). Commenting on the paradoxical structure of Descartes' stated use of a national "natural language" to appeal to universal "'natural reason,'" Jacques Derrida ties *discours* back to *traité*: "this work becomes then also . . . a discourse *on* its own language as much as *in* its own language, that is, a 'treatise' on discourse, since the word 'discourse' in the title *Discours de la méthode*, maintains, among other meanings, that of 'Treatise'" ("La philosophie dans sa langue nationale," in *Du droit à la philosophie* [Paris: Galilée, 1990], p. 287).

13. Pascal, "Discours sur les passions de l'amour" (1652–53?), Corneille, "Discours sur le poème dramatique" (1660), Bossuet, *Discours sur l'histoire universelle* (1681). On the historical usage of *discours*, cf. Friedrich, *Descartes und der französische Geist*, p. 12n4.

none that succeed it.[14] "Discours *sur* la méthode" would have conveyed Descartes' "design" of "talking about" method; the (untranslatable) difference in meaning conveyed by "Discours *de* la méthode" combines a definitive ("Traité *de* . . .") with a discursive ("*Discours* sur . . .") sense of method, a methodical and practical approach to the "design" of "talking about" method itself.[15]

Suggesting a "traité" but describing a "discours," the equivocal "de" of Descartes' *Discours de la méthode* brings discourse together with method, but even its discursive and methodological components are difficult to characterize. "Method," understood to refer solely to the four cursory rules of procedure offered in Part Two, would exclude not only the overtly autobiographical discourse of Parts One and Two but also the "three or four maxims" for conducting one's life stipulated in Part Three, the narration of the *cogito* and argument for the existence of God in Part Four, the laws of nature and description of the human body based on the unpublished *Le monde* and *L'homme* in Part Five, and the apology for not publishing that double treatise and introduction of the *Dioptrique* and *Météores* in Part Six. Even—or especially—if they are so isolated from the rest of the *Discours,* the four rules are generally recognized to summarize or simplify the more fully explicated, if unfinished, *Regulae*.[16] "Short and unimpressive" when

14. Cf. Ronsard's *Discours des misères de ce temps* (1562–63) and La Boétie's *Discours de la servitude volontaire* (published by Montaigne in 1571). Leibniz's *Discours de métaphysique* (1686) would be a notable exception to the lexical shift described here.

15. In the only references I have found to Descartes' choice of prepositions, Jean-Luc Marion significantly interprets this "de" as an ablative of origin—"*Le Discours de la Méthode* should not be understood as a discourse *on* [*sur*] method but as a discourse which originates in method [*un discours à partir de la méthode*] in view of the project which engenders and sustains it" ("Ouverture," *Problématique et réception,* p. 16)—while Evert van Leeuwen, noting that Descartes' "phrase leaves more than one possibility for the genitive," suggests "it might be the case that the discourse is spoken *by* the method," a view he considers briefly as "more than a little odd," but suggestive of the common purpose of discourse and method (see "Method, Discourse, and the Act of Knowing," in *Essays on the Philosophy and Science of René Descartes,* ed. Stephen Voss [Oxford: Oxford University Press, 1993], p. 226). Without similarly ascribing agency to method, the present analysis investigates the origin of method *in* discourse, Descartes' "talking about."

16. On the substantial agreement of the rules of Part Two with the *Regulae,* see Lewis J. Beck, *The Method of Descartes: A Study of the Regulae* (Oxford: Clarendon, 1952), pp. 1–8, and Peter A. Schouls, *The Imposition of Method: A Study of Descartes and Locke* (Oxford: Clarendon, 1980), pp. 52–87, 256–57. On their status as "pale shadows" of

considered in isolation, the rules comprise a method that would hardly justify the "discourse" devoted to it.[17] Furthermore, Descartes situates the procedural rules within the discursive context of his autobiographical narrative, suggesting that he developed them to correct the defects of the individual methods he was taught at La Flèche.[18] If such contextualization defeats the notion of isolating method from discursivity in a discourse "on" method, perhaps Descartes' *Discours de la méthode* is more literally, if unusually, a discourse belonging to or inhering in method and a method originating in discourse, not in the sense of etiology but rather of articulation: the discourse *of* the method. What then would be *discours,* and what, *méthode?*

---

the *Regulae* and reinterpretation as a mode of analytic comparison, see Jakko Hintikka, "A Discourse on Descartes's Method," in *Descartes: Critical and Interpretive Essays,* ed. Michael Hooker (Baltimore: Johns Hopkins University Press, 1978), p. 74. In "Science and Certainty in Descartes" (also in Hooker, *Descartes*), Daniel Garber singles out the criteria of "clearness and distinctness" as "substantially new in the *Discourse*" (p. 119), a view he maintains but modifies in "Descartes et la méthode en 1637" by identifying essential agreement between the two works and locating the turning point in Descartes' interest in method in the inadequate relation of the previously written *Essais* to the newly completed *Discours* whose method they are stated to demonstrate (in Grimaldi and Marion, *Le discours et sa méthode,* pp. 73, 80, 83–87). The accepted chronology of the *Essais* is as follows: the *Dioptrique* may date from as early as 1629, the *Météores* is a revised part of *Le monde* (1633), and the *Géométrie* dates from Descartes' solution of the Pappus problem, communicated to him by Golius in 1631. Cf. *OP,* 1:549–50; Leon Roth, *Descartes' Discourse on Method* (Oxford: Clarendon, 1937), pp. 17–20; Gilbert Gadoffre, "Sur la chronologie du *Discours de la Méthode,*" *Revue d'histoire de la philosophie et d'histoire générale de la civilisation* Jan.–Mar. (1943): 45–70; Gadoffre, *Introduction au Discours de la Méthode* (Manchester: University of Manchester Press, 1947); Gadoffre, "Réflexions sur la genèse du *Discours de la Méthode,*" *Revue de Synthèse* 22 (1948): 11–27.

17. Garber, "Descartes et la mèthode," p. 65; cf. Ferdinand Alquié, "Introduction," *Le Discours de la Méthode et les Essais, OP,* 1:564.

18. *OP,* 1:584–86.

2 Autobiographical Discourse: "Fable" as "Tableau"

It is a commonplace in histories of Western philosophy and culture that the *Discours de la méthode* marks the beginning of modern thought. As if to inaugurate that consensus, the first self-styled "moderns" took Descartes as a model of antitraditionalism in the *querelle des anciens et des modernes* which, beginning in 1650 (the year of Descartes' death), pervaded French arts and letters for the remainder of the century.[1] The consequences of the independence of thought theorized by Descartes were to find their most pronounced practical expression in the advocacy of the modern in architecture: the Académie Royale d'Architecture debated in specifically Cartesian terms the bases of the rules of architectural form, an issue we will return to later. But in general it may be observed that, just as if in rebuke to the historicist polemic of the *querelle* many of the *modernes* have not lived to tell their stories, while such *anciens* as Racine, Boileau, La Fontaine, and La Bruyère survived and continue to survive seventeenth-century modernity quite well, the classically modern *Discours,* which may have initiated a different way of defining *discours,* started something it could not finish.[2]

1. See Hans Robert Jauss, "Ästhetische Normen und geschichtliche Reflexion in der 'Querelle des Anciens et des Modernes,' " "Introduction" to Charles Perrault, *Parallèle des anciens et des modernes* (Munich: Eidos, 1964), pp. 8–64.
2. The modernity of the *anciens* can be recognized not just by pure dint of posterity. As Jauss points out, it was the *anciens* who served as the very models for the argument made by many *modernes,* that the accomplishments of the authors of the *grand siècle* surpassed those of the ancient Greeks: "[Charles Perrault] makes the paradox of French classicism evident: its greatest representatives stand on the side of the *anciens* in the *querelle,* even though they are the very *modernes* in whose works Perrault seeks to demonstrate the superiority of the contemporary over ancient art" (ibid., p. 48). On the other hand, the thesis of the "incomparable" status of ancient works advocated by the *anciens* can be seen to inaugurate our own modern or postromantic sense of the

However one chooses to define the polemical thrust of the modern, the theoretical modernity of the *Discours de la méthode* (as contrasted, for example, with the posthumously published *Regulae*) is the dispute or *querelle* it contains within itself.

Beginning with its title, that dispute constitutes the discourse of the *Discours,* whose heterogeneity of content continues to provoke debates. The striking disunity of the concerns voiced in the various parts of the *Discours* has led to reinvestigations of its date(s) of composition and the conclusion that the work is actually a temporal patchwork whose confusing assemblage reflects distinct periods in Descartes' intellectual life.[3] This thesis has been countered by the assertion that, while the *Discours* may combine different moments in the chronology of Descartes' intellectual development, "each part of the *Discours* respond[ing] to a past attitude of his consciousness," the "coherence" of the *Discours* lies precisely in its identity as a "narrative" or "story" ("récit" or "histoire") of those moments, rather than as a "system" of method.[4] By this account the *Discours* is essentially an autobiographical text whose modernity is marked by its identity as such, the identification of the thinking subject as the seat of reason in the *cogito* represented on the discursive level by a narrative of the self.[5] The addi-

---

ineradicable singularity of historical experience, a shift which, in Jauss' view, brings with it the end of the *querelle* (see ibid., pp. 52, 54, 58, 60–61, 64; also see *OP,* 1:572–73 (cited in note 9 below), for the language of the "incomparability" of ancient works already used in the *Discours*).

3. Cf. Gadoffre, "Réflexions sur la genèse." Whether or not one accepts Gadoffre's claim that the heterogeneity of the *Discours* must owe to the discontinuous history of its composition, his basic observation—that this grounding text of modern philosophy is extremely difficult to grasp in coherent, formal terms—cannot be stressed enough: "Far from it being the case that the coherence and homogeneity of the *Discours* impose themselves as self-evident, one must only peruse the text without preconceived ideas to be struck by the arbitrary nature and the oddness [*bizarrerie*] of its plan" (p. 11). See also Roth, *Descartes' Discourse,* pp. 23–27.

4. See Alquié's commentary, *OP,* 1:553: "The *Discours de la Méthode* is, above all, a story. It is the story of the thoughts of Descartes. And the coherence which we can find in it is that of a narrative, not of a system." Ibid., p. 560: "the *Discours,* one must recall, is, above all, the history of the thought of Descartes."

5. "Regarding the ensemble of the *Discours,* one can say at the very most that Descartes, unifying his thoughts only in relating them to the history of the subject who formed them, appeals to a kind of historical *cogito,* the unconscious *cogito* of the self of which the metaphysical *cogito* later will be only the reflexive coming to consciousness.

tional fact that Descartes names the "life story" ("histoire") he is about to narrate a fiction or "fable" secures his place in a literary confessional tradition while ensuring that its modernity is and will remain unassailable.[6]

The "fable" Descartes narrates, or his representation of his life "[in this discourse] as in a tableau" ("d'y représenter ma vie comme en un tableau")—a distinction in representational modes whose theoretical significance Descartes appears to gloss over—recounts his experiences first as a student at La Flèche and then as a volunteer soldier in Holland under Prince Maurice of Nassau.[7] Related in Part One, continued and recapitulated in Part Two, and referred to again in Part Three, these experiences compose a story of ostensible disunity as well, a tale of intensive study cut off by itinerant military adventures. They are united by their common aspect of an encounter with writing or representation. In a narrative which repeatedly doubles back on itself chronologically, and which, by the light of its own explanation, makes Descartes' decision to travel seem more rather than less improbable, Descartes describes the story of his life as a turn from the books of study to what he famously calls "the book of the world." His disenchantment with the former is stated within the first sentences of his narrative:

His first work is the story of his thinking self. The second will reveal that the affirmation of the thinking self is the condition of all other affirmations. In the one case as in the other, Descartes is the philosopher who says 'I' " (Ibid., p. 553). On autobiography as both vehicle for the *cogito* and persuasive, literary strategy of the *Discours,* cf. Friedrich, *Descartes und der französische Geist,* pp. 13–14; Paul Valéry, *Les pages immortelles de Descartes* (Paris: Chastel, 1961), pp. 28, 46–49; Rée, *Philosophical Tales,* pp. 10–16, and Dalia Judovitz, *Subjectivity and Representation in Descartes: The Origin of Modernity* (Cambridge: Cambridge University Press, 1988), esp. pp. 131–35.

6. *OP,* 1:571. On the modern, philosophical status of the autobiography as "fable," cf. Judovitz, *Subjectivity and Representation,* pp. 132–33: "By negating its own exemplarity, the didactic function of the *Discours* is cancelled and subsumed by autobiography. . . . The *Discours* as autobiography presents only the conditions of the subject's self-invention as representation." See also Jean-Luc Nancy, "Mundus est fabula," in *Ego Sum* (Paris: Flammarion, 1979): "Descartes proposes his *Discours as a fable.* This is not a comparison; his work does not borrow, by imitation, the allure of a literary genre. It is given *by virtue* of a fable and it must be used *as* a fable. In truth . . . from now on, it will only be a question of this: how a certain change in the use of fiction is the operator of the truth of the subject . . . '*Discours de la Méthode*' means, in a very rigorous sense, '*Fable de la Méthode*' " (pp. 101–5).

7. *OP,* 1:570–71.

J'ai été nourri aux lettres dès mon enfance, et parce qu'on me persuadait que, par leur moyen, on pouvait acquérir une connaissance
claire et assurée de tout ce qui est utile à la vie, j'avais un extrême désir
de les apprendre. Mais, sitôt que j'eus achevé tout ce cours d'études,
au bout duquel on a coutume d'être reçu au rang des doctes, je changeai entièrement d'opinion. Car je me trouvais embarrassé de tant de
doutes et d'erreurs, qu'il me semblait n'avoir fait autre profit, en tâchant de m'instruire, sinon que j'avais découvert de plus en plus mon
ignorance.[8]

I have been raised on letters from my childhood, and because I was
persuaded that by means of them one could acquire clear and certain
knowledge of all that is useful in life, I had an extreme desire to learn
them. But, as soon as I finished this whole course of studies, at the
end of which one is usually received into the ranks of the learned, I
changed my opinion entirely. For I found myself embarrassed by so
many doubts and errors that it seemed to me the only profit in trying to instruct myself was that I had increasingly discovered my own
ignorance.

This brief narrative account appears clear and straightforward until one
realizes that it is, precisely, *too* clear and straightforward; Descartes, we
might say, is getting ahead of himself, concluding his "story" almost as
soon as it begins. The time between the expectant beginning of his studies
and the complete reversal of his opinion of what studies bring is immediately eclipsed by the conjunction "as soon as," referring to the moment
those studies came to an end. A future moment in the chronology of the
"story" (to be told) is made past by the backward glance cast from a narrating position future to the story itself. The diachronic development of
Descartes' autobiography is flattened by a temporal and narrative short
circuit, a projection ahead to an already represented end. The *Discours*
will then proceed to reverse this projection, filling in, over the next seven
paragraphs (that is, up to the last paragraph of Part One) the experiences
skipped over in Descartes' two-sentence sequence of beginning and end.
That filling-in takes place in more or less, but never exactly, chronological sequence, the forward movement of autobiographical description—
forward or forward-looking in the senses both of linear temporal development and of the personal optimism described—irregularly accompanied

8. Ibid., p. 571.

by the movement of retrospection, the backward glance both of futurity
and disenchantment. We read Descartes' "fable" from its beginning, in
other words, "as in a tableau": in strikingly non-Aristotelian fashion, Descartes joins the end of his story to its beginning before he represents its
middle, proceeding (if that is still the word) backward to relate its middle
by moving between beginning and end.

   "As in a tableau" which the eye tries to see in detail and the mind tries
to grasp as a whole, the movement back to the middle sketched by Descartes takes place in no predefined order. His discursive "fable" enumer-
ates in brief, and then returns again to consider individually, the different
disciplines contained within the "whole" of his course of studies. The
"languages" useful to the reading of "ancient books," the graceful "fables"
which "awaken the mind," the "histories" whose "memorable actions"
"help us to form judgments," the works of "eloquence" of "incomparable force and beauty," the "ravishing delicacy and sweetness" of "poetry,"
the "subtle inventions" of "mathematics" whose application "facilitates all
the arts," the "writings" on "morals" which exhort to "virtue," "theology"
which teaches one to reach "heaven," "philosophy" which affords the
means of speaking convincingly ("de parler vraisemblablement") and so of
"gaining the admiration of the less knowledgeable," "law" and "medicine
and the other sciences which bring honor and wealth to those who cultivate them": all these are listed in one sentence in the following paragraph
by Descartes, an inventory of grammatically homologous clauses subordi-
nated to the single main verb, "I knew that" ("Je savais que les langues . . . ;
que la gentillesse des fables . . ;" etc.).[9] Just as the viewer of a tableau will,
at what we call a second glance, mentally note the identity of the different
objects first seen represented together, then double back, more or less at
random, to inspect them one by one, Descartes will return to comment on
his encounters with the individual disciplines, mixing praise with blame in
every case, in the six paragraphs to come (Part One, para. 8–13).[10] Rather

9. *OP,* 1:572–73.

10. "Il est bon de savoir quelque chose des moeurs de divers peuples, afin de juger des
nôtres plus sainement . . . mais lorsqu'on emploie trop de temps à voyager, on devient
enfin étranger en son pays; et lorsqu'on est trop curieux des choses qui se pratiquaient
aux siècles passés, on demeure ordinairement fort ignorant de celles qui se pratiquent
en celui-ci" (It is good to know something of the morals of diverse peoples so that
we may judge ours more soundly . . . but when one spends too much time traveling, one ends up a stranger in one's own country; and when one is too curious about

than read the story of Descartes' studies as unfolding in time, we are made, in reading, to scan it: first in a glance, grasping its "whole course," then in increasing but never narratively constrained detail, just as, moving our eye back and forth, we come to "read" progressively, but, again, not in any predetermined or given linear sense of progression, the eclectic content of a synchronic tableau.

If part of Descartes' "design" of "talking about" his method is to relate the context surrounding it—the "story" of his "life"—he presents that context in such a way as to defy the procedural laws of narrative discourse, linear representation, and temporal successivity. Not only the premoder-

---

the practices of past centuries, one usually remains completely ignorant of those in this one) (Part 1, para. 8). "J'estimais fort l'éloquence, et j'étais amoureux de la poésie; mais je pensais que l'une et l'autre étaient des dons de l'esprit, plutôt que des fruits de l'étude" (I admired eloquence greatly and was in love with poetry, but I thought that both were gifts of the mind rather than the fruits of study) (para. 9). "Je me plaisais surtout aux mathématiques, à cause de la certitude de l'évidence de leurs raisons; mais je ne remarquais point encore leur vrai usage . . . pensant qu'elles ne servaient qu'aux arts mécaniques" (I enjoyed mathematics the most because of the certainty and evidence of its arguments, but I did not yet note its true usage . . . thinking it only served the mechanical arts) (para. 10). "les écrits des anciens paiens . . . élèvent fort haut les vertus . . . mais ils n'enseignent pas assez à les connaître" (the writings of the ancient pagans . . . raise virtues very high . . . but do not sufficiently teach us how to know them) (para. 10). "Je révérais notre théologie, et prétendais, autant qu'aucun autre, à gagner le ciel; mais ayant appris . . . que les vérités révélées, qui y conduisent, sont au-dessus de notre intelligence, je n'eusse osé les soumettre à la faiblesse de mes raisonnements" (I revered theology, and intended as much as anyone else to arrive in heaven; but having learned . . . that the revealed truths that lead there are above our intelligence, I would not have dared to subject them to the weakness of my reasoning) (para. 11). "Je ne dirai rien de la philosophie, sinon que, . . . cultivée par les plus excellents esprits qui aient vécu depuis plusieurs siècles, . . . il ne s'y trouve encore aucune chose dont on ne se dispute, . . . et . . . considérant combien il peut y avoir de diverses opinions, touchant une même matière, . . . sans qu'il y en puisse avoir jamais plus d'une seule qui soit vraie, je réputais presque pour faux tout ce qui n'était que vraisemblable" (I will say nothing of philosophy except that, . . . cultivated by the best minds to have lived over many centuries, . . . there was still nothing one did not dispute within it, . . . and . . . considering how many diverse opinions there could be touching the same subject, . . . without there ever possibly being more than one that could be true, I held nearly for false everything which was only probable [or "only seemed true": *vraisemblable*])" (para. 12). "Pour les autres sciences, d'autant qu'elles empruntent leurs principes de la philosophie, . . . ni l'honneur, ni le gain qu'elles promettent, n'étaient suffisants pour me convier à les apprendre; . . . et quoique je ne fisse pas profession

nity of Montaigne's *Essais*[11] but also the ultramodernity of Mallarmé's "Coup de dès" may be read in Descartes' "represent[ation] of [his] life as in a tableau." Like the choice of the word "discours," and the "talking about" it is said to stand for, this nonsequential story—this "fable" whose entirety precedes its development—reflects the structural ambivalence of Descartes' "design." Alternately directed forward and backward, effectively modern and pre- (or post-) modern by turns, the discourse of Descartes' "discours *de* la méthode" may itself belong to or inhere in the method it is "about" by two distinct conceptions: as a narrative of the contextual formation of method, the *Bildungsroman* of its development, or as the synchronic tableau within which the method is contextualized, encompassed, or framed.

Descartes begins his expanded inventory (Part One, para. 8) by reflecting, once again from the perspective of its completion, on a time foreclosed: "mais je croyais avoir déjà donné assez de temps aux langues, et même aussi à la lecture des livres anciens, et à leurs histoires, et à leurs fables" (but I thought that I had already given enough time to languages and even to the reading of ancient books, and to their histories and their fables). Before proceeding to elaborate on the advantages and disadvantages of studying ancient *moeurs* by returning to the time preceding that conclusion, he explains the basis of the temporal closure of his studies by a comparison: "car c'est quasi le même de converser avec ceux des autres siècles, que de voyager"[12] (For it is almost the same to converse with those of other centuries as it is to travel). Here reading (ancient texts) is directly allied with (contemporary) travel, and, as the comparison continues and concludes two sentences later, both stand criticized: "lorsqu'on emploie

---

de mépriser la gloire en cynique, je faisais néanmoins fort peu d'état de celle que je n'espérais point pouvoir acquérir qu'à faux titres" (For the other sciences, inasmuch as they borrowed their principles from philosophy, . . . neither the honor nor the profit they promise were sufficient to induce me to learn them, . . . and although I did not profess a cynical contempt for glory, I nonetheless lay little store in that which I could only hope to acquire on false pretenses) (para. 13). *OP*, 1:573–76.

11. On the influence of Montaigne on the *Discours*, see Gilson, *Discours;* Friedrich, *Descartes und der französische Geist,* pp. 12, 18–21, 53; Léon Brunschvig, *Descartes et Pascal, lecteurs de Montaigne* (Neuchâtel: Baconnière, 1942), pp. 95–133; Gilbert Gadoffre, "Le *Discours de la Méthode* et l'histoire littéraire," *French Studies* 2 (1948): 301–14.

12. *OP*, 1:573. As cited in note 10, the paragraph then continues: "Il est bon de savoir quelque chose des moeurs de divers peuples" (It is good to know something of the morals of different peoples).

trop de temps à voyager, on devient enfin etranger en son pays"[13] (when one spends too much time traveling, one finally becomes a foreigner in one's own country). The real or present world of immediate experience is represented here as no more (nor less) real than the world of books. The ostensible clarity of the comparison owes to its equation of the foreign with the foreign, the unknown with the unknown, regardless of mode. For not only does Descartes equate written representations of the foreign with its first-hand experience, but also, and almost unnoticeably, he equates past foreignness with present. Excluding the differentiating media of discursivity and temporal change, his equation of the reading of ancient texts ("convers[ing] with those of other centuries") with first-hand travel in the present echoes the gesture of conflation effected in his earlier equation, by default, of "fable" and "tableau."

We soon learn that the pre-announced reversal in the course of Descartes' life is, more precisely, the exchange of one form of bookishness for another. The comparison of travel with study reappears toward the end of Part One (para. 14). Having completed his description of each discipline, Descartes recapitulates the change of opinion already stated previous to these detailed descriptions (para. 8), or indeed any description, in the second sentence of his "story."[14] Once again he states the refrain of his complete change of mind: "c'est pourquoi, sitôt que l'âge me permit de sortir de la sujétion de mes précepteurs, je quittai entièrement l'étude des lettres"[15] (this is why, as soon as age permitted me to leave the subjection to my precepters behind, I left the study of letters entirely). Now condensed in the form of a metaphor, the comparison between books and travel is used to describe not a timeless cognitive equivalence between the two but a different and future course of action. Taking a picaresque turn, Descartes' "fable" continues: "et me résolvant de ne chercher plus d'autre science, que celle qui se pourrait trouver en moi-même, ou bien dans le grand livre du monde, j'employai le reste de ma jeunesse à voyager"[16] (and

---

13. *OP,* 1:573–74.
14. See ibid., p. 571.
15. Ibid., pp. 576–77.
16. Ibid., 577. Gadoffre notes that the phrase "livre du monde" had already appeared in Charles Sorel's novel *Francion* (1623) and that Descartes' use of it reflects the rejection of an education in classical letters which he shared with the *moderne* Sorel. He does not note, however, that Descartes importantly rejects the world of experience as well; his position in this regard cannot be explained, following Gadoffre, as an

resolving not to seek further any science other than that which could be found in myself, or, just as well, in the great book of the world, I spent the rest of my youth traveling).

The clarity of the earlier comparison it consolidates makes the metaphor, "the great book of the world," appear an entirely appropriate vehicle for the new experience it describes. At the same time, it represents an impending course of action as regressive and self-defeating. For the knowledge granted by this transparent figure also forecloses, from the beginning, our expectancy that such action could have any intrinsic value in the "fable" Descartes recounts. Deriving from both things compared, the foreclosure enforced by Descartes' metaphor is overdetermined, double: "travel" in the world has already been used figuratively to describe the estrangement from knowledge enforced by books, and travel in a metaphoric "book of the world" is bound to be as disappointing as literal books have already been.[17] The turn to "the great book of the world" is not represented discursively as a narrative change in life but, rather, as a detail contained and delimited from the beginning within a life represented "as in a tableau."

Although Descartes qualifies his search for science "in the great book of the world" as being roughly equivalent to a search within himself ("en moi-même"), the metaphor of the book tells us in advance that this search, like the "whole course" of his studies, will lead nowhere. Like the "fable which ends just as it begins," and whose reading resembles the scanning of a synchronic tableau, Descartes' turn from books to the "book of the world" is progess in regress, a figurative reference to discursive representation which defeats the purpose of discursive representation, an undermining of the process of telling a story that was already undermined in the process of living it. Whether composing a "fable," "reading fables," or traveling in the world as in a book, the self progresses in knowing neither the world nor itself. At first Descartes explains his decision "to travel, to see

---

adherence to the "lieux communs" of the *modernes*, even as "the modernist ideology was flowering into rationalism." See Gilbert Gadoffre, "Le *Discours de la Méthode* et la Querelle des Anciens," in *Modern Miscellany: Presented to Eugène Vinaver*, ed. T. E. Lawrenson, F. E. Stucliffe, and G. F. A. Gadoffre (Manchester: University of Manchester Press, 1969), pp. 81, 83.

17. Cf. John D. Lyons' similar interpretation of these passages in "Subjectivity and Imitation in the *Discours de la Méthode*," *Neophilologus* 66 (1982): 514.

courts and armies, to frequent people of different humors and conditions, to gather different experiences, and to test myself in the encounters which fortune proposed to me" ("à voyager, à voir des cours et des armées, à fréquenter des gens de diverses humeurs et conditions, à recueillir diverses expériences, à m'éprouver moi-même dans les rencontres que la fortune me proposait") by contrasting what he would observe in the eventful "book of the world" to the private and, for that reason, inconsequential "speculations" artificially produced by a "man of letters":

> Car il me semblait que je pourrais rencontrer beaucoup plus de vérité, dans les raisonnements que chacun fait touchant les affaires qui lui importent, et dont l'événement le doit punir bientôt après, s'il a mal jugé, que dans ceux qui fait un homme de lettres dans son cabinet, touchant des spéculations qui ne produisent aucun effect, et qui ne lui sont d'autre conséquence, sinon que peut-être il en tirera d'autant plus de vanité qu'elles seront plus éloignées du sens commun, à cause qu'il aura dû employer d'autant plus d'esprit et d'artifice à tâcher de les rendre vraisemblables.[18]

> For it seemed to me that I could encounter much more truth in the reasonings that each person makes concerning the matters which are important to him, and for whose coming to pass, if he has judged badly, he will have to pay soon after, than those made by a man of letters in his study concerning speculations which produce no effect, and which will bear no other consequences for him, except, perhaps, that he will derive as much vanity from them as they are removed from common sense, since he will have had to use that much more artifice in order to render them probable [or, make them seem true].

Here Descartes clearly distinguishes between practical "reasonings," whose validity or fraudulence will be proven quickly by empirical experience (their "coming to pass"), and purely discursive "speculations," whose apparent truth is the contrived effect of the "artifice" that instead isolates them from the world. Yet even this positive contrast between "reasonings" of the individual ("chacun") which are put to the test by experience and a "man of letters" spinning "vraisemblance" merely to gratify himself, is bound by the metaphor of the world as book to be short-lived. *Ending* on a note of expectancy whose formulation echoes exactly the *beginning* of

18. *OP,* 1:577.

the story of his studies—"et j'avais toujours *un extrême désir d'apprendre* à distinguer le vrai d'avec le faux, pour voir clair en mes actions, et marcher avec assurance en cette vie"[19] (and I always *had an extreme desire to learn* to distinguish true from false, so as to see the way of my actions clearly and to go with certainty in this life)—Descartes' narrative of his experience of "the book of the world" does not proceed to offer a more detailed inventory of the many chapters (courts, armies, diverse peoples and conditions, etc.) analogous to the different disciplines of his "whole course of study," which this other course of study entailed. Just as the metaphor of travel as reading "the book of the world" offered a condensed version of the comparison of reading ancient texts and contemporary travel, and just as the shared message of that comparison was that either activity increased one's ignorance of one's own land, or, to complete the comparison, one's self, there is not much to say about "the book of the world" as "fable"—"je n'y trouvais guère de quoi m'assurer" (I found hardly anything in it to assure me)—except that it taught Descartes not to take particular customs for truth, much as reading had taught him at La Flèche.[20] Descartes concludes Part One with what appears to be the close of his narrative discourse:

> mais après que j'eus employé quelques années à étudier ainsi dans le livre du monde, je pris un jour résolution d'étudier aussi en moi-

---

19. Ibid. (my emphasis). Cf. *OP*, 1:571 (my emphasis): "J'ai été nourri aux lettres dès mon enfance, et parce qu'on me persuadait que, par leur moyen, on pouvait acquérir une connaissance claire et assurée de tout ce qui est utile à la vie, *j'avais un extrême désir de les apprendre*" (I have been raised on letters since my childhood and because I was persuaded that by means of them one could acquire a clear and certain knowledge of all that is useful in life, *I had an extreme desire to learn them*).

20. *OP*, 1:578: "En sorte que le plus grand profit que j'en retirais était que, voyant plusieurs choses qui, bien qu'elles nous semblent fort extravagantes et ridicules, ne laissent pas d'être communément reçues et approuvées par d'autres grands peuples, j'apprenais à ne rien croire trop fermement de ce qui ne m'avait été persuadé que par l'exemple et par la coutume, et ainsi je me délivrais peu à peu de beaucoup d'erreurs, qui peuvent offusquer notre lumière naturelle, et nous rendre moins capables d'entendre raison" (Thus the greatest profit that I derived from my travels was that, seeing many things which, although they seem to us highly extravagant and ridiculous, are nonetheless commonly accepted and approved of by other great peoples, I learned not to believe anything too firmly that I had only been persuaded to believe by example and by custom, and thus I freed myself little by little from many errors which can darken our natural light and render us less capable of understanding reason).

même. . . . Ce qui me réussit beaucoup mieux, ce me semble, que si je ne me fusse jamais éloigné, ni de mon pays, ni de mes livres.[21]

but after I had spent several years studying in this way in the book of the world and trying to acquire some experience, I took the resolution one day to study in myself as well. . . . This seems to have been more successful than if I had never left either my country or my books.

This is the celebrated stopping point in Descartes' "fable," probably the most celebrated in the story of Western philosophy as well. Narrated at the beginning of Part Two, Descartes' single day of reflection in a stove-heated room in an unknown corner of Germany has been canonized in its spiritual and material aspects like the circumstances of a saint's vision, the pagan Augustine's hearing of voices, or the adult Marcel's consumption of a *madeleine*. Indeed, in its very modality, as we shall see, this conversion to philosophy lies precisely between the turn from the sensory world through scripture, and to a scripted world through the senses, that mark the origin of autobiography in Augustine's and Proust's confessional texts, the stories of their conversions to religion and fiction.

Yet toward the conclusion of Part Three we learn that Descartes' "resolution" is an inconclusive rest stop, directly followed by a return to the book of the world. Furthermore, this world is itself now recognized as a play of mere appearances, or fictive *vraisemblance*, the place of theatrical representations, or "comédies." After formulating his moral "maxims" in Part Three, Descartes returns to the now familiar narrative pattern of chronological and thematic regression, turning back to the stopping point in Germany as an interruption succeeded by no further scientific or philosophical development. Its direct effect, instead, is to make him seek "conversation" with others in travel, the already discredited book of the world:

je jugeai que, pour tout le reste de mes opinions, je pouvais librement entreprendre de m'en défaire. Et d'autant que j'espérai en pouvoir mieux venir à bout, en conversant avec les hommes, qu'en demeurant plus longtemps renfermé dans le poêle où j'avais eu toutes ces pensées, l'hiver n'était pas encore bien achevé que je me remis à voyager. Et en toutes les neuf années suivantes, je ne fis autre chose que rouler

21. Ibid.

ça et là dans le monde, tâchant d'y être spectateur plutôt qu'acteur en toutes les comédies qui s'y jouent.[22]

I judged that, as regarded the rest of my opinions, I could undertake freely to rid myself of them. And since I expected to better be able to arrive at this goal by conversing with men rather than remaining enclosed in the stove-heated room where I had had all these thoughts, the winter was not yet over when I set out again to travel. And in all the nine years following I did nothing but circulate here and there in the world, trying to be a spectator rather than an actor in all the comedies that are played out there.

From the room which Descartes is said to have "entered as a soldier and left as a philosopher"[23] on November 10, 1619, the "philosopher" returns to the discursive world of error, the world of conversation and theater, of representational appearances. The narrative discourse surrounding the "method" is interrupted by a single day in an enclosed space where, deprived of "conversation" with others—"trouvant aucune conversation qui me divertît" (finding no conversation which diverted me)—Descartes "had the leisure to converse with [his] own thoughts": "j'avais tout loisir de m'entretenir de mes pensées."[24] But if Descartes' "design" of "talking about" method is composed in some measure of the contextualizing autobiographical discourse of a "fable" narrated "as in a *tableau*"—the life of "conversation" in the world or, as Descartes equates the two, with books— we may ask what discourse would be, and what would be method, when that context is severed: when neither the books of study nor the book of the world is a partner in discourse. At this moment what Descartes thinks, rather than reads in conversation with books or the world, is a thought opposed to conversation as such.

If what we may call *the method of Descartes' discourse* is the undermining of the discursivity of discourse, its structural and literary foreclosure through the foreshortening of narrative perspective and semantically conflating use of metaphor, then the way in which Descartes recounts his "conversation with [his] own thoughts" must bear no resemblance to the narrative and representational discourse which he, as autobiographical

22. Ibid., pp. 598–99.
23. Gilson, *Discours*, p. 156; cf. Adrien Baillet, *La vie de Monsieur Des Cartes*, 2 vols., reprint (New York: Garland, 1987) 1:51.
24. *OP*, 1:579.

writer, has already led us to distrust, the discourse from which we have been taught to expect nothing. Such discourse identifies conversing as the way of the world, its "philosophies" no less than its "comedies," a way which only produces the illusion of change by producing further discourse. Descartes' autobiographical discourse cancels the premises of anticipation and interpretive attention which make narrative and representation, fable and tableau, hermeneutically effective. Its method of presentation enforces, rather than suspends, our disbelief: we learn immediately that we will learn no more from reading his "story" than he learned from its actual experience. No less than Descartes' "suppos[ition]" of an "evil genius" intending to deceive him—the "design" announced at the close of the First Meditation[25]—the autobiographical discourse of Descartes' *Discours* compels us to be skeptical of the "design" of "talking about" method, and yet it does this precisely by way of that "design." The cognitive impasses that Descartes' "fable" reiterates, instructing us that the "design" of contextualizing, of "talking about" method will never define method, achieve their own representation in the physical impasse of the stove-heated room. In the autobiographically delimited time and physically enclosed space of a self-enclosed conversation, a discoursing with thoughts encountered neither in books nor in the book of the world, another kind of design comes to light.

25. *OP,* 2:412 (my emphasis): "Je supposerai donc qu'il y a, non point un vrai Dieu, qui est la souveraine source de vérité, mais un certain mauvais génie, non moins rusé et trompeur que puissant, qui a employé toute son industrie à me tromper. . . . Mais ce *dessein* est pénible et laborieux, et une certaine paresse m'entraîne insensiblement dans le train de ma vie ordinaire" (I will suppose then that there is not a true God, who is the sovereign source of truth, but an evil genius, as cunning and deceptive as he is powerful, who used all his industry to deceive me. . . . But this *design* is painful and laborious, and a certain laziness draws me insensibly into the course of my ordinary life).

3 The "Discourse" of Thinking:
  Architectural Design

___

Taking place in physical isolation at a temporally isolated moment within the autobiographical narrative of the *Discours,* the moment of Descartes' thinking also marks the point in this specifically discursive work when representational discourse will give way to the formulation of universal rules and maxims. In both mimetic and diegetic terms—the very terms whose conventional methodological distinction is disqualified by Descartes' narration of a "fable" "as in a tableau"—Descartes' thinking occurs as an anomaly. It takes neither literary nor experiential mimetic form; nor is it method. If it is discourse, it is also the nondiscursive, a discourse of one. What Descartes *thinks* takes the image of what an architect *does.* Alone in his room, "one of [his] first thoughts" is of the "buildings" undertaken by an architect working alone:

> je demeurais tout le jour enfermé seul dans un poêle, où j'avais tout loisir de m'entretenir de mes pensées. Entre lesquelles, l'une des premières fut que je m'avisai de considérer que souvent il n'y a pas tant de perfection dans les ouvrages composés de plusieurs pièces, et faits de la main de divers maîtres, qu'en ceux auxquels un seul a travaillé. Ainsi voit-on que les bâtiments qu'un seul architecte a entrepris et achevés ont coutume d'être plus beaux et mieux ordonnés que ceux que plusieurs ont tâché de raccommoder, en faisant servir de vieilles murailles qui avaient été bâties à d'autres fins. Ainsi ces anciennes cités, qui, n'ayant été au commencement que des bourgades, sont devenues, par succession de temps, de grandes villes, sont ordinairement si mal compassées, au prix de ces places régulières qu'un ingénieur trace à sa fantaisie dans une plaine.[1]

I remained all day enclosed in a stove-heated room, where I had

1. *OP,* 1:579.

the leisure to converse with my own thoughts. Among these, one of the first was to counsel myself to consider that there is often not as much perfection in works composed of several pieces, and made by the hands of several masters, as there is in those on which a single master has worked. Thus one sees that buildings which a single architect has undertaken and completed are usually more beautiful and better ordered than those which several architects have attempted to rework, using old walls that had been built for other ends. Thus these ancient cities, which, having only been large villages, became great cities with the passage of time, are normally so poorly proportioned,[2] compared with the well-ordered towns and public squares[3] that an engineer traces on a vacant plain according to his free imaginings [or, fancy].[4]

The image of a single architect drawing a comprehensive plan on a "vacant plain" is the "thought" Descartes opposes both to travel and to reading, the terms of the pseudo-opposition between the figurative book of the world and literal book learning. As compared by Descartes in Part One,[5] traveling and reading are both kinds of "conversation;" refigured in

2. "Compassées" is glossed as "proportionées" in Gilson's commentary; see Gilson, *Discours*, pp. 161–62.

3. Descartes' use of "places" here is usually glossed as "towns" or "cities" ("villes," see Alquié, *OP,* 1:579n4). Gilson notes that, while Descartes would have seen few if any of the planned cities built in the early seventeenth century (such as Charleville) at the time he wrote the *Discours*, "this conception of the modern city was too generalized to have been unknown to Descartes." Yet Gilson also maintains the theoretical and historical significance of understanding Descartes' "places" literally, noting helpfully that the *"places publiques* (the Place Royale, Place Dauphine, etc.)" of Descartes' day "were inspired by the same ideal as the cities" (see Gilson, *Discours*, p. 162).

4. In translating the important phrase *à sa fantaisie* I follow Gilson, who interprets it to mean in the manner of imagination unencumbered by any material constraints: "Without any accident of terrain or any already existing construction imposing any constraint on his imagination" (ibid., p. 163). While "fancy" translates "fantaisie," its secondary status to imagination in English since Coleridge's *Biographia* runs counter to the strong sense of *imagination arbitrarily free to reason* conveyed by "fantaisie" in Descartes and, as discussed further on, other seventeenth-century French "rationalists," including the Port Royal grammarians in their description of sign formation, and "modern" theorists of the beautiful, such as Claude Perrault. See chapter 9 and Epilogue below.

5. See chap. 2, n.12.

the terms of the architectural imagery of Part Two, they would be "works composed of several pieces, and made by the hands of several masters." Descartes' "design," as he explained it to Mersenne, was not "to teach" *la méthode* but to discourse on it, "to talk about it," a proposition he restates in Part One: "ainsi mon dessein n'est pas d'enseigner ici la méthode que chacun doit suivre pour bien conduire sa raison, mais seulement de faire voir en quelle sorte j'ai tâché de conduire la mienne" (thus my design here is not to teach the method that everyone must follow in order to conduct his reason correctly, but only to show [literally, make visible: *faire voir*] how I have tried to conduct my own).[6] Here "talking" takes the form of an autobiographical demonstration which, though private in scope, would show itself as self-evident, requiring that it be neither "taught" nor "imitated" to be transmitted.[7] Such a direction of reason toward its own self-evidence would necessarily shun its own imitation in that it understands *itself* to be modeled on a *non*-imitative act. In the "Réponses" to the "Objections" published in the second edition of the *Méditations,* Descartes later summarizes his efforts to find the "solid ground" on which he posed "the foundations" of his philosophy ("une terre ferme sur laquelle j'ai posé les fondements de ma philosophie"), as the attempt made throughout his writings to imitate architects: "je tâchais partout d'imiter les architectes."[8]

After relating his "thought" of an architect drawing freely, Descartes further redescribes his "design." Denying that he ever aimed in writing at

---

6. *OP,* 1:571.

7. Cf. *OP,* 1:582: "Que si, mon ouvrage m'ayant assez plu, je vous en fais voir ici le modèle, ce n'est pas, pour cela, que je veuille conseiller à personne de l'imiter" (If, my work having sufficiently pleased me, I show you the model of it, it is not for that reason that I wish to counsel anyone to imitate it). Judovitz interprets Descartes' disassociation of the *Discours* from teaching and imitation as "a falling back on the authority of sincerity": "rather than intending the method for instructional purposes, Descartes now presents it solely as his private education or exercise" (*Subjectivity and Representation,* pp. 130–31). The motives of sincerity and privacy are not, I think, adequate for understanding what is involved for Descartes in the nonimitative act of "faire voir," or "drawing on an empty plain," or, as we shall see, "method." All these Descartes opposes to the representational and persuasive book learning from which his "essai" takes distance as it attempts to "build on a foundation that is entirely [his] own" (*OP,* 1:582; see the discussion of this passage immediately following). That building is not a private structure but rather (as analyzed in chapter 7) the universal method enacted in the *cogito.*

8. *OP,* 2:1044–45. Cf. Payot, *Le philosophe,* p. 116: "Descartes imitates architects precisely in that, self-producing [*auto-géniteurs*], architects imitate nothing."

any kind of public reformation, and declaring he would not have published the *Discours* ("cet essai") if he thought his intention could be so
construed, he asserts the selfhood essential to his efforts in specifically nondiscursive terms. To the desire to transform the public realm through published discourse he opposes his own "design" in the *Discours,* now defined
as an attempt "to build" upon himself alone: "jamais mon dessein ne s'est
étendu plus avant que de tâcher à réformer mes propres pensées, et de bâtir
dans un fonds qui est tout à moi"[9] (my design never extended further than
the attempt to reform my own thoughts, and to build upon a foundation
that is entirely my own).

Such a "foundation" removed from all public conversation would be *la
méthode.* Yet the narrative "design" in which method is contained, the contextual sequence of private reformation and "build[ing]," requires *discours.*
Unlike an imagined architect designing "places regulières" without any
external or historical encumbrance whatsoever, Descartes' discoursing on
or "talking about" method is both historical and projected forward, both
representational and intentional. Descartes' stated "design" (*dessein*), his
intention or motive, is thus not the "design" (*dessin*), outline, or ground
plan the architect draws "à sa fantaisie."[10] Yet these two kinds of "design"
require each other. Viewed in terms of the "discourse" which includes
them both, Descartes' "design"—by which I mean neither term alone but
rather his use of and reliance on the two terms individually—takes place in
the exchange between *dessein* and *dessin,* or discourse and architectonics,
without which there would be no "method."

While Descartes commonly uses *dessein* in the *Discours* and elsewhere

9. *OP,* 1:582.
10. Etymologically, the two words, of course, are one: *dessein* and *dessin* share a common source, the Italian *disegno,* and were variants of each other until the eighteenth
century. The verbal forms, *desseigner* and *dessigner,* used into the fifteenth century,
reflect the alteration by the Italian *disegnare* of the Latin *designare.* The accident of
differently spelled verbal forms seems to have been the basis for the separate formations of *dessein* and *dessin,* whose distinction came to mean the difference beween a
mental and a physical plan (on the single etymology of the two words, see Wartburg's
Französiches Etymologisches Wörterbuch). This history of the lexical distinction between
discursive and linear intentionality sheds an ironic light on a contemporary French
Anglicism: the increasingly frequent use of the word *design* (already standard in Italian)
to fill the gap left by the conceptual and verbal split between a subjective purpose and a
purposeful object, between temporal intention and spatial fabrication, in graphic and
industrial art as well as everyday discourse.

when stating his speculative plan or intention, he first uses *dessin,* an architect's plan, when, after presenting the four rules of procedure, he describes what one must do "to rebuild a house" in addition to "having carefully traced its ground plan (*dessin*).[11] In this first paragraph of Part Three—as we shall see later on in chapter 7—Descartes develops and significantly alters the image of the act of architectural drawing he had "thought" of in his stove-heated room.

To say that Descartes "thought" of an "image" is already partially, if necessarily misleading. For it is precisely not a drawing per se but the act of freely drawing an architectonic shape that Descartes, in "conversation with [his own] thoughts," thinks. This hybrid "thought" of the act of nonfigural delineation, this image without particular mimetic characteristics, may indeed be the only adequate transcription of a conversation with thoughts unrelated to the world. Still discursive in part, such a conversation would not be pure thinking—that is, thinking independent of any object, the activity Descartes identified with the intransitive verbal form *cogito* (and which, ever since Descartes, we have most identified with him)—but, rather, as Descartes writes, it would be a "reform[ation]" of his "own thoughts," their reshaping. When Descartes fully objectifies the act of free, imaginative drawing in the image of the accomplished plan (*dessin*), his "design" (*dessein*) of reshaping his thoughts has already begun. This same process of self-reformation will ultimately include his description of the *cogito* in Part Four. But before the relation between the derivation of Cartesian epistemology and the transformation of the act of drawing into a plan can be described, the place of Descartes' architectonic "thought" in his discursive "design" must be more carefully defined.

Situated in the autobiographical *discours* at its complex "turning point" —just before the formulation of the four rules, after which Descartes' "fable," instead of proceeding forward on a different path, returns inexplicably to the way of the world—the act of architectural drawing that Descartes thinks of in solitude is the image of a nonconversational and nonrepresentational design. Produced within a discursive context, it is the "thought" of a nondiscursive method: a synchronic, rather than his-

---

11. *OP,* 1:591: "Et enfin . . . ce n'est pas assez, avant de commencer à rebâtir le logis où on demeure . . . d'en avoir soigneusement tracé le dessin" (And finally . . . it is not enough before beginning to rebuild the house where one resides . . . to have carefully drawn the design).

torically reworked drawing, but still not a tableau; a self-defining whole, rather than piecemeal representation, but, nonetheless, not a fable. Autonomous, self-circumscribing architectonic design is the counterdesign to "talking about" in the *Discours de la méthode*. Not a "tableau," "story," "fable," or any other form of representation, it is a structure in which conception is instead identical with manifestation.[12] That is to say, the identity of the structure does not preexist, but comes into existence with its presentation.

The act of architectural drawing that Descartes describes is the outlining of a form that was not one before. That form would combine reason ("qu'un ingénieur") with imaginative freedom ("trace à sa fantaisie"). It is not only new to the world, but intervenes in a space where nothing was, on a surface ("dans une plaine") where nothing else is. The order of its "places regulières" is the image of imagination engineering a method that is free of historical and intellectual as well as physical constraints. Yet, what can it mean to have "thought" such an image in one's own mind, rather than to have read, seen, or heard it elsewhere, in the course of conversation, which is to say, already *as* representation? To pose this question is to ask, in epistemological and literary terms, not only what Descartes "did" in a stove-heated room—what critical act he effected—but also why the "thought" of architectonic structure plays a formative role in the founding of modern discursive philosophy. It is to ask again, in another form, what the title of Descartes' "design" means; to pose anew the question, what is the "discours *de* la méthode"?

12. Cf. by contrast Jacques Lefebvre's *critique* of the "illusion of transparency" in space which views "design" as the fusion of mental intention and spatial plan, a pure embodiment of thought: "Here space appears as luminous, as intelligible, as giving action free rein. What happens in space lends a miraculous quality to thought, which becomes incarnate by means of a *design* (in both senses of the word). The design serves as a mediator—itself of great fidelity—between mental activity (invention) and social activity (realization); and it is deployed in space" (*The Production of Space*, trans. Donald Nicholson-Smith [Oxford: Basil Blackwell, 1991], pp. 27–28). With Lefebvre the present analysis stresses that such an apparent transparency of thought in "design" requires a productive context; in the case of Descartes, that context is "discourse," and, as we shall see later, the empirical subject in space and time.

4 The Things a Thinking Thing Thinks

It has been suggested that Descartes includes "imagining" under the self-defining activity of "thinking" whenever imagination includes self-reflective thought.[1] The point of reference for this argument is Descartes' central and strikingly problematic definition in the Second Meditation of what a "thinking thing," i.e., an "I," is: "Mais qu'est-ce donc que je suis? Une chose qui pense. Qu'est-ce qu'une chose qui pense? C'est-à-dire une chose qui doute, qui conçoit, qui affirme, qui nie, qui veut, qui ne veut pas, qui imagine aussi, et qui sent"[2] (What am I then? A thing which thinks. What is that? A thing which doubts, understands, affirms, denies, wills, is unwilling, and also imagines and feels). While the first of these activities may be ascribed more or less easily to thinking, the last require the recognition that thinking is their "common denominator."[3] Another way of putting this, however, would be to recall that the irreducible denominator of "thinking" is "thing." Thinking, in other words, is never thought of as disembodied (as it will be in Hegel) in Descartes.[4]

A "thinking thing" thinks embodied thoughts, even when what it thinks is the negation of bodily limits, as in Descartes' contested deduc-

---

1. John Cottingham, "Descartes on Thought," *Philosophical Quarterly* 28 (1978): 208–14.

2. *OP,* 2:420–21.

3. Cottingham, "Descartes on Thought," p. 214. Cottingham defines that "common denominator" as follows: "the reflective awareness of the mind that it is being presented with a datum of some kind: this alone is what qualifies as a *cogitatio* proper" (p. 213).

4. Cottingham makes this important point, albeit, I think, redundantly, by distinguishing a (hypothetical) "pure *res cogitans*" from a bodily one: "A human body is not a pure *res cogitans,* he is a *res cogitans* mysteriously united with a body" (ibid.).

tion of "the only idea" of which the self ("moi-même") is not "the cause," God.[5] Although Descartes insists that the idea of God is *not* the product of negation, it is his "imagination" that he negates in so insisting: "et je ne me dois pas imaginer que je ne conçois pas l'infini par une véritable idée, mais seulement par la négation de ce qui est fini, de même que je comprends le repos et les ténèbres par la négation du mouvement et de la lumière" (and I must not imagine to myself that I don't conceive the infinite by way of a true idea, but only by way of the negation of what is finite, just as I understand rest and shadows by the negation of movement and light).[6] Descartes' argument that the idea of an infinite and perfect being could not have its origin "in himself" ("en moi"), a "finite substance," and, thus, *as origin of this idea,* God must exist, is finally an argument by negation (of finite experience) analogous to the argument of the *cogito,* except that the vector of doubt, instead of pointing "inside" to identify its origin in a "thinking thing," points "outside" it: "car il est de la nature de l'infini, que ma nature, qui est finie et bornée, ne le puisse comprendre"[7] (for it is of the nature of the infinite, that my nature, which is finite and limited, cannot understand it).

Interested to argue against an earlier concept of divine ideas that he found as detrimental to religious belief as to scientific practice, Descartes can only confirm the existence of God and affirm his identity as "a thinking thing" by insisting that, at least in part, both the idea of God and of sensory objects "come from outside" him ("viennent de dehors").[8] Since

5. Third Meditation ("Of God; that he exists"); see esp. *OP,* 2:441–54. See also Gassendi's discussion of this argument in his "Objections" to the Third Meditation in *OP,* 2:739–47.

6. *OP,* 2:445.

7. Ibid., pp. 419, 445, 447.

8. Ibid., p. 435. The view—traditional since the British empiricists—that Descartes understood "ideas" as innate simplifies Descartes' inconsistent use of a term whose "equivocation" of reference is best demonstrated, according to Descartes, by the very problem of the origin of the idea of God; see the "Préface de l'Auteur au Lecteur" of the *Méditations* in which Descartes defends his notion of the "idea" ("of a thing more perfect than me") as both within him and indicative of that thing's (i.e., God's) real existence: "dans ce mot d'*idée* il y a ici de l'équivoque: car, ou il peut être pris matériellement pour une opération de mon entendement, et en ce sens on ne peut pas dire qu'elle soit plus parfaite que moi; ou il peut être pris objectivement pour la chose qui est représentée par cette opération, laquelle, quoiqu'on ne suppose point qu'elle existe

externality makes the dialectic of doubt possible in one case (I may be dreaming or otherwise imagining a *false* external world based on a real one[9]) and, according to Descartes, impossible in the other (it does not matter whether I am awake or dreaming: two plus three will always add up to five;[10] just as the three angles of a triangle will always equal two right angles even if no triangle exists in the world, so, too, must the perfect being, God, exist[11]), the rationale for radical empirical skepticism is the same as for religious belief. Externality which can be perceived, and so *may*

---

hors de mon entendement, peut néanmoins être plus parfaite que moi. . . . or, dans la suite de ce traité je ferai voir plus amplement comment, de cela seulement que j'ai en moi l'idée d'une chose plus parfaite que moi, il s'ensuit que cette chose existe véritablement" (in the word *idea* there is an equivocation here, for it can be taken materially for an operation of my understanding, and in this sense one cannot say it is more perfect than me; or it can be taken objectively for the thing which is represented by this operation, which, even if one does not suppose that it exists outside my understanding, can nonetheless be more perfect than me. . . . now in what follows in this treatise I will show more fully how, from the sole fact that I have in me the idea of a thing more perfect than me, it follows that this thing does truly exist) (*OP,* 2:391 [emphasis in text]).

On the pervasive "ambiguity" of the term "idea" in Descartes, "which means sometimes an act and sometimes its object," "a mental image, the exercise of a concept or the occurrence of an experience," see Anthony Kenny, "Descartes on Ideas," in *Descartes: A Collection of Critical Essays,* ed. Willis Doney (Notre Dame, Ind.: University of Notre Dame Press, 1968), pp. 249, 237. See also Stephen Gaukroger, "Descartes and the Doctrine of Ideas," in Antoine Arnauld, *On True and False Ideas,* Introduction and translation by Stephen Gaukroger (Manchester: University of Manchester Press, 1990), pp. 22–26, which cites Descartes' proposition in *Le monde,* chap. 1, that the momentary combination of sense perception and intellect in an idea could be compared, on the model of language, to a perceived "sign" of "nature": "why could nature not also have established some sign, which would make us have the sensation of light, even if the sign contained nothing in itself which is similar to the sensation?" (p. 24). According to Gaukroger, our ability to read such signs would be tantamount to "innate ideas," but these ideas must be understood to be formed in "reciprocity" with sensory experience (p. 25). Such an understanding of ideas as the ability to read would indeed provide for the equivocal or ambiguous situation in which what is "innate" would also be dependent on external perception. Yet precisely, and perhaps only, such an impure understanding of "ideas" remains irreducible to the nonintellectual models of causal and imaged relationships between internal and external experience which Descartes worked to deny.

9. First Meditation, *OP,* 2:406–8; cf. Part Four, *Discours, OP,* 1:607.

10. First Meditation, *OP,* 2:408.

11. Part Four, *Discours, OP,* 1:608.

be a delusion, shares the same deductive status as externality which cannot be perceived, and so—by Descartes' rejection of syllogistic reasoning[12] (I

12. Like Kant later, Descartes criticized syllogistic logic, which he, too, called dialectics. While their resulting epistemological theories could hardly have been more different—Kant's "Copernican turn" in philosophy pronouncing the necessity and a priori schematization of the sensory basis of knowledge Descartes rejected—both rejected syllogisms as illusory (Kant) or purely rhetorical (Descartes) forms of knowledge. See, in particular, Rule X of the *Regulae,* in which Descartes describes the use of syllogism, by which a mere form of reasoning confirms a truth one knew to begin with, as reason gone "on vacation": "dialecticiens . . . prétendent gouverner la raison humaine en lui prescrivant certaines formes d'argumentation, qui concluent avec une telle nécessité que la raison qui s'y confie a beau se dispenser, se mettant en quelque sorte en vacances, de considérer d'une manière évidente et attentive l'inférence elle-même, elle peut aboutir tout de même à une conclusion certaine par la seule vertu de la forme. . . . C'est pourquoi, ayant ici pour principal souci d'éviter que notre raison ne reste en chômage le temps que nous recherchons la vérité sur quelque sujet, nous rejetons ces trop fameuses formes d'argumentation comme contraire à notre intention" (*OP,* 1:128–29) (dialections pretend to govern human reason by prescribing to it certain forms of argumentation which conclude with such necessity that reason, going in a way on vacation, may well believe it can dispense with considering the inference in an attentive and clear manner, and arrive in any event at a certain conclusion by virtue of the form alone. . . . This is why, our main preoccupation being to avoid that our reason rest unemployed during the time we search for the truth about some subject, we reject these too famous forms of argumentation as contrary to our intention).

It should be noted, however, that the form of syllogism, if "useless" philosophically, is close literarily to Descartes' narrative strategy in the *Discours.* Descartes' condemnation of syllogism sheds critical light on his own autobiographical discourse while making the case *made in the context of that discourse* for the inauguration of a new method in philosophy. For, like a "fable" represented as in a *tableau,* syllogism displays a foregone conclusion, and for this very reason, Descartes determines, belongs more properly to rhetoric than to philosophy: "les dialecticiens ne peuvent construire selon les règles un seul syllogisme dont la conclusion soit vraie . . . s'ils ne connaissent pas à l'avance cette même vérité qu'ils y déduisent. . . . d'où il ressort . . . que la dialectique telle qu'on l'entend communément est parfaitement inutile à ceux qui désirent explorer la vérité des choses, et qu'elle ne peut servir . . . qu'à exposer plus facilement aux autres des raisonnments déjà connus; et que, pour cette raison, il faut la transférer de la philosophie à la rhétorique" (ibid., 1:129–30) (according to the rules, dialecticians cannot construct a single syllogism whose conclusion would be true . . . if they didn't know in advance the very same truth that is thus deduced. . . . thus it is that . . . dialectic, as one commonly understands it, is perfectly useless to those who wish to explore the truth of things, and that it can only serve . . . to display more easily to others already known reasonings; and that, for this reason, it must be transferred from philosophy to rhetoric). On Descartes' rejection of the syllogistic method

perceive reality; I perceive a man walking down the street; this man is really a man, and not a dummy moved by springs[13]) — cannot be a delusion. The ideas we have of the real world may be true, clear, and distinct, or they may be chimeras, dreams, empty beliefs to which we attribute a body, "puisque imaginer n'est autre chose que contempler la figure ou l'image d'une chose corporelle"[14] (since to imagine is nothing other than to contemplate the figure or the image of a bodily thing). But ideas that are not mental representations of bodily things must either be purely rational and innate (i.e., mathematical ideas) or derive from an indubitable external source (i.e., a perfect being). Due to their "foreign" source and independence from visual imagination, the idea of God may be compared with ideas of things: like "those ideas . . . of the kind that I call foreign [étrangères], and which come from outside, . . . like . . . this idea of heat [which] is produced in me by a thing different from me, . . . this foreign thing [which] . . . sends and imprints in me its likeness," so, too, God "put this idea [of God] in me, so that it would be like the mark of the craftsman imprinted on his work."[15]

What is remarkable in Descartes' description of the source of the idea of the infinite is not only that, deduced as being necessarily "outside" him, it would be analogous to a physical source of sensation—God is to the idea of the infinite as fire is to warmth[16]—but that God is thereby inevitably

---

of proof, cf. O. Hamlein, *Le système de Descartes* (Paris: Félix Alcan, 1921), pp. 57–59; Beck, *Method of Descartes*, pp. 102–7; Jean-Louis Allard, *Le mathématisme de Descartes* (Ottawa: Editions de l'Université d'Ottawa, 1963), pp. 38–41; Daniel Garber, "Science and Certainty in Descartes," in Hooker, *Critical and Interpretive Essays*, pp. 114–51; Cottingham, *Descartes*, p. 6; and M. E. W. Beth, "Le savoir déductif dans la pensée cartésienne," in *Descartes: Cahiers de Royaumont. Philosophie No. II* (London: Garland, 1987), pp. 141–65.

13. Second Meditation, *OP*, 2:427.

14. Ibid., p. 420.

15. *OP*, 2:435: "ces idées sont du genre de celles que j'appelle étrangères, et qui viennent de dehors, . . . comme . . . ce sentiment ou bien cette idée de la chaleur est produite en moi par une chose différente de moi, . . . cette chose étrangère envoie et imprime en moi sa ressemblance." Ibid., p. 453: "on ne doit pas trouver étrange que Dieu, en me créant, ait mis en moi cette idée [d'un être souverainement parfait] pour être la marque de l'ouvrier empreinte sur son ouvrage."

16. *OP*, 2:439: "l'idée de la chaleur, ou de la pierre, ne peut pas être en moi, si elle n'y a été mise par quelque cause, qui contienne en soi pour le moins autant de réalité, que j'en conçois dans la chaleur ou dans la pierre" (the idea of heat, or of a stone, cannot be in me, if it was not put there by some cause, which contains in itself at least as much reality, as I conceive in heat or in a stone).

substantialized. For "ideas" themselves, Descartes states, "are like images": "les idées étant comme des images, il n'y en peut avoir aucune qui ne nous semble représenter quelque chose"[17] (ideas, being like images, there can be no idea which does not seem to represent to us something). Thus, in a back-and-forth movement of induction and deduction (or synthesis and analysis) similar to the projection forward and doubling back of an auto-biographical narrative conducted "as in a tableau," God must exist, on the one hand, as the cause of the "idea" of God in Descartes, and on the other, as the effect of that idea as "image," as the thing it represents. By this characteristically Cartesian description, thinking and imaging are indeed brought together: God is a craftsman who "produced [Descartes] in his image," and that produced "likeness . . . contains within it the idea of God."[18] Furthermore, for being infinite, God is not an abstract "being": "being" God in Descartes means being, like Descartes, a "substance," even if an infinite one.

The grotesque image of God as "an infinite substance"[19] could only have been the "idea" of Descartes, much like the image of an archi-

17. OP, 2:443. As will be discussed further, the nature of mental "representation" in Descartes is anything but obvious, given the ability of "ideas" to "represent" "things" that are or are not present, to be "like images" but not like actual pictures, and to extend to sensory as well as abstract objects. On the complex involvement of "ideas" in acts of representation, cf. Kenny, "Descartes on Ideas," p. 236: "[Descartes'] ideas have some of the properties of material pictures, some of the properties of mental images, and some of the properties of concepts. Like material and mental pictures, they are representations which exhibit things. Like mental pictures, and unlike cerebral pictures, they are not made out of any matter. More, they can represent immaterial things (e.g. God) without doing so by representing something material (e.g. a bearded sage)." See also Stephen Gaukroger, "Descartes' Project for a Mathematical Physics," in *Descartes: Philosophy, Mathematics and Physics,* ed. Stephen Gaukroger (Sussex: Harvester, 1992), p. 119: "Ideas are not *simply* acts of the thinking subject. These acts also represent; they are acts with objects."

18. OP, 2:453: "Mais de cela seul que Dieu m'a créé, il est fort croyable qu'il m'a en quelque façon produit à son image et semblance, et que je conçois cette ressemblance (dans laquelle l'idée de Dieu se trouve contenue) par la même faculté par laquelle je me conçois moi-même" (From the fact alone that God created me, it is highly believable that he produced me in some way in his image and appearance, and that I conceive this likeness [in which the idea of God is contained] by the same faculty by which I conceive myself).

19. Ibid., p. 445; on Descartes as "substance" ("a thing or a substance which thinks") see ibid., pp. 449–50.

tect drawing the design of method "à sa fantaisie." Both are thoughts thought as images whose "likeness" ("semblance") can only be detected in the things produced after them: René Descartes, buildings and cities, "places régulières." Descartes represents God, buildings represent architectonic drawing. But that representational relationship is *not* reciprocal: God and architectonic drawings do not represent the substances produced in their images. Thus the bringing together of idea and image in Descartes never achieves a synthesis that would finally accrue to the image. The conjunction of idea and image is instead a kind of embodiment without a specific body (a drawing), a thing without bodily dimensions (an infinite substance), a writing and not a representation. Substance and idea, *res* and *cogitans,* architectonic drawing and thought occur *in terms of one another,* but they are *not identical with one another.* As writing is to intentionality, the architectural design of which Descartes thinks is not the same as his "design": the two are never united iconographically in a formal, representational image. Descartes' pivotal thought occurs in the image of a manifest form, a visible drawing or extension, but it does not manifest mimetic properties: it is not—nor could there be—a picture of method.

Yet it is a manifestation. Nowhere is the thought of method as free, architectonic drawing—the thought that a thinking thing thinks—more manifest in Descartes' writing than in his *Géométrie,* for the *Géométrie* is Descartes' *writing of geometry,* a method of articulating images which reason, freed *by writing,* can think. "The method" of the *Discours* is also the *thinking together* of two kinds of mathematics, geometry and algebra, so that the language of abstract analysis provided by algebra could be used to refer to the corporeal world.

This was Descartes' great innovation as a mathematician.[20] It was also his limitation as a physicist, for Descartes' *Géométrie* creates a writing of bodies in mathematical terms to which the substantial properties of bodies do not conform.[21] Yet Descartes' treatment of bodies as geometrical forms

20. As some have argued, this innovation at once foreshortened Descartes' mathematical vision. See Carl B. Boyer, *The History of the Calculus and Its Conceptual Development* (New York: Dover, 1949), pp. 167–68; Boyer, *A History of Mathematics* (New York: Wiley, 1968), pp. 373, 379; Yvon Belaval, *Leibniz critique de Descartes* (Paris: Gallimard, 1960), pp. 278–368; Jean-Marie Beyssade, *La philosophie première de Descartes: Le temps et la cohérence de la métaphysique* (Paris: Flammarion, 1979), pp. 347–50.

21. Cf. Stephen Gaukroger, "Descartes' Project for a Mathematical Physics," pp. 132–35.

transcribable on the one hand as pure extensions (lines) and on the other as the discursive symbols of algebraic equations (letters) does not only offer, as Descartes stated, a practical demonstration of "method."[22] It also indicates why there must be a "discours de la méthode." While opposed to the discourse of narrative and representation, the *Géométrie* is not drawing alone. In the innovations and limitations of the *Géométrie,* Descartes' architectonic "thought" is stated and his discursive "design" is shown.

22. See chap. 1, n.3.

TWO.   THE DISCOURSE OF METHOD

5 Letters and Lines: Algebra and Geometry in Descartes' *Géométrie*

The *Géométrie* opens with the following proposition concerning mathematical methodology:

> Tous les Problesmes de Geometrie se peuvent facilement reduire a tels termes, qu'il n'est besoin par après que de connoistre la longeur de quelques lignes droites, pour les construire. Et comme toute l'Arithmetique n'est composée, que de quatre ou cinq operations, qui sont l'Addition, la Soustraction, la Multiplication, la Division, & l'Extraction des racines, qu'on peut prendre pour une espece de Division: Ainsi n'at'on autre chose a faire en Geometrie touchant les lignes qu'on cherche, pour les preparer a estre connuës, que leur en adioster d'autres, ou en oster.[1]

Any problem in geometry can easily be reduced to such terms that a knowledge of the lengths of certain straight lines is sufficient for its construction. Just as arithmetic consists of only four or five operations, namely, addition, subtraction, multiplication, division and the extraction of roots, which may be considered a kind of division, so in geometry, to find required lines all one has to do is to add or subtract other lines.

With disarming simplicity, Descartes signals a revolution in the method of solving geometrical and related physical problems. He will arithmetize extended bodies, thereby making them amenable to the mathematical

1. *The Geometry of René Descartes,* facsimile of the first edition (1637), with notes and translation into English from the French and Latin by David Eugene Smith and Marcia L. Latham (Chicago: Open Court, 1925), pp. 2, 3 (original orthography; my translations are based on Smith and Latham with modifications aimed at maintaining original vocabulary).

operations he lists: "addition, subtraction, multiplication, division and the extraction of roots." But in order to do this, he must write geometrical problems concerning the formal disposition of lines as algebraic problems concerning symbolically designated unknowns. Thus Descartes' attempt to create a "mathematical physics" by translating geometry, the art of posing problems representative of the physical world, into mathematical terms, and by configuring mathematical problems in geometrical, graphic form, entailed an interaction, on the basis of method of representation, between the conceptual modes of geometry and algebra.[2]

Precisely this use of one conceptual mode to represent another (and vice versa) has generated a historical controversy as to where Descartes' true theoretical affiliation as a mathematician lay, with geometry or with algebra. The historical view, that in formulating analytic, or coordinate geometry, Descartes was more interested in discrete values and their algebraic designation in equations than in the continuous magnitudes of geometry—that the creation of Cartesian coordinates, by which geometric curves could be written for the first time as equations in two unknowns, betrayed his desire to constitute an ideal mathematics, independent of geometrical form[3]—has been countered by the view that graphic repre-

2. Excellent accounts of Descartes' combination of mathematical domains are provided in Gaukroger, "Descartes' Project for a Mathematical Physics," and Emily Grosholz, "Descartes' Unification of Algebra and Geometry," in *Descartes: Philosophy, Mathematics and Physics,* ed. Stephen Gaukroger (Sussex: Harvester, 1992), pp. 156–68. See esp. Gaukroger, pp. 97–98: "For Galileo, the problem of mathematical physics is that of 'mathematizing' physical problems. His central concern is that of setting up physical problems in such a way that they become amenable to geometrical treatment, and the crucial problem that of showing that the kind of questions one is dealing with in mathematical physics actually are *physical* problems and not simply mathematical idealizations. Descartes, by contrast, wants both to 'mathematize' physics and to 'physicalize' mathematics in one and the same operation. He does not simply want to use mathematics in physics, he wants to *unify* mathematics and physics in certain crucial respects." For a similar view to Gaukroger's, see Jacob Klein, *Greek Mathematical Thought and the Origin of Algebra* (Cambridge, Mass.: MIT Press, 1968, p. 197. See also Pierre Boutroux, *L'imagination et les mathématiques selon Descartes* (Paris: Félix Alcan, 1900), esp. pp. 12, 24; Carl B. Boyer, "Descartes and the Geometrization of Algebra," *American Mathematical Monthly* 66 (1959): 390–93; Boyer, *History of Mathematics,* pp. 371–73; Boyer, *History of Analytic Geometry* (Princeton Junction: Scholar's Bookshelf, 1988, pp. 74–102; and Allard, *Le mathématisme,* esp. pp. 147, 160.

3. For the classic statement of this view, see Léon Brunschvig, "Mathématiques et métaphysique chez Descartes," *Revue de métaphysique et de morale* 34 (1927): esp. pp.

sentation remained the "indispensable auxiliary" to Cartesian algebra, and that, in order to "unify" the two, Descartes in fact "geometrized" algebra, refusing to consider equations abstractly as purely functional relations.[4]

After the publication of the *Géométrie,* Descartes wrote to Mersenne:

> je n'ai résolu de quitter que la Géométrie abstraite, c'est-à-dire la re-
> cherche des questions qui ne servent qu'à exercer l'esprit; et ce afin
> d'avoir d'autant plus de loisir de cultiver une autre sorte de Géomé-
> trie, qui se propose pour questions l'explication des phénomènes de la
> nature. Car . . . toute ma Physique n'est autre chose que Géométrie.[5]

> I have resolved to give up only abstract geometry, that is to say, the
> study of questions which serve only to exercise the mind; and I do
> this for the purpose of having more free time to cultivate another
> kind of geometry, one which takes for its questions the explication of
> phenomena of nature. For . . . all my physics is nothing other than
> geometry.

After developing the "abstract geometry" published with the *Discours,* Descartes will leave mathematics for physics and, most significantly, meta-physics. But, staying for a moment with the mental "exercise" which Des-cartes viewed as an "experiment" in the "method" "talked about" in the *Discours,* one might well ask, borrowing Descartes' formulation, *whether*

286–90. See also Julian Coolidge, "The Origin of Analytic Geometry," *Osiris* 1 (1936): 231–50; John Shuster, "*Mathesis universalis,*" and Ian Hacking, "Proof and Eternal Truths: Descartes and Leibniz," both in Gaukroger, *Descartes: Philosophy, Mathematics and Physics,* esp. pp. 79–80 and 170–71. On Fermat's methodologically distinct con-tribution to the study of equations in two unknowns, see Boyer, *History of Analytic Geometry,* pp. 74–82.

4. Gilson, *Discours,* p. 220 (see also p. 190); Boyer, "Descartes and the Geometrization of Algebra"; and Boyer, *History of Mathematics,* p. 379. Cf. Belaval, *Leibniz critique de Descartes,* esp. pp. 289–91; Wolfgang Röd, *Descartes: Die Genese des cartesianischen Rationalismus,* 2nd ed. rev. (Munich: C. H. Beck'sche Verlagsbuchhandlung, 1982, pp. 72–73; Gaukroger, "Descartes' Project," esp. pp. 109–10; Gaukroger, "The Nature of Abstract Reasoning: Philosophical Aspects of Descartes' Work in Algebra," in *The Cambridge Companion to Descartes,* ed. John Cottingham (Cambridge: Cambridge University Press, 1992), pp. 91–114; and Grosholz, "Descartes' Unification," esp. p. 160: "[Descartes] made use of algebraic notation in proofs, but only if each equation could be geometrically constructed; and he never introduced a curve by means of an alge-braic equation alone."

5. Descartes, Letter of 27 July 1638, *AM,* 2:362–63.

Descartes' Géométrie "is nothing other than geometry." Or would the *Géométrie* have been more properly entitled *Algèbre?*[6] On this question turns one's understanding of Descartes not only as a mathematician but also as a metaphysician, a correlation which may initially be posed as follows: either Descartes prepared or he blocked the way for the consideration of the "mechanical" (now called transcendental) curves which he excluded from his *Géométrie,* in that, "sometimes straight and sometimes curved," they could not be expressed by algebraic equations[7] (but would be by derivatives, as their quadrature would be achieved by integrals)—in short, either he foresaw or forestalled the path to the infinitary logical procedures of the calculus;[8] and either he prepared or he blocked the way to a contemplative

6. Cf. Michael S. Mahoney, "The Beginnings of Algebraic Thought in the Seventeenth Century," in Gaukroger, *Descartes: Philosophy, Mathematics, Physics,* p. 141: "The title of the *Geometry* is deceptive, for the work is in large part a treatise on algebra."

7. Descartes excluded transcendental curves from his algebraicized geometry for the same reason that he judged them of no practical significance: they could not be "known" in the terms of the only mode that defined mathematics for him, "proportion." See *Géométrie,* Second Book, pp. 90–93: "car encore qu'on n'y puisse reçeuoir aucunes lignes qui semblent a des chordes, c'est a dire qui deuient tantost droites & tantost courbes, a cause que la proportion, qui est entre les droites & les courbes, n'estant pas connuë, & mesme ie croy ne le pouuant estre par les hommes, on ne pourroit rien conclure de là qui fust exact & assuré" (geometry should not include lines that are like strings, in that they are sometimes straight and sometimes curved, since the proportion between straight and curved lines is not known, and I believe cannot be known by men, and one can therefore conclude nothing which would be exact and certain). Cf. Boyer, *History of Mathematics,* pp. 375–76, on Descartes' exclusion of curves which cannot by "*exactly* described" by a determinate ratio. Deleuze's study of Leibniz contends, by contrast, that Descartes indeed sought the "secret of continuity," only along the wrong—"rectilinear"—paths: "Si Descartes n'a pas su résoudre [le labyrinthe de la liberté dans l'âme et ses prédicats], c'est parce qu'il a cherché le secret du continu dans des parcours rectilignes, et celui de la liberté dans une rectitude de l'âme, ignorant l'inclinaison de l'âme autant que la courbure de la matière" (If Descartes did not know how to get through the labyrinth, it was because he sought its secret of continuity in rectilinear tracks, and the secret of liberty in a rectitude of the soul. He knew the inclension of the soul as little as he did the curvature of matter) (Deleuze, *Le pli,* p. 5; *The Fold,* p. 3).

8. Cf. Boyer, *History of the Calculus;* Jules Vuillemin, *Mathématiques et métaphysique chez Descartes* (Paris: Presses Universitaires de France, 1960), pp. 55–73; Belaval, *Leibniz critique de Descartes,* pp. 135–36, 289, 299–303, 332; Allard, *Le mathématisme,* pp. 161–62; N. I. Styazhkin, *History of Mathematical Logic from Leibniz to Peano* (Cam-

metaphysics freed from both the sensory constraints of geometry and the mechanical laws of "mathesis universalis."[9] Our view of Cartesian mathematics entails our view of Cartesian metaphysics, for the mathematics of the *Géométrie* is also an "experiment" in the "method" whose discursive formulation will include the *cogito.*

Even in historical accounts that seek to emphasize the dual nature of the achievement of the *Géométrie,* a striking exchange or reversal of terms can mark the evaluation of which mathematical mode—geometry or algebra—took precedence in and was furthered by Descartes' work. The recent assessment of a particularly lucid commentator is worth citing in this regard at some length:

> What the mathematicians of antiquity had was not an especially abstract algebraic interpretation of arithmetic but an especially concrete geometrical interpretation of it. The abstract interpretation comes only when the resources of arithmetic and geometry are combined to produce something far more powerful and abstract than either of

---

bridge, Mass.: MIT Press, 1969), p. 71; Grosholz, "Descartes' Unification," pp. 162–67; Hacking, "Proof and Eternal Truths." Vuillemin, Styazhkin, Grosholz, and Hacking all see links to infinitary procedures in Descartes' analytic geometry, although Descartes dismissed the possibility and, moreover, the interest of our ever securing such procedures (see preceding note). At the same time that he presents the opposing view, Belaval shows the difficulty of drawing a line (so to speak) between analytic geometry and the calculus: "with regard to its content, Cartesian mathematics does not go beyond the domain of Greek mathematics. . . . With the ancients, Descartes still conceives of irrationals in the form of right angle segments (hypothenuses); Leibniz will conceive of them in the form of series. It would be better to reserve for Leibniz the expression of 'analytic geometry,' and, for Descartes, the expression of 'algebraic geometry.' For . . . his *Geometry* limits itself to describing curves by coordinate points, it fixes positions, it proceeds by static equations, it excludes the infinite" (p. 135).

9. On the evolution of Descartes' abandonment of the project of *mathesis universalis,* see Shuster, "Mathesis universalis." In *Descartes und die Philosophie* (Berlin: de Gruyter, 1937), pp. 42–47, Karl Jaspers finds that Descartes failed to distinguish between the "methodical mechanization of proof" promised by the "universal method" of *mathesis universalis* and the active "*discovery* of new truth": "the sense of actually creative discovery and invention, of the incalculable, which first leads to method but does not necessarily come from method, is lost to him" (p. 46). Opposing views regarding the relationship between Cartesian philosophy and the kind of mathematics Descartes practiced are developed in Brunschvig, "Mathématiques et métaphysique chez Descartes," and Allard, *Le mathématisme.*

them, and this is Descartes' achievement. He inaugurates (with Vieta and others) what I have identified as the first stage in the development of algebra, namely the freeing of number from spatial intuitions. This opened the way to the second stage, the freedom of algebra itself from an exclusively numerical interpretation. . . . His chief aim was to develop a mathematical physics and mathematics is, ultimately, algebra for Descartes. Well aware, at least after his early "universal mathematics" phase, that it could not just be a matter of applying a system as abstract as algebra to something as concrete and specific as the real world, he tried to establish that they do have one crucial thing in common: geometry. The only real properties of matter are those that can be understood wholly in geometrical terms, and algebra is represented in the imagination in purely geometrical terms. It is therefore geometry that ties the two together.[10]

This description comes at the conclusion of a study which begins as follows: "No one contributed more to the early development of algebra than Descartes. In particular, he was able to unify arithmetic and geometry to a significant extent, by showing their mutual connections in terms of an algebraic notation. . . . The aim [of the first book of the *Géométrie,* the most important as far as the fundamentals of algebra are concerned] is to show how, if we think of them in algebraic terms, we can combine the resources of the two fields."[11]

Unmistakable shifts take place repeatedly in this careful account of Descartes' contribution. There is no vacillation in the description of what Descartes did (i.e., combine the resources of arithmetic and geometry), but, rather, on the question of how he did it, and on what first principle or foundation. Algebra is described as the sphere of Descartes' unparalleled contribution and interest ("mathematics is, ultimately, algebra for Descartes") even as geometry is defined as "the one crucial thing" which, in Descartes' view, relates algebra to the "real world" in which he was most interested. Why, when interpreting Descartes as departing from algebra ("if we think of them in algebraic terms, we can combine the resources of the two fields"), do we end up with geometry ("algebra is represented in the imagination in purely geometrical terms. It is therefore geometry that

10. Gaukroger, "Nature of Abstract Reasoning," pp. 112–13.
11. Ibid., pp. 91–93.

ties the two together")? If the problem posed by the *Discours de la méthode* is, what is this discourse—a "discours sur" or a "discours de," a "discours" or a "traité," the account of a life or of a method, and, if autobiographical, a "fable" or a "tableau"—the problem posed by the *Géométrie* is, what is its method; what did Descartes do to what in order to translate between algebra and geometry?

Whether viewed as departing from or culminating in the mathematical precedence of algebra or geometry, Descartes' reconceptualization of the two modes necessarily involved new techniques of expression. At the same time as they render difficult a coherent narrative account of Descartes' mathematical development vis-à-vis his goals and preferences, these techniques are the indispensable origin of that development. With them Descartes modernizes mathematics, and, it can be demonstrated, nonmathematical deduction as well. For, the method introduced in the *Géométrie* also represents the complex "design" that inaugurates the "modern" in Descartes' *Discours:* the tableau-like form of its "fable," its interruptive "thought" of architectonics,[12] and, finally, the nontraditional origin and structure of the *cogito.* A brief recapitulation of Descartes' innovative mathematical method can help us pinpoint the discursive crux of his philosophy.

Descartes' first and most conspicuous contribution to the modernization of mathematics in the *Géométrie* was his resolution of the problem

---

12. It is worth recalling that in one of the first theoretical works to reflect philosophically on the historical forms of (epic) discourse—Lukács' *Theory of the Novel,* written during the onset of twentieth-century "modernism"—the decisive turn from (a hypothetical) ancient unity of thought and expression to modern techniques of representation is defined, precisely, as "architectonic" in character. See Lukács, *Theory of the Novel: A Historico-Philosophical Essay on the Forms of Great Epic Literature,* trans. Anna Bostock (Cambridge: MIT Press, 1971), pp. 67–68: "The way Homer's epics begin in the middle and do not finish at the end is a reflexion of the truly epic mentality's total indifference to any form of architectural construction [*architektonischen Aufbau*], and the introduction of extraneous themes—such as that of Dietrich von Born in the Song of the Nibelungs—can never disturb this balance, for everything in the epic has a life of its own and derives its completeness from its own inner significance. . . . Dante is the only great example in which we see the architectural clearly conquering the organic, and therefore he represents a historico-philosophical transition from the pure epic to the novel." On the "architectonic significance" of the newly contingent parts of novels and the "architecture of the system" which alone can "transcend" them by uniting them "compositionally," see pp. 76–77, 80.

dating from the Pythagoreans of the numerical incommensurability of linear magnitudes. Greek mathematics conceived of numbers as natural or rational integers, discrete units whose relation to one another in analogous ratios were thought to express the spatial proportions of the natural world. The physical world was viewed on the model of geometrical forms, and the discovery that the relationship of the magnitudes of two commonplace line segments given in geometry—the side and the diagonal of a square—could *not* be expressed in a ratio of integers, no matter how small the unit of measure applied, contradicted the ancient tenet of the numerical order of nature, setting off a mathematical and philosophical crisis of an order matched in modern times by the development of non-Euclidean geometry, or by the methodological paradoxes identified at the origin of quantum physics.[13]

13. That is, Einstein's discovery of the (logically disconnected) wave/particle "duality" of light, Heisenberg's formulation of the "uncertainty" relations reciprocally limiting the knowledge of variables in an experiment, and Bohr's even more greatly destabilizing concept of the "complementarity" of mutually exclusive wave and particle descriptions. The reluctance of his contemporaries to consider "the real relation of commensurability and incommensurability to one another" was already criticized by Plato: "a man must be able to distinguish between them on examination, or else must be a very poor creature" (*Laws* VII.819e-820d, *Complete Dialogues of Plato*, pp. 1389–90). On the historical effect of the discovery of incommensurability, cf. Hermann Weyl, *Philosophy of Mathematics and Natural Science* (Princeton: Princeton University Press, 1949), pp. 38–39, 68; Boyer, *History of the Calculus*, pp. 19–21; Boyer, *History of Analytic Geometry*, pp. 6–8, 16, 20; Leo Zippin, *Uses of Inifinity* (New York: Random House, 1962), pp. 38–39; Herbert Meschkowski, *Probleme der Mathematikgeschichte*, 2 vols. (Zurich: Bibliographisches Institut Wissenschaftsverlag, 1979), 1:71–76; Jeremy Gray, *Ideas of Space: Euclidean, Non-Euclidean, and Relativism* (Oxford: Clarendon, 1989), pp. 15–16; and Gaukroger, "Nature of Abstract Reasoning," pp. 98–99. On complementarity and the Bohr-Heisenberg, Bohr-Einstein collaborations and debates, see David Bohm, *Quantum Theory* (New York: Dover, 1989); Abraham Pais, *Subtle Is the Lord* (Oxford: Oxford University Press, 1982); Pais, *Inward Bound* (Oxford: Oxford University Press, 1986); Pais, *Neils Bohr's Times, in Physics, Philosophy, and Polity* (Oxford: Clarendon, 1991), pp. 300–74, 425–51. On description in quantum physics and in contemporary literary theory, see Ronald Schliefer, "Analogy and Example: Heisenberg, Negation, and the Language of Quantum Physics," *Criticism* 33 (1991): 285–307; Schliefer, Robert Con Davis, and Nancy Mergler, *Culture and Cognition* (Ithaca, N.Y.: Cornell University Press, 1993), pp. 140–47. See also Arkady Plotnitsky, *Reconfigurations: Critical Theory and General Economy* (Gainesville: University of Florida Press, 1993), and Plotnitsky, *Complementarity: Anti-Epistemology after Bohr, Bataille, and Derrida* (Durham, N.C.: Duke University Press, 1994), for critically sophisticated, scientifically fluent

When the diagonal of a square (simply, the square root of two) is treated as a rational number (i.e., the ratio of two integers, a finite number of a finite unit of measure) in a basic computation of the ratio of the diagonal to a side, it turns out to be irrational—that is, on the one hand, an odd, and on the other, an even number.[14] Inexpressible in integers, the "ratio" between the diagonal and side of a square would always relate an irrational to a rational number, thereby expressing instead an apparently insoluble paradox: the measurement by discrete number of a continuous magnitude.[15] The dilemma of the incommensurability of continuous magnitudes was compounded by Zeno's paradoxes of motion. Roughly contemporaneous with the discovery of the incommensurability of magnitudes (around the mid-fifth century B.C.),[16] Zeno's paradoxes demonstrated the incommensurability of spatial analysis with motion. Just as an *irrational* number

discussions of the unsettling insight into the systemic production of identity that links Bohr's notion of complementarity to Bataille's "general economy," Nietzsche's "re-evaluation of all values," and Derrida's nondialectical *différance*.

14. The switch from odd to even derives from the rational treatment of the side and diagonal as prime integers (indivisible by any common integral factor). Once the square root of two enters the equation (as equal to the ratio of the diagonal "a" to the side "b": $a^2 = 2b^2$; $2 = a^2/b^2$; $\sqrt{2} = a/b$), both a and b turn out to be even (divisible by 2), hence not prime ($a = b\sqrt{2}$; $a^2 = 2b^2$, or a is an even integer; if $a = 2c$, then $4c^2 = 2b^2$; $2c^2 = b^2$, or b is an even integer).

15. Cf. Florian Cajori, *A History of Mathematics,* 3rd ed. (New York: Chelsea, 1980), p. 22: "[The Greeks] used the word ['number'] in the same sense as we use 'positive integers.' Hence numbers were conceived as *discontinuous,* while magnitudes were *continuous.* The two notions appeared, therefore, entirely distinct. The chasm between them is exposed to full view in the statement of Euclid that 'incommensurable magnitudes do not have the same ratio as numbers.' . . . The transfer of the theory of proportions from numbers to magnitudes (and to lengths in particular) was a difficult and important step." As described in what follows, that transfer is effected by Descartes' *Géométrie.*

16. The discovery was reportedly kept secret by the Greeks. It is traditionally attributed to Hippasus, who, so one story goes, paid with his life in a shipwreck for having disclosed it (Cajori, *History of Mathematics,* p. 57; Boyer, *History of Analytic Geometry,* p. 7; Meschkowski, *Probleme,* p. 75). An even more memorable version of events has Hippasus banished from the community of Pythagoreans "and a tomb . . . erected for him as though he was dead" (Howard Eves, *An Introduction to the History of Mathematics,* 3rd ed. [New York: Holt, Rinehart and Winston, 1976], p. 66). Heinrich Vogt describes a less dramatic, historically staggered development of the concept, beginning with the late Pythagoreans, in "Zur Entdeckungsgeschichte des Irrationalen," *Biblioteca Matematica* 14 (1913): 9–29.

results from the "ratio" of incommensurable lines—lines that share no common unit of measure—the traversal of any line segment (or ultimately any point) could never be accomplished in terms of discrete measurement, so the paradox goes, in that it must cross infinite subdivisions of the segment; indeed, in those same terms, such motion could not even begin. Conversely, since temporal changes in position can only be measured discretely, with respect to an infinite number of discontinuous points, only instants of stasis are measured: of no point in space can we say that it is also motion.[17] As a result of the discovery of incommensurable magnitudes and the absolute impasse posed by Zeno's infinitesimal paradoxes, number and line were disassociated in Greek mathematics and infinite series were excluded from the study of line.[18] When Eudoxus, a student of Plato, redefined the theory of proportions in the fourth century B.C., basing ratios on integral equimultiples of paired line segments (or any other geometrical quantity),[19] rather than on the numerical measurement of line to line, the problem of incommensurability was "resolved" insofar as the multiplied quantities were viewed synthetically and the illogical analysis of ratios into irrational numbers could be avoided.[20]

Descartes posed another solution to the problem of relating numerical and geometrical proportions: algebraic equations. As observed in the commentary cited earlier, the use of algebraic notation in the *Géométrie* freed arithmetic from its "especially concrete geometrical interpretation" in antiquity. This description of a progressive movement away from the

17. Cf. Florian Cajori, "History of Zeno's Arguments on Motion," *American Mathematical Monthly* 22 (1915): 1–6, 39–47, 77–82, 109–15, 143–49, 179–86, 215–20, 253–58, 292–97; Cajori, "The Purpose of Zeno's Arguments on Motion," *Isis* 3 (1920): 7–20.

18. Cf. Richard E. Goodkin's discussion of Zeno's paradoxes as manifested and, in a sense, surpassed by another modern, Proust, in "Proust, Bergson, and Zeno, Or, How Not to Reach One's End," chapter 3 of *Around Proust* (Princeton: Princeton University Press, 1991), pp. 65–88. Goodkin's analysis of Proust's representation of the relationship of infinitesimal division to continuous movement, both in the story of "Un amour de Swann" and the structure of the Proustian period, helps clarify, by contrast, Descartes' exclusion of the infinitesimal from *geometrical* representation.

19. Roughly, $A(x)$ is to $B(y)$ as $C(x)$ is to $D(y)$, where A, B, C, and D are geometrical magnitudes of the same kind (line segments, angles, areas, or volumes), and x and y are integers.

20. Cf. Weyl, *Philosophy of Mathematics*, pp. 31, 39, 45; Boyer, *History of the Calculus*, pp. 30–31; Boyer, *History of Analytic Geometry*, pp. 16–17; Eves, *History of Mathematics*, pp. 19–22.

concrete in Cartesian mathematics follows the pattern—familiar since Descartes—of viewing progress as increasing abstraction from matter. But the account given in the description of how such progress was made most closely resembles the progress of mind (in all domains) described not by Descartes but by Hegel. Descartes, it is suggested, effected a classically Hegelian *Aufhebung,* or surpassing synthesis, of mutually opposed conceptual modes: "combin[ing the resources of arithmetic and geometry]," the *Géométrie* "produce[d] something far more powerful and abstract than either of them, and this is Descartes' achievement."[21] Regarding the specific context of Descartes' *Géométrie,* however, we would do well to ask precisely what "this"—"Descartes' achievement"—is: is it the combination of different resources or the abstraction produced beyond them? If the latter, then this "something far more powerful" would be algebra: "mathematics is, ultimately, algebra for Descartes." Yet algebra is also there from the beginning: "if we think of [arithmetic and geometry] in algebraic terms, we can combine the resources of the two fields." Algebra would then be the means to the end of producing algebra—but is it? For, finally (or is it also so at the beginning?), "algebra is represented in the imagination in purely geometric terms. It is therefore geometry that ties the two ['something as concrete and specific as the real world' and 'a system as abstract as algebra'] together."

Depending on how one identifies what Descartes' *Géométrie* does, both the aim and means of the dialectical progress of his mathematics change. When its "achievement" is posed in purely mathematical terms, "the two" opposing terms are arithmetic and geometry, combined algebraically to produce algebra. When posed in terms of a mathematical physics, whose development was Descartes' "chief aim," "the two" are the concrete, real world and abstract algebra, combined by way of geometry: the imaginative representation of algebra in "purely geometric terms." Descartes' "inaugurat[ion]" of "the first stage in the development of algebra, namely the freeing of number from spatial intuitions," is undertaken by way of algebraic notation; his "chief aim" of relating mathematics to the material world is undertaken by way of geometry, the imagining or materialization of algebraic notation as line. *Is* geometry superseded in the *Géométrie;* should it have been named *Algèbre?* Or is "the first stage" never com-

21. This and the following quotations are from Gaukroger, "Nature of Abstract Reasoning," pp. 112–13.

pleted (in Hegelian terms, *aufgehoben,* "sublated") by Descartes? "This," his "achievement," would then be an act of combination or conjunction whose more complex power lies in its inability to become algebra, completely abstract.

That an account of Descartes' decisive contribution to the development of algebra should conclude with an account of the decisive contribution of geometry to that development is indicative not of a description that is conceptually flawed but rather of the discourse and method, the practical "design" of Descartes. To emphasize the co-presence of geometry in the development of algebra in an experiment in method entitled *Géométrie* may seem like stretching the point, but this, too, is Descartes' doing, and not only in a figurative sense. In the Second Meditation, Descartes describes the physical effects of stretching a bit of wax in order to demonstrate the truth of the *cogito.* He relates this narrative of changing sensible forms to the possibility of true knowledge by the following reasoning: if the bit of wax is not bound by its shape, then it is "nothing but something extended, flexible, and changeable" ("rien que quelque chose d'étendu, de flexible et de muable"),[22] and the "human mind" which alone can "conceive" of the wax "in this way" is not bound by particular perceptions of shapes.[23] Like the body of the bit of wax which Descartes can "consider *toute nue,*" revealing, through a series of transformations, its only positive existence, as extension, and his only positive existence, as thinking thing, "just as if [he] had stripped it of its clothing" ("tout de même que si je lui avais ôté ses vêtements")[24] and stripped himself of sensory imagination, Descartes experiments on the body of geometry until it is stripped of its bodies and can

22. *OP,* 2:424.
23. Ibid., pp. 425–26: "je ne concevrais pas clairement et selon la vérité ce que c'est que la cire, si je ne pensais qu'elle est capable de recevoir plus de variétés selon l'extension, que je n'en ai jamais imaginé. Il faut donc que je tombe d'accord, que je ne saurais pas même concevoir par l'imagination ce que c'est que cette cire, et qu'il n'y a mon entendement seul qui le conçoive (I would not conceive what the wax is clearly and according to the truth if I did not think that it was capable of taking on more varieties of extension than I have ever imagined. I must then agree that I could never even conceive what the wax is by way of imagination and that only my understanding alone conceives this). Cf. *OP,* 2:427–28.
24. Ibid., p. 427.

be considered as nothing but something extended, flexible, and change-able, something made as naked of shape, as purely thinkable, as algebra.

This appeal to universal nudity in thinking (applying equally to things and the human mind) did not meet with universal approval, even when the necessarily misplaced, if all the more conspicuous, metaphors on which it relies were accepted with a complicitous wink. While the imaging of a bit of wax and the mind that perceives it on the model of a clothed or a naked body might add luster to the long tarnished image of Carte-sian rationalism today, Gassendi first objected to Descartes' metaphorical "stripping of the wax" by arguing that "clothed" or unclothed, figured in one form or another, the bit of wax is still a body, "something extended and spatial," and must be insofar as it is perceived by Descartes at all.[25] For Descartes, the *Géométrie* that changed the course of mathematics by developing algebra in such a way as to make infinitary, nonalgebraic equa-tions (in which Descartes saw no interest) inevitable—for Descartes, the *Géométrie* is still geometry. In his "Objections" to the *cogito* of the Second Meditation, Gassendi (whose materialism did not want humor) initiated the practice of taking Descartes at his word, addressing him rhetorically as a disembodied "soul" or "mind" in apostrophic exclamations ("Dites-moi, je vous prie, ô âme!;" "ô esprit" [Tell me, I beg you, oh soul; oh mind]).[26]

25. Pierre Gassendi, *Cinquièmes objections [traduction]*, "Contre la Seconde Médita-tion," *OP*, 2:708–23 (French translation from the Latin based on the Clerselier version in the 1647 edition of the *Méditations*): "C'est pourqoui je m'étonne que vous disiez qu'après avoir ainsi dépouillé la cire de toutes ses formes, ni plus ni moins que de ses vêtements, vous concevez plus clairement et plus parfaitement ce qu'elle est. . . . Car cela ne vous est pas rendu manifest, comme un homme le peut être de qui nous avions seulement aperçu la robe et le chapeau, quand nous venons à les lui ôter pour savoir ce que c'est ou quel il est. En après, puisque vous pensez comprendre en quelque façon quelle est cette chose, dites-nous, je vous prie, comment vous la concevez? N'est-ce pas comme quelque chose d'étendu et de spatial? . . . Et partant, votre intellection est une espèce d'imagination" (pp. 719–20) (This is why I am astonished that you say that after having stripped the wax of all its forms, neither more nor less than of its clothing, you conceive more clearly and perfectly what it is. . . . For this is not made manifest to you as a man can be of whom we have only perceived the coat and hat, once we strip him of these in order to know what or which man he is. Furthermore, when you think you understand in some way what this thing is, tell us, I ask you, how do you conceive it? Is it not as something extended and spatial? . . . Hence, your intellection is a kind of imagination).

26. *OP*, 2:709, 721.

In his "Réponses" Descartes identifies this "agreeable figure of rhetoric" as "prosopopeia" and responds in kind, addressing Gassendi from that point on as "flesh" ("Dites-moi donc, je vous prie, ô chair, ou qui que vous soyez;" "ô très bonne chair" [Then tell me, I beg you, oh flesh, or whoever you are; oh very good flesh]).[27] "Mind" and "flesh," metaphysician and Epicurian, Descartes and Gassendi meet only in the crossed swords of these appelations, staging verbally the communication of mind with matter for which Gassendi argued. Led into a rhetorical thrust and parry in response to the very objections whose publication he wanted to repress,[28] Descartes, one could say, surrenders to "flesh" in so addressing Gassendi.

But in the *Géométrie,* as in the example of the "naked" body of a bit of wax, the claims of matter invest those of mind by Descartes' own devising. The *Géométrie* is still geometry for Descartes because it rests not on extendability but on extension, the line. The opening of Book One continues:

> Ainsi n'at'on autre chose a faire en Geometrie touchant les lignes qu'on cherche, pour les preparer a estre connuës, que leur en adiouster d'autres, ou en oster, Oubien en ayant une, que ie nommeray l'unité pour la rapporter d'autant mieux aux nombres, & qui peut ordinairement estre prise a discretion, puis en ayant encore deux autres, en trouver une quatriesme, qui soit à l'une de ces deux, comme l'autre est a l'unité, ce qui est le mesme que la Multiplication; oubien en trouver une quatriesme, qui soit a l'une de ces deux, comme l'unité est a l'autre, ce qui est le mesme que la Division; ou enfin trouver une, ou deux, ou plusieurs moyennes proportionelles entre l'unité, & quelque autre ligne; ce qui est le mesme que tirer la racine quarrée, ou cubique, &c. Et ie ne craindray pas d'introduire ces termes d'Arithmetique en la Geometrie, affin de me rendre plus intelligible.[29]

> So in geometry, to find the lines one is looking for, all one has to do is to add or subtract other lines; or else, taking one line which I shall call unity in order to relate it as closely as possible to numbers, and which can in general be chosen arbitrarily, and having given two other lines, to find a fourth line which shall be to one of the given lines as the

27. Ibid., pp. 793, 795, 799, 801, 802, 832.
28. On the publication history of the *Méditations,* the *Objections,* and the *Réponses,* see ibid., pp. 377–81.
29. *Geometry,* pp. 2–5.

other is to unity (which is the same as multiplication); or, again, to find a fourth line which is to one of the given lines as unity is to the other (which is equivalent to division); or, finally, to find one, two, or several mean proportionals between unity and some other lines (which is the same as extracting the square root, etc., of the given line). And I shall not hesitate to introduce these arithmetical terms into geometry, in order to render myself more intelligible.

Descartes will treat given lines arithmetically, adding, subtracting, multiplying, and dividing them as if they were numbers. The Greeks treated natural numbers as specific line lengths in specific geometrical configurations, whose vocabulary is still our own: any line length *squared* meant the construction of a square; any line length *cubed* meant the construction of a cube. We may now say a number (or variable) to the second, third, fourth, and fifth power (and so forth to *n*) because Descartes conceived of lines purely as lines, and of exponents as expressions of purely *proportional* "relations" of magnitudes unrelated to specific figures (i.e., 1 is to x as x is to x^2 as x^2 is to x^3, and so on).[30] The new notational system introduced in the *Géométrie* uses letters to designate lines, numbers to indicate quotients of letters, and exponents to count the number of "relations," or multiples of itself, a line contains: "souvent on n'a pas besoin de tracer ainsi ces lignes sur le papier, & il suffit, de les designer par quelques lettres, chacusne par une seule. Comme pour adioster la ligne BD a GH, ie nomme l'une *a* & l'autre *b*, & escris $a + b$; . . . Et *aa*, ou a^2, pour multiplier *a* par soy mesme; a^3, pour le multiplier encore une fois par *a*, & ainsi a l'infini"[31] [often it is not necessary thus to draw the lines on paper, but it is

---

30. See Mahoney, "Beginnings of Algebraic Thought," p. 144: "[Descartes] replaced the last vestiges of a verbal algebra with a particularly revealing symbolism. Insead of writing 2 *A cubus*, he wrote $2x^3$, for which he gave the following justification: x and x^3 are quantities linked to one another and ultimately to a unit by means of certain relations. . . . Three relations lead from 1 to x^3, and the number of these relations is given by the upper index number. It is here characteristic for a new mode of thought that Descartes does not say something like, x^3 represents a cube constructed on side x, but that he considers this quantity simply as a quantity." Cf. *Geometry,* p. 5n6; Boyer, *History of Analytic Geometry,* pp. 84–85; Boyer, *History of Mathematics,* p. 371; Gaukroger, "Nature of Abstract Reasoning," pp. 102–3.

31. *Geometry,* pp. 4–7. Cf. Rule XVI, *Regulae:* "Nous les ferons souvent précéder [les lettres] des signes numériques 1, 2, 3, 4, etc., pour exprimer leur multiplicité, et nous leur joindrons aussi le nombre des relations que l'on devra comprendre en eux: par ex-

sufficient to designate each by a single letter. Thus, to add the lines BD and GH, I call one *a* and the other *b*, and write $a + b \ldots$; *aa*, or a^2, [will indicate] that *a* is multiplied by itself; a^3 that this result is multiplied by *a*, and so on, indefinitely). Just as lines may be "designated" rather than "drawn," exponents are a technical shorthand for the number of *proportional* "relations" of a designated magnitude to itself.[32] Proportions here are divested of their figural content; rather than applied to construct the sides of a two- or three-dimensional figure, these magnitudes can now be thought of as single line lengths, extensions in one dimension whose "relations" are inherently commensurable in that the first term of the series of proportional relations summarized by the exponent is one. Descartes' notation, then, substitutes letters for lines but also substitutes lines themselves for proportional relations previously represented and limited by forms in Euclidean space.[33]

Descartes' pivotal introduction of an "arbitrarily chosen" *line* "unit" also functions on this new basis of proportionality, producing a relation between two equations by departing from another version of one, a line

---

emple, si j'écris $2a^3$, ce sera comme si je disais, le double de la grandeur désignée par la lettre *a*, et contenant trois relations" (*OP*, 1:186) (we will precede [letters] by numerical signs 1, 2, 3, 4, etc., to express their multiplication, and we will also attach to them the number of relations that should be understood in them: for example, if I write $2a^3$, this will be as if I said: the double of the magnitude designated by the letter *a*, and containing three relations).

32. On the relational (i.e., proportional) rather than intuitive or realist basis of Descartes' exponential symbolism, see *OP*, 1:103n, 105n2, 187n2.

33. On the modernization of mathematics effected by Cartesian notation, see Salomon Bochner, "Why Mathematics Grows," in *The Collected Papers of Salomon Bochner*, 4 vols., ed. Robert C. Gunning (Providence, R.I.: American Mathematical Society, 1992), 4:191–214. Bochner suggests that the difference between Greek and Cartesian uses of letter symbols, and "the failure of Greek mathematics to install coordinate systems," is tantamount to "the difference between two levels of abstraction": "the Greeks rarely ventured beyond abstractions from actuality, in mathematics, in natural philosophy, and in other philosophy; and we wish to state, with emphasis, that the absence of algebraic symbolism from Greek mathematics was a symptom of a general Greek limitation, and not the cause of it" (pp. 20, 23). The Greek abstraction from the diameter of an extended physical object to the zero diameter of a geometrical line would be such an "abstraction from actuality," or "one-step abstraction" typical of "ancient" mathematics; the introduction of a coordinate system of graphic representation would be a "second-level abstraction from abstraction" of the "modern" kind, and "evolved out of the *Géométrie* of Descartes" (pp. 20–21).

segment posed as a fixed unit of measure.[34] The unit and one given will stand in proportion to each other as another given stands in proportion to an unknown fourth term: "puis sans considerer aucune différence entre ces lignes connuës, & inconnuës, on doit parcourir la difficulté, selon l'ordre qui monstre le plus naturellement de tous en qu'elle sorte elles dependent mutuellement les unes des autres, iusques a ce qu'on ait trouvé moyen d'exprimer une mesme quantité en deux façons: ce qui se nomme une Equation" (then, making no distinction between known and unknown lines, we must examine the difficulty by traversing it according to the order that shows most naturally the relations between these lines, until we find it possible to express a single quantity in two ways. This is what is called an equation).[35] This artificial construction of proportional terms as a method of problem-solving—by which any line segment in a known proportional relation with another could be used as the standard unit to solve for a fourth term—was to trigger a fundamental conceptual problem in architectural theory after Descartes. For in granting proportionality first importance, it also put into question the referential status of architectonic proportions whose unit of measure was posited by man. At the same time, the proposition that line represent an arbitrarily known number ("unity"), rather than an unknown to be measured in numbers, enabled Descartes to think of x in terms of y, and so to plot the *loci* or lines of equations in two unknowns. Beginning with his positing of an arbitrary linear unit, Descartes not only solved the Pappus problem,[36] upon which he first focused, but also developed the working elements of the coordinate system.[37] The

34. According to Deleuze, Leibniz creates "baroque mathematics" by rejecting the elemental notion of unit of measure here carried to the level of invention by Descartes. See Deleuze, *Le pli*, pp.8–9, 24, 28–28n12, on Leibniz's substitution of "continuity" for the "unit" and "continuous repetition of . . . point of . . . view" ("la répeitition continue . . . du point de vue") for "extension [that] consists of measurable lengths" ("l'étendue [qui] consiste en grandeurs measurables").

35. *Geometry*, pp. 6, 8, 9.

36. Cf. Boyer, *History of Analytic Geometry*, pp. 87–88; Gaukroger, "Nature of Abstract Reasoning," pp. 95–97; Grosholz, "Descartes' Unification," pp. 157–59.

37. Because it allows Descartes to conceive of line as "the site of its points, the analytic punctual equation" ("la ligne cartésienne comme lieu de ses points, l'équation ponctuelle analytique"), Deleuze considers the coordinate system part and parcel of the Cartesian "error" and opposes it to the plastic "genetic element of the variable curve"—the "fold" or "inflection" which instead fuses point and line in a "point-fold" ("point-pli"): "[inflection is] the pure Event of the line or of the point, the Virtual,

formulation of the x and y axes, the bases of the blueprint for plotting multivariable equations which now bear Descartes' name, is, however, not the only medium required for his translation of equations from number to line.

By conceiving of "squared" and "cubed" not as actual two- and three-dimensional figures but as multiplications of a line by itself, Descartes broke the barrier of nature that limited polynomial equations to the order of three. Understood to represent extensions in one dimension, orders could now be written for any value, while the use of one dimension to carry the different orders freed the other dimensions to represent another aspect of equations, variables. If Descartes remains interested in the reality of physical space, defined as dimension and magnitude, Descartes' re-writing of orders as magnitudes made the graphic resource of dimension available in a new way. The reconception of orders of equations as exten-sions thus not only made polynomial equations of an order higher than three, and of mixed orders, possible,[38] but also, in linking dimension to variables, made multivariable equations graphable. In short, Descartes' geometry could map far richer equations than could ancient geometry, just as it could convert geometrical figures into equations without being lim-ited by linear incommensurability.[39] It could do this because of a technical change in notation based on a changed perception of the relationship be-tween number and space.

In relating architectonic, geometrical form to discursive, algebraic nota-tion, Descartes extended both conceptual modes beyond their previous limitations. In this sense the modern mathematics of the *Géométrie* recre-ate the link between discourse and method posed by the *Discours*. For, by transforming the ancient notion of what orders represented, Descartes could freely *draw* figures previously unrepresentable in two dimensions;

---

ideality par excellence. . . . it is the world itself, or rather its beginning. . . . it does not refer to coordinates" ("[elle est] le pur Evénement de la ligne ou du point, le Virtuel, l'idéalité par excellence. . . . elle est le Monde lui-même, ou plutôt son commence-ment. . . . Elle ne renvoie pas à des coordonées") (Deleuze, *Le pli*, pp. 8–9, 20–22; *The Fold*, pp. 6, 14–15).

38. As Boyer states succinctly, "It permits one to write with impunity such an expres-sion as a^2b^2-b" (*History of Analytic Geometry*, p. 84).

39. I am indebted in these remarks on Descartes' transformation of the relation be-tween algebraic and graphic representation to clarifying discussions with Antonio C. Romero and Joseph J. Kohn.

and by developing a new technique for *talking about* those figures—equations in two unknowns—he could refer the abstract discourse of algebraic notation to a method for knowing the physical world. Descartes' combined conceptual and technical transformation increased the power of mathematics to describe the external world as he perceived it—that is, as shapes which could be drawn with a straight edge and compass, given an arbitrarily determined quantity (the line segment unit), two unknowns, and their disposition along coordinate axes—Descartes' "places regulières." The arbitrarily small, indeterminate quantities treated by limit functions would have no place in this project, in which algebraic abstraction and bounded geometric forms must be, at every moment, analogous. But in addition to maintaining the practical purpose and increasing the power of mathematics to refer outside itself—to "explicat[e] . . . phenomena of nature"[40]—Descartes' coordination of algebra and geometry practically increases the power of thinking: Cartesian notation saves time for the mind.

40. Descartes, Letter of 27 July 1638, *AM,* 2:362–63.

6   Writing and Intuition

Descartes' description of his notational method in the *Regulae* is preceded by an explanation of the part played by writing in intuition:

> parmi les dimensions innombrables qui peuvent se peindre en notre fantaisie, on ne doit pas en contempler plus de deux différentes en une seule et même intuition, qu'il s'agisse d'intuition visuelle ou d'intuition intellectuelle; aussi importe-t-il de retenir toutes les autres, afin qu'elles se présentent aisément à nous, chaque fois que de besoin; et c'est à cette fin, semble-t-il, que la nature a institué la mémoire. Mais celle-ci est souvent fuyante; et pour que nous ne soyons pas contraints d'immobiliser une partie de notre attention pour lui rendre sa fraîcheur, tout en vaquant à d'autres pensées, l'art y a très heureusement ajouté l'usage de l'écriture; grâce au secours de cette dernière, nous ne confierons ici absolument rien à la mémoire, et nous préserverons tout entière notre fantaisie libre pour les idées présentes, en inscrivant sur le papier tout ce qu'il faudra retenir; et cela par des signes très concis afin de pouvoir les passer distinctement en revue l'un après l'autre, . . . les parcourir tous ensuite par un mouvement très rapide de la pensée, . . . et prendre du plus grand nombre possible d'entre eux une intuition simultanée.[1]

> among the innumerable dimensions which can paint themselves in our fancy, one must not contemplate more than two different ones in a single intuition, whether a visual or an intellectual intuition; in addition, one must retain all the others so that they present themselves easily to us, each time we need them; and it is to this end, it seems, that nature instituted memory. But memory is often fleeting; and so that we not be forced to immobilize a part of our attention in

1. Rule XVI, *OP,* 1:185–86.

order to refresh it while evacuating other thoughts, art has very happily added the use of writing. Thanks to the help of the latter, we will confide absolutely nothing to memory here, and we will keep our entire fancy free for present ideas in inscribing on paper everything that should be retained; and we will do this by way of very concise signs, so that we may be able to review one after the other distinctly, . . . then traverse them all by a very rapid movement of thought, . . . and take from the greatest possible number of them a simultaneous intuition.

Writing for Descartes is not an "aide-mémoire," an inessential yet potentially dangerous supplement;[2] nor are signs the negative means which spirit or intelligence produces so as to return to itself in thought.[3] Writing, for Descartes, is the way supplied by "art" to obviate memory altogether, allowing the mind to work entirely in the present. Substituting, for the benefit of "fancy," for the function of memory supplied by "nature," the "very concise signs" of algebraic notation are also to be understood oppositely to the signifying structure of syllogistic rhetoric. If during the time of the inattentive use of syllogism our "reason rests unemployed" ("en chômage"), in employing too much of our "attention" in the effort of remembering, we run the counterrisk of leaving reason with no time to work at all.[4] Reason is not put out of work by individual signs as it is by the sophis-

2. The ambivalent argument for the dispensability of written signs doubles as an argument against their pernicious effect on spirit. The seminal discussions of the problematic status of writing—as nonintuitional materiality—in philosophies of spirit are Jacques Derrida's *La voix et le phénomène* (Paris: Presses Universitaires de Frances, 1967); Derrida, *De la grammatologie* (Paris: Minuit, 1967); and Derrida, *L'écriture et la différence* (Paris: Seuil, 1967).

3. See Hegel's discussion of the inassimilable externality of signs learned by rote, in which alone the subject is said to think, sec. 458–464 of the *Enzyklopädie der philosophischen Wissenschaften im Grundrisse*, ed. Friedhelm Nicolin and Otto Pöggeler (Hamburg: Felix Meiner, 1969), pp. 368–77. Cf. Paul de Man, "Sign and Symbol in Hegel's *Aesthetic*," *Critical Inquiry* 8 (1982): 761–75; de Man, "Hegel on the Sublime," in *Displacement: Derrida and After*, ed. Mark Krupnik (Bloomington: Indiana University Press, 1983), pp. 139–53.

4. See chap. 4, n.12. On Descartes' potentially confusing use of the single term "mémoire" to signify both "reminiscence" (the kind of memory he wants to obviate) and "retention" (made possible by writing), see A. K. Stout, "The Basis of Knowledge in Descartes," in *Descartes: A Collection of Critical Essays*, ed. Willis Doney (Notre Dame, Ind.: University of Notre Dame Press, 1968), pp. 169–91. Placing Descartes' discus-

tic structure of syllogism, through which conclusions are foretold. Rather, it gains the freedom of "fantaisie" to move quickly between discrete elements and, in so doing, to structure them virtually without knowing it, what Descartes calls "tak[ing] from . . . them a simultaneous intuition." In Descartes' first published work, no less than in Husserl's posthumously published "Origin of Geometry," the objectivity of geometrical intuition originates in writing. Both the historical origin of phenomenology in Cartesian "intuitionalism" and its conceptual end in Husserl's "origin of geometry"—the turn from a theory of present, intentional acts of perception, to one of written linguistic embodiment and its historical transmission as the basis for affirming the possibility of "ideal" objectivity—derive equally from the art of writing introduced as integral to thinking in Descartes' *Géométrie*.[5]

---

sion of memory in the context of the intuitional certainty at which he aims, Stout argues that "retention" provides no greater certainty than "reminiscence," since "sensible [signs] . . . cannot prove that you are right in remembering the process to have been self-evident" (187n). Here the point of Descartes' use of signs *as signs rather than as a process of thought* is significantly overlooked. "Concise signs" can be taken in at a glance precisely because they are themselves as self-evident as—in themselves— they are meaningless. The two kinds of memory Descartes distinguishes as the act of remembering instituted by nature ("mémoire"), and the act of retaining ("retenir") written signs added by art, correspond to Hegel's explicit distinction in the *Enzyklopädie* between *Erinnerung* (memory as internalization of experience) and *Gedächtnis* (the mechanical memorization of arbitrary signs). The addition or supplement (of nonintuitional writing) upon which, as analyzed by Derrida, metaphysical concepts and statements depend is the "art" or technical means of thinking as defined by Descartes, whose introduction into the intuitive field of geometry he calls "method."

5. See Edmund Husserl, "Der Ursprung der Geometrie als intentional-historisches Problem," ed. Eugen Fink, *Revue internationale de philosophie* 1 (1939): 203–25; Husserl, *The Crisis of European Sciences and Transcendental Phenomenology*, trans. and with an introduction by David Carr (Evanston, Ill.: Northwestern University Press, 1970), Appendix VI, pp. 353–78; Husserl, *L'origine de la géométrie*, trans. and with an introduction by Jacques Derrida (Paris: Presses Universitaires de France, 1962). In this extraordinary late work Husserl redefines "linguistic embodiment" as the only "means" by which the "merely intrasubjective structure" at the origin of geometry becomes "objective structure." Here geometry stands for all "ideality" that must also be the "objective world," "one structure common to all"—in short, for the possibility of phenomenology itself: "How, by contrast [with descriptive sciences], is a science like geometry possible? How, as a systematic, endlessly growing stratified structure of idealities, can it maintain its original meaningfulness through living reactivatability if its cognitive thinking is supposed to produce something new without being able

Descartes' definition of an "intuition" in the *Regulae* is worth recalling in this context:

> Par *intuition* j'entends, non point le témoignage instable des sens, ni le jugement trompeur de l'imagination qui opére des compositions sans valeur, mais une représentation qui est le fait de l'intelligence pure et attentive, représentation si facile et si distincte qu'il ne subsiste aucun doute sur ce que l'on y comprend; ou bien, ce qui revient au même, une représentation inaccessible au doute, représentation qui est le fait de l'intelligence pure et attentive.[6]

> By *intuition* I understand not the unstable testimony of the senses, nor the deceiving judgment of the imagination, which effects compositions without any value, but a representation which is the act of the pure and attentive intelligence, a representation so ready and distinct that no doubt subsists as to what it comprehends; or, what comes

---

to reactivate the previous levels of knowledge back to the first?" (Husserl, *Crisis*, pp. 357–60, 363). The question Husserl poses with respect to the future of the "first" or "original" cognitions upon which the further development of geometry depends, repeats, on an overarching historical plane, Descartes' indication of the "help" that must be given to memory in the individual act of deduction. His answer to the question is Descartes' as well. First made possible through "linguistic expression, as geometrical speech, as geometrical proposition" (p. 358), geometry, Husserl reasons, is ultimately made science through writing: "written . . . expression . . . makes communications possible without immediate or mediate personal address; it is, so to speak, communication become virtual. Through this, the communalization of man is lifted to a new level" (pp. 360–61). Moving even further from intentionalism, Husserl describes the reactivation of "original meaningfulness"—which, like Descartes' thinking aided by "signs," can "produce something new" because it does not exhaust itself in the constant effort of memory—as the convergence of thinking with "historicity." The origin of *geometry*, i.e., of the psychic *object*, made possible by writing, is both an event for the individual mind and the "inner structure of meaning" of "history" in the largest sense: "making geometry self-evident . . . is the disclosure of its historical tradition. . . . such self-evidences result in nothing other and nothing less than the universal a priori of history" (p. 371). Derrida's early observation that, given the temporal origination of each so-called synthetic act of transcendental intentionality, "the absolute idealism of [Husserl's] *Ideen*" is "in a certain sense, purely methodological," could be applied equally to Descartes, were method understood as no less impure than the "passive," temporal origin of perception it is supposed to efface. See Derrida, *Le problème de la genèse dans la philosophie de Husserl* (Paris: Presses Universitaires de France, 1990), pp. 37–39; cf. pp. 118–24.

6. Rule III, *OP,* 1:87.

to the same, a representation inaccessible to doubt, a representation which is the act of pure and attentive intelligence.

An "intuition" is a "representation." Contrary to philosophies of representation since Plato, contrary to expectations formed by those philosophies—indeed, one could almost say, counterintuitively—Descartes defines "intuition" as a "representation inaccessible to doubt." Such a representation is produced neither by the "senses" nor by the "imagination" they contaminate, but by "the pure and attentive intelligence." Yet such a representation must be produced in a medium. Algebraic signs are the language of "intuition," the discursive means with which "pure and attentive intelligence" enacts a "representation." Since they themselves are representations only in the most external, abstract or arbitrary, and least mimetic of senses—because they have, strictly speaking, no representational value whatsoever apart from their "use" in denoting values, both known and unknown, during the life of an equation—the signs that are the discursive means of the intelligence cannot be used by the imagination to effect "compositions without any value." Those "compositions" are the stuff of book learning and the "book of the world," representational forms repeatedly pronounced valueless by Descartes. Yet it is those compositions—"philosophies" as well as "comedies"—to which Descartes repeatedly returns, and whose experience composes much of the nonintuitional, autobiographical discourse of the *Discours de la méthode*.

In view of Descartes' explications of intuition and the use of writing, the use of narrating such experience "as in a *tableau*" begins to become evident. A life story cannot be intuited, but if represented concisely, without mimetic narrative development, its first and last terms may be grasped nearly simultaneously. Such autobiographical discourse would imitate the life not of a subject but of an equation. What *is* grasped in Descartes' "fable," that of a "life represented as in a tableau," is precisely the failure of "compositions" representing experience to provide the textual grounds for "intuition."

Method, too, is not an intuition, but it should provide, unlike autobiography, the order that makes the "tak[ing]" of an "intuition" from "the largest number" of discrete elements possible. Method is the order for effecting those representations of elements we may call intuitions, but *in order for there to be a method, those elements must be written:* abstracted from sensory experience and imagination, abbreviated to such a degree that the mind need not even remember them. In scanning writing rapidly, the "pure and attentive intelligence" acts.

In fact, the "concise signs" of algebraic notation preserve reality as the medium of intelligence in altered form. Signs maintain the identity of the lines they name. Mathematical operations performed on numbers immediately sever those numerical designations from the referents they measure in the physical world. Individual letters remain individually visible; as the legible signs of a value, unlike a value, they cannot be transformed. Regardless of the operations performed on them, they remain, *as signs,* the same; and for the life of the equation, whenever the mind scans it, the linear quantities signs represent remain visualizable *as lines.* In the substitution of letters for linear magnitudes, as in exponential and coordinate notation, the increased abstraction of algebra from geometry *maintains* the concrete elements of geometry; in the discursive language of intuitions, letters represent lines:

> nous utiliserons les lettres *a, b, c,* etc., pour exprimer les grandeurs déjà connues, et les lettres A, B, C, etc. pour les inconnues; nous les ferons souvent précéder des signes numériques 1, 2, 3, 4, etc., pour exprimer leur multiplicité. . . . Pour comprendre plus clairement tout cela, il faut remarquer d'abord que, si les arithméticiens ont l'habitude de désigner chaque grandeur par plusieurs unités, c'est-à-dire par un nombre, nous ne faisons au contraire pas moins abstraction ici des nombres eux-mêmes que nous le faisions un peu plus haut des figures géométriques, comme de n'importe quel autre sujet. Et nous le faisons autant pour éviter l'ennui d'un calcul fastidieux et superflu, que pour obtenir, et c'est le principal, que les parties du sujet qui touchent à la nature de la difficulté restent toujours distinctes, et ne s'enveloppent pas dans des nombres inutiles: par exemple, si l'on cherche l'hypoténuse d'un triangle rectangle dont les côtés donnés sont 9 et 12, un arithméticien dira qu'elle est $\sqrt{225}$, c'est-à-dire 15; nous, au lieu de 9 et de 12, nous poserons *a* et *b,* et nous trouverons que l'hypoténuse est $\sqrt{a^2 + b^2}$, en laissant distinctes ces deux parties, a^2 et b^2 qui dans le nombre sont confondues.[7]

we will use the letters *a, b, c,* etc., to express already known magnitudes, and the letters A, B, C, etc., for those unknown; we will often

7. Rule XVI, *OP,* 1:186–87; for missing text indicated by ellipses, see chap. 5, n.31.

have the numeric signs, 1, 2, 3, 4, etc., precede them to express their multiplication. . . . To understand all this more clearly, it must first be noted that if mathematicians have the custom of designating every magnitude by many unities, that is to say, by a number, we, on the contrary, abstract no less here from numbers themselves than we did above from geometrical figures, as from any other subject. And we do this as much to avoid the time-consuming trouble of a fastidious and superfluous calculation, as—and this is the principal motive—to make it so that the parts of the subject that touch the nature of the difficulty always remain distinct, and do not become enveloped in useless numbers: for example, if one is looking for the hypotenuse of a right triangle whose given sides are 9 and 12, a mathematician will say that it is $\sqrt{225}$, that is to say 15; instead of 9 and 12 we will pose a and b, and we will find that the hypotenuse is $\sqrt{a^2 + b^2}$, in leaving distinct the two parts, a^2 and b^2, that are confused in the number.

In the *Regulae* Descartes had argued that he would prefer the expression "extension occupies space" ("l'étendue occupe le lieu") to "that which is extended occupies space" ("ce qui est étendu occupe le lieu") because the latter entailed the "ambiguity" of referring equally to two kinds of bodies, simple objects and animate beings.[8] The expression "the body has extension" ("le corps a de l'étendue") entails similar semantic confusion by distinguishing extension from a subject as its possession, or "distinct" quality.[9] At the same time, Descartes states, he would not subscribe to an understanding of extension as the negation of body ("l'étendue n'est pas le corps") because no "idea in fancy would correspond to it" ("aucune idée qui lui soit propre ne lui correspond dans la fantaisie"), thereby compelling us, paradoxically, to give it a body, since any idea requires "the representation of a body" in order to be thought.[10] Just as line or extension occupies a

8. Rule XIV, *OP*, 1:173.
9. Ibid., 1:173–74.
10. "Enfin, si l'on dit: *l'étendue n'est pas le corps,* on prend alors le mot d'étendue dans un tout autre sens que ci-dessus; et en ce nouveau sens, aucune idée qui lui soit propre ne lui correspond dans la fantaisie; cette assertion dans son ensemble est l'oeuvre de l'entendement pur, qui seul possède la faculté de séparer des entités abstraites de cette espèce. C'est là que la plupart des gens trouvent une occasion de se tromper: ne remarquant point que prise en ce sens, l'étendue ne peut être comprise par l'imagination, ils se la représentent par une véritable idée [corporelle; editor's addition]; et comme une pareille idée enveloppe nécessairment la représentation d'un

middle ground between "bodies" and the "idea" of extension,[11] letters provide a middle ground between (numerically) incommensurable lines and the (nonlinear) abstraction of number. Letters and lines are the technical intermediaries that make the comparison of the otherwise incommensurable domains of number and figure possible. What geometric figures lose in concreteness by being reduced to one-dimensional lines, numbers gain by being designated by concrete signs. The individuality of the sign that remains uneffaced in computation permits the mind both to visualize equations at any moment as lines drawn on a two-dimensional plane and to traverse equations without stopping to remember other "dimensions."[12] The "very concise signs" of method enable the eye to move rapidly; like the discursive context of a life represented "as in a tableau," the mind apprehends its own movement across notation *as* "a simultaneous intuition."

This is how letters, standing for lines, create mental extensions. That is to say, Descartes uses *discontinuous,* written signs, individually visible to the eye, to effect a *continuous,* and therefore, strictly speaking, invisible movement in the mind. External line and a line of thought—Descartes' "visual or intellectual intuition"[13]—are both "represented" in equations of discontinuous forms. But here discontinuity is not a natural number; it is

---

corps, ils ne peuvent dire que l'étendue ainsi conçue n'est pas le corps sans se trouver imprudemment engagés dans cette contradiction, que *la même chose serait simultanément corps et non corps* (Rule XIV, ibid., p. 174) (Finally, if one said, *extension is not the body,* one would be taking the word extension to mean something completely different from the meaning given above; and in this new meaning, no idea that would be proper to it would correspond to it in the fancy [*fantaisie*]; on the whole this assertion is the work of pure understanding, which alone possesses the faculty of separating abstract entities of this kind. This is where most people have occasion to deceive themselves: not remarking that, taken in this way, extension cannot be understood by the imagination, they represent it to themselves by way of an actual idea; and as such an idea necessarily envelopes the representation of a body, they cannot say that extension so conceived is not body without finding themselves imprudently involved in the contradiction, that *the same thing would be simultaneously body and not body*). On "ideas" as the "representation" of a body in the "imagination," cf. *OP,* 2:420, 2:443, and chapter 4, n. 14 and n. 17, above.

11. On Descartes' pivotal conception of *de l'étendue* and the infinite perspective within space it inaugurated, see Hubert Damisch, *L'origine de la perspective,* 2nd ed. rev. (Paris: Flammarion, 1993), pp. 12, 119–20.

12. Rule XVI, *OP,* 1:185–86.

13. Ibid.

rather an extra-arithmetic form, the discursive sign or letter. The incommensurability of continuous magnitudes and discontinuous units of measure is surpassed, or circumvented, by way of a detour into the discursive. In the "experiment" in "method" that is Descartes' *Géométrie,* nonarithmetic signs make the method possible, letters are the only means of representation that make the view of "representation" as "intuition" tenable: the age-old problem of incommensurability is mediated neither by natural nor numerical means, but by written signs. Signs ensure the freedom of "fantaisie" to take from discrete elements an intuition, to make a representation of the "pure and attentive intelligence." [14] In the *Géométrie* the "use" of "writing" "added" to thought by "art" is the "discours *de* la méthode." [15]

The uninterrupted continuity of thought provided by discontinuous discursive means pertaining neither to geometry nor to algebra as such must occur "free" from reflection in the thinking subject. Only in the rapidity of reading signs like exponents, without remembering the objects (lines) or relations (proportions of lines) they stand for, can the mind conceive the parts of an equation and series of equations as an "intuited" whole. In the discourse of the method of Descartes' *Géométrie,* arbitrary representations can be *viewed* as "representation[s]" which are "act[s]" of "intuition" when the successivity of their reading seems synchronic to the reading subject—when, as in the autobiography of the *Discours de la méthode,* a diachronic form of representation is itself presented as if it were self-present. Like the *Discours de la méthode,* the discourse that is indispensable to the *Géométrie* is a way of "talking about" a method of procedure which also inheres in the geometry practiced. Not itself method, nor intuitional, it is the con*text* in which intuitions based on method are enacted, just as the "thought" which is the image of method in the *Discours*—"freely imagined" architectonic drawing—occurs in the context of an indispensable, if markedly arbitrary, life story. What, then, would be the method of arriving at knowledge of which discursive signs are an indispensable part?

Intuitions which employ discursive signs occur by way of comparisons:

> ce n'est que par une comparaison que nous connaissons précisément la vérité. Par example, dans le raisonnement suivant: tout A est B,

14. Rule III, *OP,* 1:87.
15. Rule XII, *OP,* 1:185–86.

tout B est C, donc tout A est C, on compare entre eux le terme cherché et le terme donné, savoir A et C, sous ce rapport que l'un et
l'autre sont B, etc. Mais puisque les formes du syllogisme, comme
nous l'avons déjà fait plusieurs fois remarquer, ne sont d'aucun secours pour apercevoir la vérité des choses, le lecteur fera bien de les re-
jeter complètement, et de bien comprendre que d'une façon générale,
toute connaissance qui ne s'obtient pas par l'intuition simple et pure
d'une chose isolée, s'obtient par la comparaison de deux ou plusieurs
choses entre elles. Et presque tout le travail de la raison humaine consiste sans doute à rendre cette opération possible: car lorsqu'elle est
facile et simple, on n'a besoin d'aucun secours artificiel, il suffit de la
seule lumière naturelle pour voir par intuition la vérité qu'elle permet
d'obtenir.[16]

it is only by way of a comparison that we know the truth precisely.
For example, in the following chain of reasoning: every A is B, every
B is C, therefore all A is C, we compare among them the term
searched for and the given term, i.e., A and C, according to the relationship that both one and the other are B, etc. But since the forms
of syllogism, as we have often remarked, are of no assistance in per-
ceiving the truth of things, the reader would do well to reject them
completely, and to understand that, in a general manner, all knowledge that cannot be obtained by the simple and pure intuition of an
isolated thing is obtained by the comparison of two or more things
among themselves. And almost all the work of human reason consists, without doubt, in making this operation possible, for since it is
ready and simple, we have no need for any artificial assistance; natural
light alone suffices to see by intuition the truth that it allows one to
obtain.

As Descartes' use of signs in the rudimentary example "all A is B, all
B is C" already indicates, the operation of comparison requires "artificial
assistance" if it is to work at all. The "artificial assistance" Descartes criticizes is syllogistic. But in order for "two or more things" to be compared
"among themselves" such that their comparison may be seen by "natural
light" to constitute the truth of "intuition," they must themselves stop
being themselves and be represented in the artificial light of discursive
symbols. If "almost all the work of human reason consists, without doubt,

16. Rule XIV, *OP,* 1:168.

in making this operation possible," the discursive designation of things, without doubt, makes all this work possible; the signs introduced in the *Géométrie* as integral to its method are no less integral to the posing and solution of any nonmathematical problem of knowledge. Without these means, neither discursive nor nondiscursive, metaphysical nor physical problems could be posed, let alone "intuited" as solved, at all.[17]

That discursive symbols are useful to the solution of logical problems is, of course, a commonplace since Aristotle, whose definitions of syllogistic forms of reasoning and demonstration in the *Organon* are the *loci classici* of the logic of pure and applied procedural norms.[18] But while Descartes never doubted the category of truth, he never conceived it as a *logical* category. His early discussion of a "possible" universal language which would sharé the calculatory ambitions of Leibniz's *Ars Combinatoria* already pointed out the practical problems in a purely grammatical production of truth, and denied specifically that such a language would ever come into "use" ("usage"). Consistent with his own practical focus on the means and order of investigation, method, Descartes suggested that, with respect to language users, any invented language would do best to establish "an order among the thoughts that enter the human mind," while, with respect to linguistic meaning, the employment of a single artificial language would require "great changes in the order of things."[19] In historic contrast

17. Cf. the important discussion of comparison in Gaukroger, "Descartes' Project," p. 99: "It is a comparison of this kind, which becomes an immediate act of the intuition, that forms the basis for the solution of 'perfectly well comprehended problems.' In this respect, which can be termed *methodological,* the procedures for posing mathematical and nonmathematical problems are the same." In focusing on the *discursive* means by which "comparison . . . becomes an immediate act of the intuition," the present discussion questions whether, given those means, "becoming" and "immediacy," or "comparison" and "intuition," can coincide as identical.

18. *Prior Analytics* I.1.24b.18–26b.34; *Posterior Analytics* I.2.72a.25–73a.20, in *The Basic Works of Aristotle,* ed. Richard McKeon (New York: Random House, 1941), pp. 66–70, 113–15: "A syllogism is discourse in which, certain things being stated, something other than what is stated follows of necessity from their being so. . . . That one term should be included in another as in a whole is the same as for the other to be predicated of all of the first" (*Prior Analytica,* I.1.24b).

19. Letter to Mersenne, 20 November 1629, *AM,* 1:89–93. Descartes concludes of the "possible" new language: "Mais n'espérez pas de la voir jamais en usage; cela présuppose de grands changements en l'ordre des choses, et il faudrait que tout le Monde ne fût qu'un paradis terrestre, ce qui n'est bon à proposer que dans le pays des romans" (Do not hope to ever see it in use; that presupposes great changes in the order of

to Leibniz, who considered syllogisms among "the most beautiful" "invention[s]" of "the human mind," Descartes saw no intellectual attraction in
formal or symbolic logic, whose grounding in syllogism could only serve to
remove the mind further from the *practical* pursuit of truth, an "intuition"
achieved only in a present act of "attention."[20]

---

things, and the World would have to be a terrestrial paradise, which it is only good to
propose in the land of novels) (1:93).

   That such a language and such a "terrestrial paradise" are no less alien in "the land of
novels" is the subject matter of two romantic works that largely repeat Descartes' conclusion here, Kleist's *Über das Marionettentheater* (1810) and *Die Marquise von O . . .*
(pub. 1810). In the latter Kleist represents Descartes' imperfect "order of things"—
the "fragile order of the world" ("gebrechlich[e] Einrichtung der Welt")—as a kind of
theater of the impossibility of cognition, while his discussion of "grace" as mathematically true movement in the *Marionettentheater* ends with a Cartesian emphasis on the
necessary failure to arrive at true knowledge through terrestrial experience, *combined
with* a Pascalian reflection on the infinite nature of mental effort toward that end.
See Heinrich von Kleist, *Sämtliche Werke und Briefe*, 2 vols., 7th ed. rev., ed. Helmut
Sembdner (Munich: dtv, 1987), 2:104–43, 338–45. On the discrepancies among dis-
cursivity, cognition, and mathematically true movement in the two works, cf. my
"Whatever Moves You: 'Experimental Philosophy' and the Literature of Experience in
Diderot and Kleist," in *Traditions of Experiment from the Enlightenment to the Present:
Essays in Honor of Peter Demetz*, ed. Nancy Kaiser and David E. Wellbery (Ann Arbor:
University of Michigan Press, 1993), pp. 17–43. On Descartes' practical objections to
the project of a universal language, see Belaval, *Leibniz critique de Descartes*, pp. 181–
83. Cf. Derrida's suggestion, in "Les romans de Descartes ou l'économie des mots," *Du
droit à la philosophie*, that such a language was Descartes' own theoretical ambition:
"the language of paradise and the language of the method would share a common universal transparency. There would no longer even be a method to desire" (p. 341).
20. On the bases of Leibniz's and Descartes' opposing views of syllogistic, formal
logic, see Beck, *Method of Descartes*, pp. 272–78, 286–87: "[Descartes'] very definition
of intellectual intuition, *intuitus mentis purae et attentae*, includes within it the vital
factor of attention not only to the form of the argument, or its *connexio*, but to the very
nature of the content itself. . . . The definition of truth cannot therefore lie in some
purely formal equation; it cannot be defined apart from the actual awareness or apprehension of it in the act of intellectual intuition. . . . Leibniz . . . wishes some formal
equivalent to his own ideal of an *Ars Combinatoria*. Nothing . . . could be farther from
the Cartesian conception, with its Leibnizian presupposition of formalism and the
possibility of 'giving reason a holiday'" (pp. 275, 277, 287). See also Thomas M. Carr,
Descartes and the Resilience of Rhetoric: Varieties of Cartesian Rhetorical Theory (Carbondale: Southern Illinois University Press, 1990), in which the central Cartesian notion
of "attention" is provocatively linked to rhetoric (on the function of "attention," see
note 27, this chapter).

The empirical aspect of "attention" is never effaced by Descartes' use of notation: thus the *Regulae*, "Rules *for the Direction of the Spirit*," rather than for the construction of a mechanical system of proof defined as identical with truth; thus the "*Discours* de la Méthode," rather than the restatement of the automatisms of syllogism; thus the *Géométrie*, rather than *Algèbre*.[21] Descartes' letters designate neither the parts of a computational machine nor the sequence of premises and predicates he views as rhetorical, but, rather, specific linear magnitudes, things in the world. Descartes' "signs" signify content, and the "things" designated by those signs would have been unthinkable without them, for those signs facilitate "the work of human reason" by making our experience of the deductive act of comparison continuous:

> On peut dès lors se demander pourquoi, en sus de l'intuition, nous avons ajouté ici un autre mode de connaissance, celui qui se fait par *déduction*. . . . Il a fallu procéder ainsi, parce que la plupart des choses sont l'objet d'une connaissance certaine, tout en n'étant pas par elles-mêmes évidentes; il suffit qu'elles soient déduites à partir de principes vrais et déjà connus, par un mouvement continu et ininterrompu de la pensée, qui prend de chaque terme une intuition claire: ce n'est pas autrement que nous savons que le dernier anneau de quelque longue chaîne est rattaché au premier, même si nous ne voyons pas d'un seul et même coup d'oeil l'ensemble des anneaux intermédiaires dont dépend ce rattachement; il suffit que nous les ayons examinés l'un apres l'autre, et que nous nous souvenions que du premier au dernier, chacun d'eux est attaché à ses voisins immédiats.[22]

> One can ask why we have added, aside from intuition, another mode of knowledge, that made by *deduction*. . . . It was necessary to proceed in this way because most things are the object of a certain cognition even if they are not evident themselves; they need only be deduced on the basis of true and known principles, by a continuous and uninterrupted movement of thought, which takes a clear intuition from each term: this is the same as knowing that the last link of a long chain is attached to the first, even if we don't see in a single

21. That is to say, rather than the nonepistemological mathematics of Leibniz. Cf. Hacking, "Proof and Eternal Truths," pp. 170–78. On Leibniz and Aristotle, see Styazhkin, *History of Mathematical Logic*, pp. 22–23.

22. Rule III, *OP,* 1:88–89.

glance the whole ensemble of intermediary links upon which this attachment depends; we only need to have examined them one after the other, and remember that from the first to the last, each one of them is attached to its immediate neighbors.

What we "remember" in the diachronic course of a deduction are the signs that make it possible for us to "preserve our entire fancy free for present ideas,"[23] that is, for precisely such a "continuous and uninterrupted movement of thought." Signs make it possible for us to view the sequential terms of a comparison as a whole, and thus to perform a deduction in a putative or effective present, "even if we don't see in a single glance" all the terms we have already "examined." The discursive means of the method remember content for us: we need not double back and replace them by the "things" for which they stand. To do so would be to break the continuous line of delimited, comparative reasoning (the "chain" connecting "first" and "last" through "intermediary links") which is the intellectual counterpart of finite, physical extension in space.

A line of thought such as produces the drawing of a line in Descartes' *Géométrie* can only be produced in abstraction from lines. This abstraction must be marked—what we in a general way call "legible"—and this is where the method set forth in the *Géométrie* spells out the unspoken process involved in all discursive experience. The abstraction from content provided by discrete letters allows the mind to "retain" them without reflection, much as more complex signs, combinations of letters, or words, make it possible for us to produce and to receive, to write and to read sentences. No sentence could be completed if its writer or reader were compelled to remember, at every moment, every word, indeed, every syllable and letter that preceded every succeeding term. Sentences, too, that is to say, are available to Zeno's paradoxes, if in a conceptually more complex way.[24] For unlike a point that is infinitely divisible, the words, syllables, and letters that we must unthinkingly retain in order to write or to read beyond them have different grammatical functions and signify different meanings. A point is a point is a point . . . : Zeno's paradoxes insist that we understand this fact not as a redundancy, but as an infinite regress of semantics and syntax, meaning here always meaning more of itself, without qualitative change. Words, however, mean something else: thanks to

23. Rule XVI, *OP,* 1:186.
24. Cf. Goodkin, *Around Proust,* pp. 85–88.

the arbitrary integrity of "concise signs," a sentence is not infinitely divisible, but the meanings of its terms are inexhaustible. No sentence would be utterable or understandable if that arbitrary integrity were made to account for its references; if we stopped to replace words with their definitions in words, let alone with specific things. Because Descartes' signs are letters, and because the things they stand for are finite lines, in addition to mechanical arithmetic operations, the mind may perform the "operation" of "comparison." Comparison—"the work of human reason"—yields a deduction, and deduction yields the effect of synchronic vision, an intuitive whole. The continuity of the intelligence enabled by discursive means ensures that comparison, although it must take place in time, will never resemble a representational "fable," and that the intuition of the whole effected in deduction will always resemble a "representation inaccessible to doubt,"[25] a *vrai,* rather than *vraisemblable,* "tableau."

"C'est une règle de la méthode, lorsqu'on a plus de deux choses différentes à comparer entre elles, de les parcourir successivement, et de ne fixer son attention que sur deux d'entre elles à la fois"[26] (It is a rule of the method, when there are more than two different things to compare, to traverse them successively and not fix one's attention on more than two of them at a time). In that it "directs" the spirit outward toward "the intuition of *évidence,*" "attention" has been described as a "bridge across the radical discontinuity of Cartesian metaphysics, the distinction between res *cogitans* and *res extensa,*" and as opening "a space that might be labeled rhetorical . . . within [Descartes'] system."[27] To this important observation it should be added that the "évidence" toward which "attention" directs the intelligence are signs—the discursive means "*de* la méthode"—and that even these "very concise signs" inhering in method must be attended to in a staggered fashion, no "more than two of them at a time." In order to effect the kind of representation Descartes calls an intuition, each deduction enacts a temporal "*discours* de la méthode."

The model for linking *res cogitans* and *res extensa,* one could say more generally, is Descartes' *Géométrie,* an "experiment" in method in which discursive rhetoric (including the "rhetoric" of logic, i.e., syllogistic form)

25. Rule III, *OP,* 1:87.
26. Rule XIV, *OP,* 1:183.
27. Carr, *Resilience of Rhetoric,* pp. 39, 4, 168.

is circumvented. Words of different and uncertain meanings representing different objects of uncertain existence—representations, in other words, that *are* accessible to doubt—are replaced by entirely abstract signs representing extension, whose objectification in one substance, finite lines, can be drawn from any point in two dimensions. Compared two at a time, the signs of the method offer a "ready" and "simple"[28] means of achieving mental certainty and continuity analogous to the physical act of drawing a line that embodies the changing values of paired variables. This is the method in which discourse inheres, the "thought" of which the architectural drawing of well-proportioned "places regulières"—the transcription of "fancy" unencumbered by objects, by the need to remember content, and by historical error—is the image. Is the *cogito* such a "thought?"

28. Rule XIV, *OP,* 1:168.

THREE. THINKING AS LINE

7   The *Cogito* and Architectural Form

The *cogito* returns us to the *Discours de la méthode,* an autobiographical discourse that describes its "story" as a "fable" and "represent[s]" the content of that fable—"ma vie"—"as in a tableau."[1] This representation has the critical effect of showing the insufficiency of learning derived from "fables." Under "fables" Descartes finally includes writings in all known disciplines whose foundations are borrowed from the imaginings of philosophy:

> d'autant que [les autres sciences] empruntent leur principes de la philosophie, je jugeais qu'on ne pouvais avoir rien bâti, qui fût solide, sur des fondements si peu fermes [. . .] ayant appris, dès le collège, qu'on ne saurait rien imaginer de si étrange et si peu croyable, qu'il n'ait été dit par quelqu'un des philosophes.[2]

> inasmuch as the other sciences derive their principles from philosophy, I judged that one could not have built anything solid upon such shaky foundations [. . .] having learned, since college, that one cannot imagine anything so strange and so unbelievable, that it has not been said by some philosopher.

Firsthand experience of the world, too, resembles a discursive "fable." First said to resemble reading, then posed as an alternative to reading, and ultimately figured, once again in terms analogous to reading, as "study in the book of the world," firsthand experience is described as the viewing of "comédies," the equivalent of an encounter with "fables" presently enacted.[3] Alternately projecting ahead of and doubling back upon itself

1. *OP,* 1:570–71.
2. Ibid., pp. 576, 583.
3. Ibid., pp. 571, 573, 577, 578, 599.

in distinctly nonlinear fashion, and undermining the significance of its stated change in direction by way of comparisons between reading and travel, this narrating or "talking about"—this discoursing which, while it is Descartes' stated "design," is also shown by Descartes to be antithetical to "the method" which those same narrated experiences teach him to seek elsewhere—resembles less a life progressively represented than a life whose "whole course" is present from the beginning. "Represent[ed] as in a *tableau*," Descartes' "fable" of his life forecloses its interest as a representational story. It is not the fictionality of that story that makes it a "fable" but rather its implication that life stories are the fiction of a single decisive change ("je changeai entièrement d'opinion"[4]), a single moment of truth (rather than "opinion"), and thus an elimination of fiction in experience to come.

To the degree that Descartes' narrative presents its own foreclosure, representing the search for truth in experience not as revelation but as "fable," reading the *Discours* is less like reading a "story" than viewing an already delimited representation, a picture. To recognize and to represent autobiographical narrative as a picture is quite the opposite, however, to formulating an epistemology which is pictorial. Rather than ascribe new truth value to subjectively generated representations, Descartes distrusts them and invites us to distrust his tableau-like "fable."[5] Its representations

4. Ibid., p. 571.

5. Ibid.: "ne proposant cet écrit . . . que comme une fable, en laquelle, parmi quelques exemples qu'on peut imiter, on en trouvera peut-être aussi plusieurs autres qu'on aura raison de ne pas suivre" (in proposing this writing . . . only as a fable, in which, among examples that one can imitate, one will perhaps find many others that one will be right not to follow). Ibid., p. 582: "si, mon ouvrage m'ayant assez plu, je vous en fais voir ici le modèle, ce n'est pas, pour cela, que je veuille conseiller à personne de l'imiter" (if, my work having sufficiently pleased me, I show it to you as a model, it is not that I want to counsel anyone to imitate it).

The view that Descartes makes pictorial representation into a philosophical model by ascribing to subjective representations the status of objective truth is argued by Judovitz in *Subjectivity and Representation*. See, in particular, pp. 188–89: "The major characteristic of the Cartesian theory of representation is that, by forcing and framing the world into a particular order, the world is reduced to an object that has the character of a picture. . . . [Representation] ceases to function as a convention and acquires the objective character of truth as certitude based on the extension of epistemological principles to the rest of philosophy. . . . In other words, representation now becomes paradigmatic of the new set of relations between Cartesian subjectivity and the world." Judovitz uses the concept of representation to describe the "modern" erasure of the

(and representations of representations) are the *matter* of his "discourse," the medium, and not the purpose, of his explicitly discursive intention or "design."

Yet that "design"—to "talk about" method—includes a non-autobiographical representation shorn of discursive context, the "thought" of architectural drawing. Taking place in intellectual and physical isolation, Descartes' "thought" of an engineer or architect drawing lines according to the free power of his intellect—"à sa fantaisie"—is discontinuous with the false continuity of book learning and worldly experience declared and demonstrated in his "fable." On the basis of this disruptive "thought" embedded within his *Discours,* Descartes criticizes not only his own "story" but the history of the world, including the intermittent, circumstantial formation, compelled by crimes, feuds, and divergent opinion, of legal statutes, religions, and knowledge. His "thought" of an architect continues:

> Ainsi je m'imaginai que les peuples qui, ayant été autrefois demi-sauvages, et ne s'étant civilisés que peu à peu, n'ont fait leurs lois qu'à mesure que l'incommodité des crimes et des querelles les y a contraints, ne sauraient être si bien policés que ceux qui, dès le commencement qu'ils se sont assemblés, ont observé les constitutions de quelque prudent législateur. Comme il est bien certain que l'état de la vraie religion, dont Dieu seul a fait les ordonnances, doit être incomparablement mieux réglé que tous les autres. . . . Et ainsi je pensai que les sciences des livres, au moins celles dont les raisons ne sont que probables, et qui n'ont aucunes démonstrations, s'étant composées et grossies peu à peu des opinions de plusieurs diverses personnes, ne sont point si approchantes de la vérité que les simples raisonnements

---

autobiographical subject of the *Discours* by the epistemological subject of the *cogito:* "the truth of the proposition 'I think' lies in the order of representation, embedded in the self-evident character of its utterance"; "the *cogito* is presented . . . as a primitive act of knowledge, one based on a *simple act of mental vision*—in other words, *intuition*" (pp. 110, 116). However, I find no basis for ascribing to Descartes the equation of pictorial representation with intuition. As the notational method necessary to the *Géométrie* demonstrates, thinking in Descartes is not a "self-evident" "representation," nor is the necessary structure of the *cogito,* described in what follows, of the "primitive" order of "a simple act of mental vision" to be conflated with a picture. Like the free architectonic drawing of which Descartes "thinks" within the context of his representational "fable," the *cogito* is an activity distinctly at odds with all pictorial representation.

que peut faire naturellement un homme de bon sens touchant les choses qui se présentent.[6]

Thus I imagined that people who, having once been half-savages, and only having become civilized little by little, made their laws only to the extent [or, according to the measure: *qu'à mesure*] that the inconvenience of crimes and quarrels constrained them to do so, would not be as well ordered as those who, from the very beginning of their coming together, observed the constitutional laws of some prudent legislator. As it is certain that the state of the true religion, whose ordinances were made by God alone, must be incomparably better ordered than all others. . . . And thus I thought that the sciences of books, at least those whose claims are only probable, and which have no demonstrations, having been composed and enlarged little by little by the opinions of many different people, do not approach the truth as do the simple reasonings which a man of good sense can make naturally concerning things that present themselves.

The history of the human endeavor to order itself, to live in society, and to know, is a tissue of partial efforts whose diachronic development ("little by little"), like the historically composite buildings produced by several different architects, can never resemble the self-regulating reasonings of a single man thinking, like a single architect drawing, alone. Finally, the errors that are part of institutional diachrony are analogous to the errors of any individual life; world history is but a longer version of each autobiography: "Et ainsi encore je pensai que, pour ce que nous avons été enfants avant que d'être hommes, et qu'il nous a fallu longtemps être gouvernés par nos appétits et nos précepteurs . . . , il est presque impossible que nos jugements soient si purs, ni si solides, qu'ils auraient été, si nous avions eu l'usage entier de notre raison dès le point de notre naissance, et que nous n'eussions jamais été conduits que par elle"[7] (And thus I thought further

6. Part Two, *OP,* 1:580.

7. Ibid., pp. 580–81. Timothy J. Reiss has argued that Descartes' "use of an architectural metaphor" at the opening of this passage shows that the "implicit goals of an ostensible 'mere' philosophical method are immediately politicized." Since architecture provides the only link between the thinking of method and its discursive manifestation, it must also stand between thinking and all historical human activity in the *Discours.* Just as method is no "mere" philosophical pursuit for Descartes, the empirical and worldly function of the architectonic in Descartes' discussion of historical and social formations is explicit. See Reiss, "Power, Poetry and the Resemblance of

that, since we have all been children before being men, and since we had
to be governed for a long time by our appetites and our teachers . . . , it
is almost impossible that our judgments be as pure and as solid as they
would have been, had we had the full use of our reason from the moment
of our birth, and only been led by her).

Descartes' modest "fable" is thus also the discourse of human civiliza-
tion. The only basis on which Descartes, as autobiographical narrator, can
"reform [his] own thoughts"[8] and formulate a method is the "thought"
of nondiscursive formation manifested in architectural drawing. But this
"thought" is not "merely" a metaphor, that is, an image understood as a
dispensable figure of an otherwise independent thought. It is the manifestation, in discourse, of the method exercised in the *Géométrie.* After briefly
stating the four rules of procedure, Descartes reminds us that it was not
his "design" to study "mathematical" sciences in particular but to identify the general way in which they regard their different objects. Finding
that mathematicians "considered nothing [in objects] other than relations
or proportions between them" ("elles n'y considèrent autre chose que les
divers rapports ou proportions qui s'y trouvent"), he then summarizes the
conceptual innovations of the *Géométrie* specifically in terms of the technique of its method:

> je pensai qu'il valait mieux que j'examinasse seulement ces propor-
> tions en général, et sans les supposer que dans les sujets qui serviraient
> à m'en rendre la connaissance plus aisée; . . . que, pour les considérer
> mieux en particulier, je les devais supposer en des lignes . . . ; mais
> que, pour les retenir, ou les comprendre plusieurs ensemble, il fallait
> que je les expliquasse par quelques chiffres, les plus courts qu'il serait
> possible.[9]

> I thought that it would be better if I only examined proportions in
> general, supposing them only in subjects which would serve to facili-
> tate my knowledge of them; . . . that, in order better to consider
> them in particular, I should suppose them [manifested] in lines . . . ;
> but that, in order to retain them, or to comprehend many of them

Nature," in *Mimesis: From Mirror to Method, Augustine to Descartes,* ed. John D. Lyons
and Stephen G. Nichols (Hanover, N.H.: University Press of New England, 1982),
p. 222).

8. *OP,* 1:582.

9. Part Two, *OP,* 1:588–89.

together, I would have to explicate them by means of the briefest possible signs.

The proportional "places regulières" drawn by an architect acting in complete autonomy are the manifestation of a rapid, mental continuity discontinuous with autobiographical or any human history. They are forms produced on an empty plain whose use is uninhibited by the remains of years and millennia that are historical memory. *But in order to become a method, drawing must be made available as discourse:* the physical content of proportional relations must be signified, so as to be forgotten, in the rapid act of the drawing of a deduction—what Descartes calls "taking an intuition of the whole." There can be no method without the discourse "about it," or within which it occurs; lines, or "things," must be designated as letters.

The *cogito* designates a "thing" "I." The *discours de la méthode* is, on the one hand, autobiographical, a representational recollection, "fable" and "tableau"; and on the other, abstract notation, a literal substitution and momentary forgetting, "deduction" and "intuition." Between these is the *cogito,* the autobiographical deduction, or self-designating intuition, that holds the *Discours* together, linking representational with abstract discourse and discourse with method. For, ultimately, the *discours de la méthode* is the statement "je pense, donc je suis."[10] The words of the *cogito* state that the reality of the physical world is knowable only from thought, and they state this with reference to a reality which is also the writer of the statement. In this *autobiographical* deduction, the "thing" which is intuited is also the thinking subject that intuits it. Cartesian dualism, the origin of the modern "mind-body problem," or, in more general terms, the break between epistemology and ontology which in large measure constitutes post-Cartesian philosophy, follows the self-containing statement of the *cogito* like the gifts of evil sprung from Pandora's box. "Follows," precisely, *in time,* but far less precisely, *from:* the self-reflexive *cogito* weds a logical problem of inference ("donc") with a concrete problem of reference ("je suis"), creating an indivisible conceptual knot of which innumerable

10. Part Four, *OP,* 1:603. Descartes calls it "the first principle of the philosophy that I was seeking" ("le premier principe de la philosophie que je cherchais" [ibid.]). Typically, this "first principle" is given *after* the prescriptive rules and maxims, at the close of the autobiographical writing, the whole of which would require certain knowledge of "I" in the first place.

efforts to locate the precise point of the mind-body split offer ongoing evidence. It is fair to say, in the true spirit of Zeno, that the literature on this topic is both inexhaustible and cannot get past a certain point; or, alternatively, that whatever analytic tools have been developed in the interim, however fine (or fuzzy) the logical and linguistic subdivisions used to describe it, the *cogito* remains ahead of its professional interpreters and cannot be overtaken. The modern analytic reception of the *cogito* resembles for the most part a history of painstaking, hairsplitting divisions tending, coincidentally, to divide among themselves between those concerned primarily with mind and those primarily considering body, the former analyzing the question of what kind of statement "je" is making in the *cogito,* the latter analyzing the nature of the existential "je" about whom it is made.[11]

11. The following sampling of refinements of the mind-body paradigm is illustrative of basic trends: Cartesian dualism is not between mind and body but between "the soul and its consciousness of its body and . . . the reality of this body outside my consciousness of it," i.e., two notions of body (Henri Gouhier, *La pensée métaphysique de Descartes* [Paris: Vrin, 1962], p. 372); it is between two notions of ontology, corporeal and "incorporeal" (Hiram Caton, *The Origin of Subjectivity: An Essay on Descartes* [New Haven, Yale University Press, 1973], pp. 141–43); it is between "pure thoughts" and "sensations" (Margaret D. Wilson, "Cartesian Dualism," in *Descartes: Critical and Interpretive Essays,* ed. Michael Hooker [Baltimore: Johns Hopkins University Press, 1978], pp. 208–11); it is between body thought of as "extensa" and as "cogitatio" (Alan Donagan, "Descartes' Treatment of Mind and Body," in Hooker, *Descartes: Critical and Interpretive Essays,* p. 191); it is between "conceivability" and "logical possibility" as between "what is a body" and "[what] is essentially a body" (Michael Hooker, "Denial of Mind-Body Identity," in Hooker, *Descartes: Critical and Interpretive Essays,* pp. 174–84); it is between a being which is the result of a finite process of reflection and one which is infinitely in process (Robert Spaemann, "Le *sum* dans le *cogito sum,*' in *Le discours et sa méthode,* ed. Nicolas Grimaldi and Jean-Luc Marion [Paris: Presses Universitaires de France, 1987], p. 283), or it is between a logical "proposition" and momentary "performance" on the one hand and a proposition and the actuality of "thought" on the other (Jean-Claude Pariente, "Problèmes logiques du *cogito,*" in Grimaldi and Marion, *Le discours et sa méthode,* pp. 241–43, 260–68); see also Beyssade, *La philosophie première,* pp. 217–30. The most interesting analyses from the point of view of the *discursive* nature of Descartes' method focus less on the splitting of mind and body than on the confusion of logical inference and reference in his central formulation. In "The Certainty of the *Cogito,*" in Doney, *Descartes: A Collection of Critical Essays,* pp. 88–107, Bernard Williams recalls Gassendi's original objection to the exclusive linking of existing with thinking—why not, "I breathe therefore I am" instead? (pp. 98–100)—and reflects on the specific nature of the statement and the "I" it pre-

If one views the *cogito,* however, as integral to Descartes' "design"—his "discours *de* la méthode"—a different understanding of its status emerges. That discourse is autobiographical and notational, representational and abstract. Both these discursive modes compose the context in which method is enacted: in the "thought" that images the free exercise of reason as self-determining architectural drawing; and in the writing of spatial extensions as letters permitting reason to grasp a deductive "chain" as a "whole," to represent physical reality in such a way as momentarily to erase and replace it in the rapid movement of an "intuition." An intuition takes place during the time that notation is read. The *cogito* reads, in context, as follows:

> à cause que nos sens nous trompent quelquefois, je voulus supposer qu'il n'y avait aucune chose qui fût telle qu'ils nous la font imaginer. Et parce qu'il y a des hommes qui se méprennent en raisonnant, même touchant les plus simples matières de géométrie, et y font des paralogismes, jugeant que j'étais sujet à faillir, autant qu'aucun autre, je rejetai comme fausses toutes les raisons que j'avais prises auparavant pour démonstrations. Et enfin, considérant que toutes les mêmes pensées, que nous avons étant éveillés, nous peuvent aussi venir, quand nous dormons, sans qu'il y en ait aucune, pour lors, qui soit vraie, je me résolus de feindre que toutes les choses qui m'étaient jamais entrées en l'esprit n'étaient non plus vraies que les illusions de mes songes. Mais aussitôt après, je pris garde que, pendant que je

---

supposes: "we may wonder whether the proposition is not formulated in such a way as to lend itself to confusion. . . . it appears . . . to be a kind of inference from one proposition that is certain to another and to be based not only on the principle of presupposition and the unique properties of the word 'I' but also on the autonomy of 'I think' " (pp. 94, 102–3). Jaakko Hintikka's seminal study of the *cogito* as inference and speech act, *"Cogito, Ergo Sum:* Inference or Performance?" focuses similarly on its ambivalent status as both a necessary inference from a proposition and the necessary performance of that proposition: "the word *cogito* has a curious double role in Descartes's dictum. On the one hand, it is a part of a proposition whose status (indubitability) is at stake. On the other hand, it refers to the performance through which the indubitability of this proposition is revealed" (see Hintikka, *"Cogito, Ergo Sum,"* in Doney, *Descartes,* p. 133). Both Williams and Hintikka depart from A. J. Ayer's important analysis of the logical "degeneracy" (or tautological "truth") of the *cogito* as statement: "Knowing that I exist . . . is having the answer to a question which is put in such a form that it answers itself" (see Ayer, " 'I think, therefore I am,' " in Doney, *Descartes,* p. 87).

voulais ainsi penser que tout était faux, il fallait nécessairement que moi, qui le pensais, fusse quelque chose. Et remarquant que cette vérité: *je pense, donc je suis,* était si ferme et si assurée, que toutes les plus extravagantes suppositions des sceptiques n'étaient pas capables de l'ébranler, je jugeai que je pouvais la recevoir, sans scrupule, pour le premier principe de la philosophie que je cherchais.[12]

since our senses sometimes deceive us, I willed myself to suppose that there was no thing which was such as our senses make us imagine it. And because there are men who are mistaken in reasoning even about the simplest matters of geometry, and commit paralogisms, judging that I was as subject to error as any other, I rejected all the arguments that I had taken for demonstrations before as false. And finally, considering that all the same thoughts that we have when we are awake can also come to us when we are asleep, without any of them being true, I resolved to pretend that all the things that had ever entered into my mind were no more true than the illusions of my dreams. But, immediately afterward, I remarked that, during the time that I wanted thus to think that everything was false, it was necessary that I, who thought this, be something. And remarking that this truth: *I think, therefore I am,* was so firm and so assured that all the most extravagant suppositions of the skeptics were unable to shake it, I judged that I could receive it, without scruple, as the first principle of the philosophy I was seeking.

That our senses may deceive us, that we may be dreaming when we believe ourselves awake, and that there can be no manner of disproving these illusions by proving them illusions: these are the well-known negative foundations of Cartesian skepticism. Less commonly recognized is the specific example of sensory error Descartes gives—that of men reasoning falsely "even about the most simple matters of geometry." Those matters are the simple elements of physical reality, and the simplest of these is extension or line, which we are led by the sensory perception of three-dimensional figures to comprehend falsely. The true nature of the most simple matter of geometry can only be known when it is represented and replaced by the simple matter of a concise sign. Geometry must be "talk[ed] about" in signs: there must be discourse if there is to be knowledge—if there is to be method. For method only "is" insofar as it is en-

12. *Discours,* Part Four, *OP,* 1:602–3.

acted. Descartes' "design" is to write a *discours,* not a *traité de la méthode;* the method can only be demonstrated in the course of its demonstrations, in the "experiment" of the *Géométrie* that *requires* the writing and reading of discursive notation.

"Je pense, donc je suis": "this truth," "the first principle of the philosophy I was seeking," or, as Descartes had already suggested in Part Two, the truth which would be both the point of departure and the realization of his "design . . . of reforming my own thoughts, and of building on a foundation which is entirely my own," is written at the intersection of Descartes' autobiography and Descartes' *Géométrie.*[13] The complex "design" of the *Discours de la méthode* suggests that "this truth" be read neither in terms of the metaphysical opposition of epistemology and ontology, which it was the purpose of method to bridge, as a way of knowing what is; nor in those of the analytic oppositions of statement and action, and of logic and substance, which it was equally the purpose of method to bridge, as a way of replacing syllogistic reasoning about verbal definitions with the performance of an "intuition" of things. Read instead in terms of the practical method for knowing that requires it, the *cogito* is the writing and reading of notation.

The *cogito* deduces the truth concerning "je": that it ("je") is—surely a strange operation to perform upon a subject. It is a thing during the time

13. As Gilson has demonstrated, it was in fact the *Géométrie* that Descartes intended to elaborate during his retreat in the stove-heated room in Germany. His ambition "to build, by means of a single method, the entire edifice of Geometry" was extended first, Gilson argues, to include "all sciences" and finally to the recognition—which Gilson identifies with Descartes' "thought" of an architect drawing—that he must "constitute the entire system within himself" ("en constituer à lui seul le système entier"). That constitution, the *cogito,* would then literally be the result of the mediation of the *Discours* by the *Géométrie*—Descartes' initial object or aim—and of the *Géométrie* by the autobiographical *Discours,* the means by which he came to understand himself as the object of the *Géométrie* (see Gilson, *Discours,* pp. 157–60).

Damisch makes the connection between the *cogito* and the *Géométrie* in a more limited sense. Viewing its "first person" as a "fixed point," he states that "in this respect alone, the *Cogito* can be held for the translation . . . of a methodical theme or structure" that "obeys demonstrative reasoning, in the sense that pertains to geometry" (*L'origine de la perspective,* p. 70). As discussed in what follows, the notion of "je" as a "point," which was developed in existential rather than geometrical terms by Jaspers, does not, I think, adequately express the fundamental extension of the "methodical structure" of the *cogito.*

that it thought all other things were false: "pendant que je voulais ainsi penser que tout était faux, il fallait nécessairement que moi, qui le pensais, fusse quelque chose" (during the time I wanted thus to think that everything was false, it was necessary that I, who thought this, was something). The temporality of the *cogito* is the temporality of an intuition. The Second Meditation will pose the question, "but how much time" is the temporality of the certainty, the intuition of "je"? (*"Je suis, j'existe:* cela est certain; mais combien de temps?")"; and answer that question in the terms of the temporality of thought given in the *Discours:* "as long as I think" ("autant de temps que je pense").[14] "During the time" that Descartes "thinks" all things are false, he is not the subject of a "fable" but the subject of a deduction, "something."[15] He is "je," the thing that is written and read in the deductive statement that is the *cogito:* "et remarquant que cette vérité, *je pense, donc je suis,* était si ferme et si assurée" (and remarking that this truth: *I think, therefore I am,* was so firm and so assured). But what kind of thing is it whose existence is assured in the form of a deductive statement?

That thing has no attributes: no body, and thus no place in the world, and certainly no history — surely a strange way to treat an autobiographical subject.[16] The context of the *cogito* continues:

> Puis, examinant avec attention ce que j'étais, et voyant que je pouvais feindre que je n'avais aucun corps, et qu'il n'y avait aucun monde,

14. Second Meditation, *OP,* 2:418.

15. On the finite temporality of deductions, cf. Carr, *Resilience of Rhetoric,* p. 40: "The attraction of *évidence* is all but irresistible and compels consent, but this consent lasts only as long as the mind continues to experience the clarity and distinctness of the idea, that is, only as long as attention is sustained. Thus, time remains its enemy."

16. It is precisely this phenomenological disappearance of the thinking subject that post-Husserlian phenomenology strove to address. Merleau-Ponty's aim of rethinking the *cogito* as the Ego "in situation" and philosophy as an activity that cannot be thought apart from its medium presented the most comprehensive turn in the direction of a "history" of the thinking, "incarnate" subject (among subjects). His *Phénoménologie de la perception* (Paris: Gallimard, 1945) can be read as an extended confrontation with the bodiless thinking "thing" of Descartes. As developed in the present analysis, Descartes also makes explicit the necessary situation of the self as subject of discourse. Yet, as argued in the epilogue to this study, the "thing[s]" that result from discourse for Descartes — line and the thinking subject — are *not* bound to bodily, historical situation in that way.

ni aucun lieu où je fusse; mais que je ne pouvais pas feindre, pour cela, que je n'étais point; et qu'au contraire, de cela même que je pensais à douter de la vérité des autres choses, il suivait très évidemment et très certainement que j'étais; au lieu que, si j'eusse seulement cessé de penser, encore que tout le reste de ce que j'avais jamais imaginé eût été vrai, je n'avais aucune raison de croire que j'eusse été: je connus de là que j'étais une substance dont toute l'essence ou la nature n'est que de penser, et qui, pour être, n'a besoin d'aucun lieu, ni ne dépend d'aucune chose matérielle. En sorte que ce moi, c'est-à-dire l'âme par laquelle je suis ce qui je suis, est entièrement distincte du corps, et même qu'elle est plus aisée à connaître que lui, et qu'encore qu'il ne fût point, elle ne laisserait pas d'être tout ce qu'elle est.[17]

Then, examining with attention what I was, and seeing that I could pretend that I had no body, that there was no world, nor any place where I was; but that I could not pretend, for all that, that I was not; and that on the contrary, from the very fact that I thought of doubting the truth of other things, it followed very evidently and very certainly that I was; whereas, had I only stopped thinking, even if all the rest of what I had ever imagined were true, I had no reason to believe that I had been. From this I knew that I was a substance whose entire essence or nature is only to think, and which, in order to be, has no need of any place, nor depends on any material thing. In this way this me, that is to say the soul by which I am what I am, is entirely distinct from the body, and even easier than it to know, and even if the body did not exist, the soul would not cease being all that it is.

In the act of thinking that takes place in the soul, "this me" ("ce moi") is recognized as "entirely distinct from the body," independent of "any place" and "any material thing." In the act of thinking, "this me, that is to say the soul by which I am what I am" becomes available to knowledge as "I," "something" that is. But what, and moreover how, can "I" — the subject of thinking — be before it is? The "I" of the *cogito* is a demonstrable subject — "ce moi" — stripped of everything it remembers and imagines about itself as an object, and about other objects, other demon-

17. Part Four, *OP,* 1:603–4. In translating this passage I have tried to maintain Descartes' unusual coordination of verbal tenses.

strable things. The "I" of the *cogito* is the subject rendered concise, the notational rendering of "ce moi": "I" is the subject transcribed as a sign which is "something" "during the time" the subject thinks.

"I," the abstract subject of thinking, is a sign that clears the way for thought. Upon this subject, or basis, thought can begin, but, to begin with, there is no basis for "I." This arbitrarily posed unity evacuates the empirical attributes of what it stands for, making the free "attention" required by thinking possible. The deduction in which it operates thus takes on the status of an intuition, knowledge which is certain. On the basis of signs, the subject can intuit the truth of its reasonings in a "representation that is the act of the pure and attentive intelligence."[18] When the thinking subject writes and reads a sign for itself thinking, it knows the truth of that "I," that "I am" — a sign, the only "thing" without demonstrable attributes at all, and thus, in its pure and rapid legibility, the vehicle of thought.

In order for something to be determined by thinking alone, there must first be an independently fixed unity designated by a sign. For a subject to determine himself in this way, he must presuppose himself, his "soul," as a sign which thinks, that is to say, a sign by which "I am what I am" — surely a strange way but perhaps the only way to avoid the presupposition of a self that precedes all self-reflexivity. In the *cogito* Descartes treats "this me" not as a given but as a subject of proof, and in order to do this he must make himself into a form of notation, a sign stripped of any attributes aside from the act of thinking. If the act of thinking lasts only as long as itself, the *cogito* is the autobiography of thought in which the notation that substitutes for *ce moi,* for all that inheres in being a self — memory, imagination, sensory experience, and doubt — denotes its writer and reader while replacing him. The cogito denotes the self so that it may intuit itself during the time it thinks nothing else is, the time of a deduction carried out in discursive notation, in which all one apprehends, compares, and deduces from are signs. In order to intuit his existence as something other than the vicissitudes of a particular body in places and in time, the vehicles of a "fable" which change and change inconsequentially, Descartes must represent himself and read himself in the form of a deduction — a strange way to treat an autobiographical subject, and the only way to know that subject not as an autobiographical subject of representation but as "a sub-

18. Rule III, *OP,* 1:87.

stance" which is. "All the essence or nature" of this "substance," the pure sign of the self, "I," is "to think."

With positive critical insight, Karl Jaspers described the "concrete" problem posed by the formulation of the *cogito* as a radical division between the absolute contraction and uncertain expansion of the thinking self:

> If thinking, for [Descartes], is, as pure thinking, *self-sufficient,* he falls into an unfilled and unfillable emptiness; if he *describes* thinking more closely, he falls into a psychological phenomenology. Taken to its logical extreme, there are two possibilities for the concrete interpretation of thinking based on Descartes:
>
> Either it has the character of divine thinking (as construed since ancient times) which is and contains in itself all being, because in *thinking it at the same time creates that which is thought.* Instead of this, however, human thinking finds in itself only the empty point of the "I think" without all-filling being. . . .
>
> Or immediately self-certain thinking would not be the identity of a unity certain of itself but rather it would be split into two, that is, into that which thinks in me and that which this thinking, as thinking, knows. Then, however, certainty is no longer immediate but rather refers to something which must, to begin with, be something else for knowing. . . . In this way thinking is *consciousness* and the being of thinking is the *being of the entirety of consciousness,* or everything that is an object of a phenomenology of consciousness. . . .
>
> Thus, when one questions the determination of the thinking Descartes means, certainty refers either to an empty point—the self thinking itself—or to the manifold, wavering reality of consciousness. In both cases . . . the origin [of philosophizing] which this first certainty should hit upon has disappeared.[19]

When taken not as consciousness but as a self-reflexive unity, the *cogito* must be an "empty *point*": "the point . . . in which consciousness of existence shrinks to a minimum"; "a point of the indubitable which bears no fruit"; "the logical point of understanding as such."[20] Determined, on

---

19. Jaspers, *Descartes und die Philosophie,* p. 12 (emphasis in text).
20. Ibid., pp. 13, 81, 83, 85 (my emphasis). Cf. Damisch, *L'origine de la perspective,* pp. 172–73, 455, on the " 'subject' . . . reduced—in the phenomenological sense—to a

the one hand, as a "point," "alien to being" ("seinsfremdes"), and, on the other, as nothing but being in all its variety, as "philosophy of consciousness and therewith psychology," the *cogito* for Jaspers is "no longer truly philosophical."[21] He judges the conjunction of these two incommunicable possibilities—a point empty of objective extension and a subjectivity extending to all objects—to be, instead, "dogmatic," stating frankly that Descartes' apparent "clarity" "appears far more like *concealment* ["Verborgenheit"] itself."[22] This "concealment," this "riddle one cannot see through" ("es ist unmöglich, dieses Rätsel durchzuschauen") likewise defies communication between concealment and revelation. The "concealment" that is Descartes is, Jaspers concludes, "uncanny, because it does not conceal something that one could interpret and which would then become revealed" ("Descartes scheint vielmehr die *Verborgenheit* selbst . . . Unheimlich ist diese Verborgenheit, weil sie nicht etwas verborgen hält, das man deuten könnte, und das dann offenbar würde").[23]

Without detracting from its irreducible opacity, or confusing it with a presupposed subjectivity with which it is incompatible, the philosophically "empty point" described in Jasper's incisive analysis of the *cogito* can be seen to take the kind of extension formulated instead in Descartes' method. Thinking—the continuous movement of the mind that requires the discursive means of abstract signs—is the intellectual equivalent of a physical line. Thinking is independent of subjectivity and objective things the way lines, in the *Géométrie*, are independent of their historical limitation to geometrical shapes. The "I" that thinks rapidly draws a line of thought through a deduction effected upon signs. For Descartes to say that only the "I" that "thinks" "is," and "is" (only insofar and as long as it "thinks") not a body in space—in other words, that "I" is not the autobiographical subject, René Descartes—is much the same as if he were to say that "I" is not a square or a cube. The "I" that can "think" that "every-

point which will inscribe itself, with Descartes, into the beginning of modern science" (p. 173), and Lyons, "Subjectivity and Imitation," p. 520: "What vanishes in the Cogito is the autobiographical 'I' of the narrative of preparation. Although the Cogito permits certainty about the existence of the subject, the latter is no longer the subject, the 'person,' we have known. The subject of the Cogito has no body, no past, no relationship to others, no project or method, no location in historical space."

21. Jaspers, *Descartes und die Philosophie*, pp. 84–85.
22. Ibid., pp. 84, 89–90 (emphasis in text).
23. Ibid., p. 90.

thing is false," and "immediately afterward" deduce ("therefore") that it "is," need only pay attention to the line of its thought, just as, in attending only to the simple substance of extension denoted as a letter for the purpose of thinking, Descartes is able to draw lines unavailable to the bodily imagination of three-dimensional figures in the *Géométrie*.[24] The *cogito* is the "chain" of "links"[25] whose continuity is held in the mind by means of signs, the line of thought that Descartes draws from thinking to being by means of the denotation "I."

It is in this sense that the *cogito* must prove maddening to logical analysis.[26] That Descartes is no logician nor cared to be is evident from this foreshortened syllogism, whose "medius terminus" (like the middle terms of Descartes' narrative) is simply missing—a structural defect noted emphatically by Hegel, who commended the *cogito* exactly as a departure from syllogistic form, the new statement of true metaphysical "context."[27]

24. While deleting from consideration—as discussed in the preface—the centrality of discursive signs to Descartes' ability to draw lines independent of geometrical figures, Deleuze does point out the parallel between "extension" in Descartes and the "I" as "thing" thought without a body: "according to Descartes . . . the thinking thing and the extended thing are in themselves, or really distinct, and thus separable" ("La chose pensante et la chose étendue sont complètes chacune, ou réellement distinctes, donc séparables, selon Descartes") (Deleuze, *Le pli,* p. 75; Conley, *The Fold,* p. 55).
25. *OP,* 1:89.
26. Cf. Caton, *Origin of Subjectivity,* pp. 141–42: "Logical truths are independent of their being thought, whereas the Cartesian principle is not; further, logical truths are not about contingent existents, whereas Descartes' thinking and existence are contingent. . . . The necessary tie between thinking and existence is . . . not a relation that constitutes one of the properties of a simple nature understood as an 'object' given prior to doubt, nor is it the case that the tie is available in the pre-philosophic experience of one's own existence. . . . Descartes' recognition of the indubitability of his existence . . . produces the certainty of his presence to his thinking; the certainty is 'unshakable' because that presence is generated by that very act of thought."
27. Hegel remarks that the *cogito* cannot be a deduction by syllogism in that it lacks a mediating premise [*Glied*]: "three parts belong to a syllogistic deduction [*einem Schlusse*]; in this case a third by which thinking and being would be mediated. This is however not the case—not I think, *therefore* I am. This Therefore is here not the Therefore of a deduction; it is only the context composed of being and thinking (*Vorlesungen über die Geschichte der Philosophie* [Frankfurt: Surhkamp, 1971], 3:131–32). The most exhaustive contemporary attempt to save the *cogito* for syllogistic form must be Helmut Brands' *Cogito Ergo Sum. Interpretationen von Kant bis Nietzsche* (Munich: Karl Alber, 1982). Using symbolic notation and the visual aid of a Venn diagram, Brand rejects both Descartes' categorical statement (in the "Réponses" to Mersenne

For Kant it was rather the absence of the "major premise: everything which thinks, exists," that either rendered Descartes' statement "tautological" (*Kritik der reinen Vernunft* [*KrV*], 1st ed.), or divested the "I" not of mediation but of a necessary "empirical representation," the "material" without which "the act, I think, would not take place" (*KrV*, 2nd ed.).[28] As Jaspers reiterated in this century: "following Descartes' own statements on the matter, the *cogito ergo sum* is no syllogism ['kein Schluss']; for a syllogism would presuppose other truths from which the *sum* would result, while the thought [stated here] means rather to be its own origin ['Ursprung']."[29] Jaspers proceeds to offer an alternative formulation that would more accurately state the self-constituting origin of thought. The statement of a momentary simultaneity, "*cogitans sum* (when I think, I am)" might have better "expressed the derivation of the extant sense of being from the fact of thinking," he reasons, but such an expression would be "nearly empty," border too closely on "temporal existence" ("das zeitliche Dasein"), and ultimately lead to an "emphasis on the *sum* alone." "Thus," Jaspers concludes, "we continue to use Descartes' formulation *cogito ergo sum* in spite of its availability to misunderstanding through the

---

[*OP*, 2:564]) that the *cogito* is "no syllogism" and Hegel's observation that Descartes "begins the new epoch in philosophy" by making being "inseparable" from thinking rather than a conclusion from premises (*Vorlesungen*, pp. 126, 131). He proceeds to "construct" just such a syllogism, consisting of the major premise, "Everything that thinks is" ("Alles, was denkt, existiert"); the *terminus medius*, "I think" ("Ich denke"); and the conclusion, "I am" ("Ich bin") (pp. 155–57). Brands' formal translation of *je pense* into a middle term and addition of a major premise are effected, however, for the final purpose of proving that the major premise can be erased: since one may substitute "the object designated 'I' [Ich]" for the larger set that includes it, "x" (= everything that thinks ["Alles, das denkt"]), the major premise, he argues, "shows itself" to be "*superfluous*," while the "logical" basis of the "conclusion"—or so he contends—remains (pp. 162–63; cf. 180). This modern logical proof ironically proves nothing so much as the persistence of Aristotelianism, for it repeats the same circular pattern Descartes observed in (and on the basis of which he rejected outright) the syllogistic logic of his day: the deduction of conclusions already known from the start which puts reason out of a job ("en chômage") (see chap. 4, n.12). Cf. Beyssade's defense of syllogism as a form for displaying intuition as articulation after the fact: "une mise en fome, rétrospective mais éclairante, qui dégage les articulations naturelles de la démarche intuitive [du *cogito*]" (*La philosophie première*, p. 243).

28. Immanuel Kant, *Werkausgabe*, 12 vols., ed. Wilhelm Weischedel (Frankfurt: Suhrkamp, 1977): *Kritik der reinen Vernunft*, A 355, IV:366; B 423, IV:355.

29. Jaspers, *Descartes und die Philosophie*, p. 10.

determined apprehension of it as a syllogism."[30] Although the *cogito* is not
a three-term syllogism, the two terms or actions that compose, in Jaspers'
words, this "incomparable act of thought" ("Denkakt")—one "which in
thinking relates back to itself and becomes aware of this relation"[31]—cannot be collapsed into one.

But neither, given the faulty logical shape of the *cogito*, could the verb
"think" have been any other.[32] It is not because the *cogito* does not work
as a logical syllogism that any act can serve equally as the premise for the
existence of "je"; it is rather the act of thinking, as Descartes understands
it, which has no use for syllogistic form. "But, as soon as I had finished
['Mais, sitôt que j'eus achevé'] this whole course of studies, . . . I changed
my opinion entirely";[33] "[b]ut, immediately afterward ['mais, aussitôt
après'], I remarked that, during the time that I wanted thus to think that
everything was false, it was necessary that I ['moi'], who thought this, was
something." The time of experience deleted from Descartes' "fable" is the
necessary time of thinking, and what follows thinking, rather than an inessential change in opinion, is a very specific knowledge of being.

"Le temps pendant"—the time during which Descartes thinks everything is false—is anything but a middle term to be gotten through on the
way to truth. That time and its "immediate" sequel compose together the
temporality of the *cogito*. Just as a line extends from one purely representational point (the coordination of two unknowns) to another (at which

30. Ibid., p. 11.
31. Ibid.
32. Cf. Descartes' remarks to Gassendi, "Réponses aux Cinquièmes Objections" *OP,*
2: 792–93: "car, quand vous dites que j'eusse pu conclure la même chose de chacune
autre de mes actions indifféremment, vous vous méprenez bien fort, parce qu'il n'y en
a pas une de laquelle je sois entièrement certain, j'entends de cette certitiude métaphysique de laquelle seule il est ici question, excepté la pensée. Car, par exemple, cette
conséquence ne serait pas bonne: *Je me promène, donc je suis,* sinon en tant que la connaissance intérieure que j'en ai est une pensée, de laquelle seule cette conclusion est
certaine, non du mouvement du corps, lequel parfois peut être faux" (For, when you
say that I could conclude the same thing indifferently from all my other actions you
are mistaken, for there is no other of which I am entirely certain, by which I mean the
metaphysical certainty solely in question here, except thought. The conclusion, *I walk,
therefore I am,* for example, would not be good, except insofar as the internal knowledge I have of it is a thought, whose conclusion is certain, and not a bodily movement,
which can sometimes be false).
33. *OP,* 1:571.

the values of those unknowns change), the *cogito* extends from one "je," coordinated verbally with the act of thinking, to another, coordinated verbally with the fact of being that, *in being extended to this second "je,"* the first coordination entails. Thinking cannot be conducted unless for every point "during the time" of the act of thinking there is a value, "I." The connection of those points into an intuitional "whole"—the representational act which thinking effects upon its activity of deductive comparison *by means of signs*—is thus less self-reflective than actually productive. An entirely functional "I" acquires substantial being only as a consequence of the extension of that function in time, and that extension can only be intuited in the mind in the way that it is graphed on axes, in the translation of an arbitrarily posed, abstract notation. Unlike the back-and-forth movement of Descartes' representational autobiography, the *cogito* is a simple, or continuous, extension of "I," produced "during the time" of an act of thinking uninterrupted by the referential and descriptive effort of memory. But like the representational autobiography, the *cogito* can only take place discursively, through the rapid traversal and comparison of representations of "I."

Abstracted from things, these signs of existence memorialize memory, stand for it, and so can be read neither as a "fable" nor even as a synchronic "tableau." An extension of "I" in time wholly delimited by its designation is intuited as an externally delineable "whole." One imagines that, rather than "reason" the *cogito* into a handbook of syllogistic logic by means of "rhetorical" contortions, Descartes would have liked to have drawn it, physically, as a finite line. Instead, he had to "talk about" being in the language of a subject thinking because, *unlike* a method for knowing the natural world, the *cogito* is the discursive means for representing and knowing the true nature of *a subject who is the vehicle of method,* the *context* in which method is articulated, "ce moi." In brief, what Descartes carries out in the *cogito*—what the denotation of "I" carries in the *cogito*—is Descartes' "design."

Finally, that context must include Descartes. In substituting for the autobiographical subject, Descartes' "I" makes Descartes, the thinking subject, into part of a deduction. "I" is extended over the course of that deduction, and this simple extension functions as linear extension functions in the *Géométrie.* Line, the fundamental intermediary between mathematics and the physical world in Descartes' attempt to produce a mathematical physics,[34] finds its counterpart in the *Discours* in "the first principle of the philosophy [Descartes] sought." Metaphysics and method are implicated in each other: what Descartes "sought" for purposes of philosophical speculation — the simple substance produced in the *cogito* — is made available by the exercise of method. Philosophy and geometry are comparable in general in this regard:

> Les hommes sont la proie d'une si aveugle curiosité qu'ils conduisent souvent leur esprit par des chemins inconnus, et sans aucune raison d'espérer, mais seulement pour courir leur chance d'y trouver par hasard ce qu'ils cherchent; comme quelqu'un qui brûlerait d'un désir si brutal de découvrir un trésor, qu'il ne cesserait de courir les rues çà et là, cherchant si par hasard il n'en trouverait pas un qu'un voyageur aurait perdu. C'est ainsi que travaillent presque tous les chimistes, la plupart des géomètres, et plus d'un philosophe. . . . Il vaut cependant bien mieux ne jamais songer à chercher la vérité sur quelque objet que ce soit, que le faire sans méthode: car il est très certain que ces recherches désordonnées et ces méditations obscures troublent la lumière naturelle et aveuglent l'esprit; et tous ceux qui s'habituent ainsi à marcher dans les ténèbres affaiblissent tant leur vue que par la suite ils ne peuvent plus supporter la lumière du jour.[35]

> Men are the prey of such blind curiosity that they often conduct their spirit along unknown paths, and with no reason to hope, but only in order to try their luck at finding what they seek by accident; like someone who burned with such a brutal desire to discover a treasure, that he would not stop running in the streets, here and there, looking to see if, by accident, he might find one that a traveler had lost. This is how almost all chemists, most geometers, and more than one philosopher work. . . . It is far better never to dream of seeking the truth about any object than to do it without method: for it is very certain that these disorderly investigations and these obscure meditations trouble the natural light and blind the spirit; and all those who thus grow accustomed to walking in the shadows weaken their sight so much, that as a consequence they cannot stand the light of day.

34. Cf. Gaukroger, "Descartes' Project," p. 110.
35. Rule IV, *OP*, 1:90–91.

Method makes it possible for us to see by the light of day, and the "first principle," the first "object" whose "truth" we see is "I." The men who run here and there in a disorderly fashion, who walk in shadows and whose meditations remain obscure because they have not first made themselves the simple subjects of deduction, are Descartes' version of the prisoners in Plato's cave. In method, no less than in the Republic, the very possibility of knowledge in this world is at stake: Descartes' well-ordered procedure offers a direct parallel to Plato's well-ordered state. If that parallel goes unnoticed, it is probably because the Platonic theory of forms appears perfectly opposed to Cartesian empirical science, and because method makes knowledge available to anyone, not just a single prisoner dragged into the daylight, a philosopher-king.[36] Yet, while the realms of truth they describe are explicitly different, the art of educating rulers to recognize truth advanced by Plato's Socrates is, in principle, Descartes' method: that of teaching the soul not specific precepts but how to "rightly direct" its vision.[37] Order in a harmonious Republic, itself a metaphor for the just or "beautiful order" of a soul whose parts are in proportion at natural harmonic "intervals,"[38] is analogous, on the model of a sensible accord, to the proportional order for effecting the representation of a whole by which Cartesian method guides the spirit. In the *cogito* Descartes links "the first principle of the philosophy" he sought with the first philosophy, insofar as both Plato and Descartes speculate on the order or "rules for directing the spirit" without which we cannot know.

By taking his own spirit as the metaphysical proving ground of method, Descartes writes the *cogito,* producing a line of thought in which spirit figures as a sign and knows itself as "substance." But the "substance" intuited in the deduction of the *cogito* cannot be drawn once and for all: Descartes cannot draw "I" according to his fancy, nor draw the *cogito* as the permanent solution to an age-old mathematical problem. By putting himself in the place of an arbitrarily defined unit, by making method speculative, Descartes also signals that the context of method, the discourse of speculative philosophy, will never be contained by the method it "talks about." For "during the time" that Descartes pretends everything is false, the time

---

36. *The Republic,* VII.514a–521d, in *The Collected Dialogues of Plato,* pp. 747–53.
37. Ibid., VII.518d5, p. 751.
38. Ibid., IV.443c9–444a7, p. 686.

succeeded immediately by the recognition that he is "something," Descartes, the autobiographical subject, must be someplace. The free translation between letter and line, the sign and substance of extension, requires nothing but an "empty plain." But there is no moment "during the time" of his own translation, *or* "immediately afterward," that Descartes does not occupy an already historical space. At the opening of Part Three of the *Discours,* Descartes refers to himself as an architect whose drawing is now seen in the past tense, as a completed "ground plan" or "design" (*dessin*):

> Et enfin, comme ce n'est pas assez, avant de commencer à rebâtir le logis où on demeure, que de l'abattre, et de faire provision de matériaux et d'architectes, ou s'exercer soi-même à l'architecture, et outre cela d'en avoir soigneusement tracé le *dessin;* mais qu'il faut aussi s'être pourvu de *quelque autre,* où on puisse être logé commodément *pendant le temps qu'on y travaillera;* ainsi, afin que je ne demeurasse point irrésolu en mes actions pendant que la raison m'obligerait de l'être en mes jugements, et que je ne laissasse pas de vivre dès lors le plus heureusement que je pourrais, je me formai une morale par provision, qui ne consistait qu'en trois ou quatre maximes, dont je veux bien vous faire part.[39]

> And finally, as it is not simply enough, before beginning to rebuild the house where one resides, to tear it down, to make provisions for materials and architects, or to practice architecture oneself, and even to have carefully drawn the *design* of it; but it is also necessary to provide for *some other,* where one can be conveniently lodged *during the time that one will be working at it;* thus, so that I don't reside irresolute in my actions while reason obliges me to be so in my judgments, and so that I don't stop living from that time as happily as I can, I formed for myself a provisional code of morals, which consisted in but three or four maxims, which I want to share with you.

In this remarkable passage directly preceding Descartes' maxims for living—situated *after* the formulation of the four rules of procedure and *before* the *cogito* in Part Four—Descartes recognizes that the "thought" of an architect drawing freely on an empty plain is not one he, its thinker, can embody.[40] Even if he were to act as the autonomous, non-"conversant" ar-

---

39. Part Three, *OP,* 1:591–92 (my emphasis).
40. In a brief reference to this passage Payot effectively conflates it with the earlier de-

chitect of method, if he traced the ground plan himself, he would have to "live" in some already delimited place during the interim of its exercise — be it that minimal, livable place, a stove-heated room — just as his building would have to be a "rebuilding" of the "house" in which he already lives. "During the time" he "works" at rebuilding knowledge, his active self — the self that produces lines of thought — must "reside" somewhere if it is not to "reside irresolute," even while his judgment, or reflective self, is suspended. "But, immediately afterward I remarked that, *during the time* I wanted thus to think that everything was false, it was necessary that I, who thought it, be something ['quelque chose']"; "it is also necessary to provide for some other ['quelque autre'], where one can be conveniently lodged *during the time* one will be working on it": the self which will be recognized as necessarily "something" *after* the time during which Descartes thinks is recognized to need "some other" thing, some other already habitable place in which to live, "during the time" of the work of thinking, the *cogito,* ahead. Just as the rules are doubled by the maxims, Descartes, the "something" or "substance," must inhabit "some other" Descartes "pendant le temps."

The discursive time of the *cogito,* of comparative deduction, of representations apprehended as intuitions, is made to appear simultaneous

---

scription of free architectonic drawing, dismissing the intervention of the recognition of time — *pendant le temps que* — that will be repeated word for word as the basis for the *cogito.* By divorcing the "metaphor" of architectonics from the necessary temporality of its context, in autobiography as well as the *cogito* — divorcing it, in short, from discourse, Descartes' "design" — he suggests in an axiomatic manner more Cartesian than Descartes that, once "the essential," "a unique foundation," has been furnished, "building is nothing more than a question of time and *of order*" (*Le philosophe,* p. 119, emphasis in text). Lyons comes closest to the view of the present argument in stating with regard to the subject of this passage: "The ethical, provisional 'I' is cut off from the central Cartesian project. . . . The two subjects are antithetical and nondialectical; no synthesis between provisional 'I' and metaphysical 'I' is projected ("Subjectivity and Imitation," p. 518). But while Lyons defines this "provisional 'I' " as "mimetic," "a performer of examples" whom "Descartes bases . . . on imitation" (pp. 518–19), I see no grounds for conflating the discursive, temporal self reintroduced into this narrative of building with a self constructed exclusively of imitative representations. Although it tends to polarize the distinction between method and discourse, or "the specular and the mimetic" (p. 519), rather than recognize the dependence of method (and the *cogito*) on discursivity (which need not be imitative), Lyons' analysis of the *Discours* remains one of the most sensitive to the verbal work of Descartes' text.

by signs, to produce a line of thought like the freely drawn proportions of a single architect's comprehensive design. The necessary *temporality* of the *cogito*—of method made self-reflexive—is spelled out by Descartes in this autobiographical fable of the need for temporary housing. *A fable of the thinking subject,* this autobiographical reflection will never be part of Descartes' past, cannot be represented as in a tableau. "To build on a foundation that is entirely my own," which is to say, in terms of Descartes' method, to construe one's self as a line—"to practice architecture oneself" upon one's self, determining "ce moi" as "dessin"—is to draw on discourse, not an empty plain. Like the disposable signs in which the material for thought must be stored if there is to be thinking, and, strictly as a consequence of thinking, the drawing of a line—the projection and designation of a foundation: the *sub-ject* (literally, "the built under," from *subicere*), "I"—the need for temporary housing indicates that the "thought" of architectural self-determination, the image of method that is the nondiscursive turning point of the *Discours de la méthode,* cannot contain speculative thinking, "I" "thinking" "I."

For the author of the *cogito,* for any architect whose "foundations" must be "à moi"—entirely his own—the thinking that draws those foundations must reside elsewhere, in "some other" place. If it is not "to stop living," if it is to extend itself during the time of thinking into being "something," thinking must become, precisely, *auto-bio-graphical,* a delineation of the self whose discursive basis is Descartes' *dessein,* the *Discours de la méthode.*

8 Staircase as Labyrinth: Eudoxe on Method

Toute la méthode réside dans la mise en ordre et la disposition des objets vers lesquels il faut tourner le regard de l'esprit, pour découvrir quelque vérité. Et nous l'observons fidèlement, si nous réduisons par degrés les propositions complexes et obscures à des propositions plus simples, et si ensuite, partant de l'intuition des plus simples de toutes, nous essayons de nous élever par les mêmes degrés jusqu'à la connaissance de toutes les autres.

C'est en ce seul précepte que se trouve l'essentiel de toute la ressource humaine, et cette règle doit être suivie par qui veut accéder à la connaissance des choses, aussi fermement que le fil de Thésée par qui voulait pénétrer dans le labyrinthe. Mais il en est beaucoup qui ne réfléchissent pas à ce qu'elle prescrit, ou qui l'ignorent totalement, ou encore qui s'imaginent pouvoir s'en passer, et qui examinent des questions fort difficiles avec souvent si peu de méthode qu'ils me semblent faire comme s'ils essayaient de parvenir, d'un seul bond, du pied jusqu'au faîte de quelque maison, en dédaignant l'escalier destiné à cet usage, ou en ne remarquant même pas qu'il en existe un.[1]

The entire method resides in the order and the disposition of the objects toward which one must turn the attention of the spirit in order to discover some truth. And we observe it faithfully if, by degrees, we reduce complex and obscure propositions to simpler ones and if, departing subse-

---

1. Rule V, *OP*, 1:100. Alquié remarks that Descartes misnames the metaphor he offers for his method; what Descartes calls "Theseus' thread," he notes, "we call (more politely) Ariadne's thread" (p. 100n). Determined by his "thought" of method, from which all conversation between the self and others (including sexual seduction) is excluded, it is fair to say that Descartes' misattribution of that guiding thread to the agent of its exercise is more self-revealing than Theseus' purposefully deceptive, self-serving use of women, Ariadne—"her" thread notwithstanding—included.

quently from the simplest intuition, we try to raise ourselves by the same degrees to the knowledge of all the others.

In this single precept one finds the main point of all human resource, and whoever wants to accede to knowledge of things must follow this rule as firmly as one who wanted to penetrate the labyrinth must follow Theseus' thread. But there are many who do not reflect on its prescription, or who are entirely ignorant of it, or even who imagine that they can do without it, and who examine highly difficult questions often with so little method that they seem to me to act as if they were trying to reach, in a single bound, from the base to the summit of some house, disdaining, all the while, the staircase meant for this use, or not even remarking that one exists.

Rule V of the *Regulae* describes method alternately as a guiding thread through the constructed confusion of a labyrinth and a staircase standing ready-made in the ordered structure of a house. The discursive method of the *Géométrie* and the *cogito* of the *Discours de la méthode* demonstrate that no such staircase "exists" prior to and independent of the "design" of "talking about it." The drawing of a line in two unknowns that embodies a necessarily mental comparison of material signs, the drawing into being of "je" across the necessarily temporal context of "moi," are staircases of a structure whose base and summit have not yet been delineated, let alone built.

"Je" and "moi," method and discourse, *dessin* and *dessein, tracer* and *penser,* support each other structurally, cannot exist independently, and never unite. The ordered steps they compose in conjunction might be better described by the famous double staircase at Chambord, in which the act of ascent or descent matters less to the formal progress of steps one takes than the prospect of a lateral coincidence of the two distinct paths at each tier. The illusory sense of the mutual approach and eventual crossing of these paths that is provided by each winding detour of the double helix-like structure proves an insuperable distance experienced over and over in the course of the curve that structure describes. If—to employ Descartes' own contradictory architectonic imagery—method, *chez Descartes,* is a staircase, a gradual means of "raising oneself" to the summit of a house of knowledge already built, that staircase is itself a labyrinth, the noncoincidence of *dessein* with *dessin,* a "design" that turns on itself.

The view of "building a new [house]" of knowledge proffered by Eudoxe to Poliandre in the *Recherche de la vérité* must prove illusory in the same way as the prospect of a single "truth" in which the strands of that (unfinished) dialogue could meet. Although Eudoxe, the principal speaker in this late work, virtually repeats the description of method in the *Regulae*—"tout le secret consiste à commencer par les premières et par les plus simples, et à s'élever ensuite peu à peu et comme par degrés jusqu'aux vérités les plus éloignées et les plus composées"[2] (the entire secret consists in beginning with the first and most simple truths, and raising oneself subsequently little by little, as by degrees, to the furthest and most complex)— he proposes, in addition, that this method requires the "demolition" of a prior structure, the "badly built house" or syllogistic "labyrinth" of "metaphysics" from which, once it is entered, there can be no exit.[3] Rather than a closed structure in the image of a standing edifice complete with built-in access to its hierarchy of knowledge, Eudoxe describes knowledge attained only in the active reversal of knowledge, the double action of destroying and building. Borrowing from Part Two of the *Discours,* Descartes' Eudoxe states that "the best way to remedy" ("je ne sais point de meilleur moyen pour y remédier") an edifice built on shaky foundations "is to raze it to the ground and build a new one from it" ("que de la jeter toute par terre, et d'en bâtir une nouvelle").[4] But this citation of the *Discours* becomes more

2. *OP,* 2:1140. In place of the image of the "staircase" used in Rule V, Eudoxe calls this method the "single link" ("même lien") by which "all truths follow one another and are united to one another" ("toutes les vérités se suivent l'une l'autre et sont unies entre elles") much like the production of an "intuition" described in Rule III (*OP,* 1:89) or its equivalent, its "representation" in a line drawn from equations in the *Géométrie.* But just as the production of a single line required indirect comparisons by way of signs, the back-and-forth movement of a staircase by which Descartes describes his "entire method" also characterizes the "discours de la méthode" entertained in this *dialogue.*

3. *OP,* 2:1123: "si je demandais, par exemple, à Epistémon lui-même ce que c'est qu'un homme, et qu'il me répondît, comme dans les écoles, qu'un homme est un animal raisonnable, et si en outre, pour expliquer ces deux termes, qui ne sont pas moins obscurs que le premier, il nous conduisait par tous les degrés qu'on appelle métaphysiques, certes nous serions entraînés dans un labyrinthe dont nous ne pourrions jamais sortir" (if, for example, I asked Epistémon himself what a man is, and he answered, as one does in the schools, that a man is a reasonable animal, and if, furthermore, in order to explain these two terms, which are no less obscure than the first, he led us by all the degrees that one calls metaphysical, we would certainly be drawn into a labyrinth we could never get out of).

4. Ibid., pp. 1117–18 (for the complete text, see epigraph).

complicated when it attempts to include the temporality of demolition and of doubt: the time—"pendant le temps que"—whose inclusion at the opening of Part Three and at the center of the autobiographical deduction of the *cogito* makes possible an indispensable self-reflexivity "après coup."

This temporality is not mere successivity but the mental context within which experience can be reflected upon and, from experience, intuitions and the subject itself can be projected. Abstract signs standing for physical extensions, lines, are remembered and compared in time, producing a "representation" unassailable by doubt. And in time an initial act of doubting sensory representations is seen *retrospectively* to have entailed the existence of "some thing," "I," abstracted from all sensory qualities whatsoever. This temporality is also, however, the physical context in which sensory qualities are experienced: "during the time" that one "works at" building method, by tearing down and rebuilding "the house in which one resides," one must reside comfortably in "some other [house]."[5] Just as abstract signs require a physical place of manifestation, an impermanent surface upon which they are produced, the "some thing" of being cannot be the same thing as building, or doubting, or razing to the ground. Precisely because it (or "je") must be somewhere (else), the dual perspective of a temporal context opens up. Thus the architectonic form of a nondiscursive *dessin* in which method is embodied must be contextualized in the discourse of a *dessein* about method; thus the line of the *cogito* in which "je" is embodied is contextualized in the discourse of an autobiographical "moi."

Like the two fundamentally dissimilar meanings contained by the preposition in Descartes' title—a discourse "inhering in" or "about [method]"—the two kinds of "design" of the *Discours* cannot be conflated. In the difference between them there emerges what Descartes calls a "foundation in my self": a method for translating between letters and lines, between thinking (independent of things) and being (a thing). The knowledge of that difference must be a recognition of what was *not* known "during the time" that an earlier identity was doubted and denied. The temporal delay between demolition and building, the time of discourse which also situates Descartes' autobiographical *Discours* between Augustine and Proust—between the verbal negation (based on a scriptural vision) and verbal recuperation (based on a visionary sensation) of

5. *OP,* 1:591.

the mundane experience of the self; between the saint's City of God and the novelist's book of the world — is reduced to an impossible simultaneity in Descartes' explicitly discursive *Recherche*.[6] When Eudoxe tells Poliandre that, "*pendant que* nous travaillerons à cette démolition, nous pourrons, par même moyen, creuser les fondements qui doivent servir à notre *dessein*" (while we work on this demolition, we can, by the same means, dig

---

6. On Descartes' relation to Augustine and Augustinian doctrine, see Gilson's authoritative synthesis of the comments of Descartes' contemporaries (*Discours*, pp. 292–99), including Descartes' own reactions to Arnauld's observation that the *cogito* resembled Augustine's affirmation of his existence in *The City of God* (Book XI, chap. 26: "For just as I know that I exist, I also know that I know"), as well as his distinction of body from soul in *On the Trinity* (297): "With respect to the text of *De civitate Dei*, Descartes declares himself content enough to be henceforth guaranteed by such an authority, but notes that Saint Augustine uses the *cogito* for ends very different from his own. With regard to the text *De Trinitate* we have no response from Descartes" ("A propos du texte du *De civitate Dei*, Descartes se déclare bien aise d'être désormais garanti par une telle autorité, mais note que saint Augustin use du *Cogito* pour des fins très différentes des siennes. A propos du texte du *De Trinitate*, nous n'avons aucune réponse de Descartes"). Gilson concludes that while Descartes must have been familiar with the "uninterrupted tradition, since Saint Augustine, which makes the immediate cognition of the soul in itself the first and most evident of our cognitions," it remains impossible to prove that Descartes actually knew the Augustinian texts: "as for proving that Descartes knew the texts of Saint Augustine himself, this remains impossible; for an analogy between texts is no proof, and Descartes never affirmed nor denied that he knew the passages from Saint Augustine that one compared to his" (pp. 297–98). Even if Descartes had been less characteristically laconic on this matter, and such a proof of familiarity were available, it would not serve to cancel the distance between Augustine and Descartes, "for Descartes," Gilson argues, "remains opposed to Saint Augustine on the most essential point of Augustinianism: the relationships of reason with faith, and generally speaking, his idea of philosophy itself": while Descartes "integrates . . . a series of Augustinian theses in his doctrine . . . , it is not the spirit of Saint Augustine that animates him" (p. 298). In summation, Gilson cites the pointed passage from *De l'esprit géométrique et de l'art de persuader*, in which Pascal states that, whether or not Descartes "learned of it in the reading of this great saint," the *cogito* that appears only after "a long and extended reflection" in his writings "is as different . . . from others that have said it in passing as a man full of life and force is different from a dead man" (p. 299 [Gilson cites here from the final section of *De l'esprit géométrique*: "Règles nécessaires pour les démonstrations"]). Without commenting on the being of thinking in Augustine, the present argument places Descartes' *cogito* between the writings of Augustine and Proust precisely on the basis of its necessary contextualization in a discursive representation of reflection in time.

the foundations which must serve our *design*), he effectively eliminates discourse from the dialogue and, "by the same means," method.[7] The *Recherche de la vérité* is not the *Discours de la méthode,* and Eudoxe, although he cites his author in part, is not Descartes, much less the Descartes designated and cited as being "I." The difference in means and in time between destroying and building, as between designating and drawing, involves architectonic form in discourse that attempts to represent the possibility of thinking. The name for that representation will not remain "method," but the name of the discourse remains modern speculative philosophy as we know it from Descartes, even when it repeats the error of Eudoxe, mistaking destroying and building for a single act.

7. *OP,* 2:1118 (my emphasis).

9   Postscript: Architectural Theory
        after Descartes

Descartes could scarcely have imagined that the "places régulières" drawn "à sa fantaisie" by an imaginary architect—the representation of self-determining thought, or linear manifestation of method, in the *Discours*— would make manifest a fundamental anxiety within the discourse and practice of architectural theory itself. Like the lines representing proportional relations in the *Géométrie*, the "well-proportioned" lines of Descartes' architectural "design" offered in themselves no incitement to controversy. But neither were lines "in themselves" at issue: the matter that made architectural theory question its own presuppositions was rather the origin or basis of their proportional relation. According to Descartes—and this is as much the discovery of the *cogito* as of the *Géométrie*—in drawing from an imagination freed of given images an architect makes visible unencumbered thought. The source and recipient of these delineations are, respectively, a mind emptied of false precepts and an "empty plain." This dual emphasis on emptiness collapses the scheme of a third or figural dimension of imagination required by hermeneutic notions of literature and art. Traditional hermeneutic theory takes the problem of interpreting the new originally posed in biblical exegesis—that is, the event of Christ as word incarnate within a textual context—as a model for understanding the productions of secular imagination. Viewed as individual figures emerging from a horizontal, historical plane, these forms of imagination are understood to mediate real change, serving, through their reception, both to relay the past from which they stand out and to bring the present into the future.[1] As the leveling or evacuating of the sites of production

1. The evolving sense of "figura"—from that of a "face" distinct from the contextual landscape, a plastic form whose vertical dimension rises from a horizontal plane, to that of a textual, grammatical form similarly available to hermeneutic reception—

and reception in the *Discours,* and the emancipation of thought from the limits of figural dimensions in the sign language of the *Géométrie* both make plain, Descartes' architect must instead take only his own thought as model, making architecture undergo its own kind of *cogito: I am thought, therefore I am.*

The first prop of thinking eliminated in such a speculative architectonics would be, precisely, the support of the senses: the sensations whose rational value is doubted in the course of the *cogito* reappear in architectural theory as conceptual, if not existential, cheats, in that they lead one to believe architecture "is" because of nature. As thinking can only know itself independent of the immediate impressions of the senses, architecture must know itself independent of objects in nature; proportions are not imitative but originary, indeed arbitrary, productions of mind. But this would mean that the rules of proportion would have no referential basis in the world and that architectonic order, like discursive method, would be an entirely human invention. Beauty, understood as the pleasing effect of proportion in architecture (and other sensory objects), would likewise be misunderstood if identified with natural causes.

Such was the view espoused by the physiologist and French translator of Vitruvius, Claude Perrault, whose writings on proportion inscribed architectural theory in the *querelle des anciens et modernes,* the debate over the necessity of classical models in the discursive arts in which Charles Perrault, Claude's younger brother, famously squared off against Boileau.[2] Member of l'Académie des Sciences, participant in l'Académie Royale d'Architecture, and one of three architects (with Le Vau and Le Brun) selected by Colbert (who also commissioned his translation of Vitruvius) to submit plans for the eastern façade of the Louvre,[3] Perrault actually authored few architectural plans. The Louvre colonnade, now widely, if not

---

already informs Erich Auerbach's seminal study of the same name ("Figura," in *Scenes from the Drama of European Literature* [Minneapolis: University of Minnesota Press, 1984], pp. 11–76).

2. Cf. Jauss, "Ästhetische Normen," pp. 43–60, for an analysis of the contradictory consequences of what Jauss takes to be that "modern's" central insight, the historicity of aesthetic production and experience, norms and taste, accomplishment and *moeurs.*

3. On the creation of the Académie Royale by Colbert and Colbert's relationship to Claude and Charles Perrault, see Louis Hautecoeur, *Histoire de l'architecture classique en France,* (Paris: Picard, 1948), 2:441–91.

exclusively, attributed to him, would constitute Perrault's only building; his main professional occupations were anatomical dissection, in which he lectured for twenty years, and mechanical construction. Followed with interest by von Haller, Buffon, La Mettrie, Maine de Biran, Leibniz, and Huygens, Perrault's physiological investigations described organic forms in terms of architectonic construction and called for the recognition of the role of reason in empirical sciences. This openly Cartesian "natural" scientist doubted that knowledge derived from the senses: "il est nécessaire de joindre toujours les observations avec le Raisonnement . . . ; il arrive souvent que l'on voit des choses, sans sçavoir qu'on les voit et l'on peut aussi sçavoir que des choses sont, bien qu'on ne les voye pas"[4] (it is necessary always to join observations with reasoning . . . ; it often happens that one sees things without knowing that one sees them, and one can also know that things are, although one does not see them).

But Perrault's Preface and Notes to Vitruvius and his later treatise on the five architectural orders were hardly destined to win him a following among theorists of architecture when he translated his view of reason to the particular sensory field of aesthetics. Perrault argued, in conformity with tradition, that our sense of beauty in architectonic construction owes largely to the presence of proportional relations. But for Perrault—and in opposition to traditional architectural and aesthetic theory—both beauty and proportional relations are "arbitrary" creations: no natural law, no

---

4. Recorded in the Register of the Academy of Sciences, 1667, cited in Wolfgang Herrmann, *The Theory of Claude Perrault* (London: A. Zwemmer, 1973), pp. 8–9n23. The present discussion is indebted to Herrmann's lucid study. Of the two book-length studies of Perrault that have followed Herrmann's, Walter Kambartel's *Symmetrie und Schönheit: Über mögliche Voraussetzungen des neueren Kunstbewusstseins in der Architekturtheorie Claude Perraults* (Munich: Wilhelm Fink, 1972) argues, I think correctly, for the ongoing modernity of Perrault's aesthetic theory (as opposed to that of his brother, Charles); Antoine Picon's *Claude Perrault, 1613–1688, ou la curiosité d'un classique* (Paris: Picard, 1989), offers a helpful overview of Perrault's varied career, in which the "classical" effect of combining an interest in specific biological forms and systematic architectural forms is stressed. The Cartesian nature of Perrault's theory can be interpreted directly from his major texts: the annotated, expanded version of his translation of Vitruvius, *Les dix livres d'architecture de Vitruve corrigez et traduits nouvellement en François, avec des notes et des figures* (1674), and his presentation and proposed systematization of the five orders of columns, *Ordonnance des cinq espèces de colonnes selon la méthode des anciens* (1683).

imitation of nature, and no natural authority determines what pleases the eye.[5] Open to innovation and imitation over time, beauty and proportion, according to Perrault, are founded solely in "fantaisie," the Cartesian term for the free drawing of order from the mind:

> L'imitation de la Nature, ny la raison, ny le bon sens ne sont donc point le fondement de ces beautez, qu'on croit voir dans la proportion. . . . De manière que ceux qui les premiers ont inventé ces proportions, n'ayant gueres eu d'autre regle que leur fantaisie, à mesure que cette fantaisie a changé, on a introduit de nouvelles proportions qui ont aussi plû à leur tour.[6]

> Neither the imitation of nature, nor reason, nor common sense is the foundation of the beauties that one believes one sees in proportions. . . . Since those who first invented these proportions had no rules other than their free imagination ["fantaisie"], to the extent that this "fantaisie" changed, one introduced new proportions, which also pleased in their turn.

The argument for the rule of "fantaisie" in *aesthetically pleasing* proportions shifts the site of Descartes' metaphysics while maintaining the parameters of method. On the one hand, the pleasure afforded by any sense perception cannot be ascribed to universal reason or even a less exalted common sense; on the other hand, architectonic beauty does not please naturally, with an exclusively sensory immediacy. If reason does not rule the aesthetics of architecture, neither does natural order—tra-

5. On the polemic to which Perrault's theory of the "arbitrary" nature of proportional beauty gave rise, both during and after his time, see Emil Kaufmann, "Die Architekturtheorie der französischen Klassik und des Klassizismus," *Reportorium für Kunstwissenschaft* 44 (1924): 206–8, and Manfredo Tafuri, " 'Architectura artificialis': Claude Perrault, Sir Christopher Wren e il dibattito sul linguaggio architectettonico," in *Barocco europeo, barocco italiano, barocco salentino: Papers from the Congresso Internazionale sul Barocco,* ed. Pier Fausto Palumbo (Lecce: Centri di Studi Salentini, 1970), pp. 375–98. As Tafuri describes it, Perrault's theory prompted a historical passage in the "discourse" of architecture from a symbolic *Ordo naturalis* to an *Ordo artificialis* (or social order), the estrangement from all references to "anthropomorphic, cosmological, gnostic-cabalistic or biblical structures" and "folding of architectonic language upon its own internal laws, stripped of *values* that transcend" them (pp. 383–84).
6. Perrault, "Préface," *Ordonnance des cinq espèces de colonnes selon la méthode des anciens* (Paris: Jean Baptiste Coignard, 1683), p. x (original orthography maintained).

ditionally identified with musical harmony—provide any prototype for the orders of proportions that please. Just as Descartes, in disassociating mathematical orders from fixed geometric forms, was able to institute proportional relations arbitrarily, and, through those relations and the signs that freed the mind from remembering them, to construct solutions to previously insoluble problems, so architects, according to Perrault, must establish the proportions they use, basing that "arbitrary" activity on free imagination, acquired knowledge, and accident. The presupposition of unchanging proportional relations analogous to natural configurations only falsifies the true grounds for the determination of architectonic form. Given, or "positive" beauty—the beauty of musical chords and other immutable "things" of nature—offers no practical or conceptual model for an aesthetics that "depends on 'fantaisie,' " "depends on us":

> les proportions des membres d'Architecture n'ont point une beauté qui ait un fondement tellement positif, qu'il soit de la condition des choses naturelles, et pareil à celuy de la beauté des accords de la Musique, qui plaisent à cause d'une proportion certaine et immuable, qui ne dépend point de la fantaisie.[7]

> the proportions of parts of architecture do not have a beauty which has such a positive foundation as would pertain to the condition of natural things, and would be like that of the beauty of musical chords, which please because of a certain and immutable proportion which does not depend on free imagination.

> il ne se trouve point, ny dans les restes des Edifices des Anciens, ny parmi le grand nombre des Architectes qui ont traitté des proportions des Ordres, que deux Edifices ny deux Auteurs se soient accordez & ayent suivy les mesmes regles.
> Cela fait connoistre quel fondement peut avoir l'opinion de ceux qui croyent que les proportions qui doivent estre gardées dans l'Architecture sont des choses certaines & invariables, telles que sont les proportions qui font la beauté & l'agrément des accords de la Musique, lesquelles ne dependent point de nous, mais que la nature a

7. Perrault, *Les dix livres d'architecture de Vitruve corrigez et traduits nouvellement en François, avec des notes et des figures,* 2nd ed. rev., corr., and expanded (Paris: Jean Baptiste Coignard, 1674), p. 106n12.

arestées & establies avec des precisions exactes qui ne peuvent estre changées sans choquer aussitost les oreilles les moins delicates.[8]

there are not to be found, either in the remains of ancient buildings or among the great number of architects who have written on the proportions of the orders, two buildings or two authors who are in harmony and have followed the same rules.

This demonstrates what [little] foundation there can be to the opinion of those who believe that the proportions that must be kept in architecture are certain and invariable things, as are the proportions that compose the beauty and the pleasure of musical chords, which do not depend on us, but which nature has arrested and established with an exact precision that cannot be changed without immediately shocking the least delicate ear.

According to Perrault, "positive beauties" that are unmistakable to the ear have their visual equivalent in architectural features whose "merit and value are easy to recognize, such as richness of material, the grandeur and magnificence of the building, the appropriateness and neatness of the execution, and symmetry, which means in French that kind of proportion which produces an evident and observable beauty . . . and . . . is immediately apparent."[9] But unlike the direct influence of the ear upon the spirit, or the proportions produced "naturally and automatically in the mechanics of moving bodies," the eye pleases "most often" indirectly, through the intervention of "knowledge," "mak[ing] known the proportion that it makes pleasing," and finding "pleasure" only in those proportions it already "knows."[10]

8. Perrault, *Ordonnance,* pp. ii–iii.
9. "les ouvrages . . . qu'il est aisé d'en connoistre le merite & la valeur, telles que sont la richesse de la matiere, la grandeur & la magnificence de l'Edifice, la justesse & la propreté de l'execution, & la symmetrie qui signifie en françois l'espece de Proportion qui produit une beauté evidente & remarquable . . . & . . . est une chose fort apparente" (ibid., pp. vi–vii).
10. Ibid., pp. iv–v: "Mais l'oeil qui est capable de faire connoistre la proportion qu'il fait aimer, ne peut faire sentir à l'esprit aucun effet de cette proportion, que par la connoissance qu'il luy donne de cette proportion; d'où il s'ensuit que ce qui est agréable à l'oeil, ne l'est point à cause de sa proportion quand l'oeil ne la connoist pas, ainsi qu'il arrive le plus souvent" [But the eye, which is capable of making known the proportion that it makes pleasing, cannot make the spirit feel any effect of this proportion except by way of the knowledge that it provides the spirit of this proportion, from which it

What the eye "knows," as distinguished from what it sees, is not sensory evidence as such but patterns it has learned to recognize, the products of an earlier manifestation of mind. This is the artificial basis of the beauties Perrault "call[s] arbitrary" and to which he scandalously accords more significance than "positive beauties," the immediately pleasing aspects of architecture comparable to natural effects.[11] Whereas the recognition of "arbitrary beauties" requires the formation of "taste," an order of aesthetic judgment directly comparable to the scientific "method" Descartes seeks by "design," "positive beauties" can be perceived by anyone possessing "good sense" ("le bon sens"), the very attribute qualified as belonging to everyone in the first words of the *Discours*.[12]

Claiming the Cartesian distinction between good, or common sense, and knowledge mediated by order and reflection for aesthetics, Perrault argues that "arbitrary beauties" are instrumental in recognizing not truth per se but "true architects": "la connoissance des beautez arbitraires est la plus propre à former ce que l'on appelle le goust, & . . . c'est elle seule qui distingue les vrais Architects de ceux qui ne le sont pas; parce que pour connoistre la plûpart des beautez positives, c'est assez que d'avoir du sens commun"[13] (knowledge of arbitrary beauties is most appropriate to the formation of that which one calls taste, and it is this knowledge alone which distinguishes true architects from those who are not; for in order to know most positive beauties, it is enough to have common sense). Although architecture as described by Claude Perrault will provide Charles Perrault with a model for distinguishing these two types of beauty in poetry, it is Claude Perrault alone who posits the singular link between the

---

follows that that which is agreeable to the eye is not so because of its proportion when the eye does not know it, which is what happens most often]. On the distinct ways in which harmony and visual proportion are apprehended, cf. Herrmann, *Theory of Perrault,* p. 41; Picon, *Perrault,* p. 144.

11. Perrault, *Ordonnance,* p. vii. On the deposing of nature in Perrault's hierarchy of beauties, see Picon, *Perrault,* p. 145; and Georges Teyssot, "Clasicismo, neoclasicismo y 'arquitectura revolucionaria,' " Introduction to Emil Kaufmann, *Trés arquitectos revolucionarios: Boullée, Ledoux y Lequeu* (Barcelona: Edición Gustavo Gil, 1980), p. 22.

12. Perrault, *Ordonnance,* pp. vi, viii, x, xii, xix. Descartes, *OP,* 1:368: "Le bons sens est la chose du monde la mieux partagée" (Good sense is the most commonly shared thing in the world).

13. Perrault, *Ordonnance,* p. xii. On Perrault's definition of "bon goût" in opposition to "bon sens," see Kambartel, *Symmetrie und Schönheit,* pp. 89–91.

recognition of arbitrary beauty—proper to forming taste—and knowledge of an object.[14]

Once freed from the false positivism of natural resemblance and good sense, aesthetic theory can describe the mechanisms by which arbitrary beauty becomes an acquired pleasure. Perrault defines two axes of pleasure in architectural form: habit, "l'accoutûmance," and contiguity, "compagnie." In the first case, pleasure is reinforced through repetition over time. In the second, it is transferred by spatial association: "the spirit" makes a "relation" ("liaison") between two different things ("deux choses de différent nature"), extending a known "value" to something else which appears beside it.[15] This principle of doubly metonymic pleasure, mixing the blind fact of circumstance with the dumb fact of familiarity, is not counterbalanced in Perrault's theory by an appeal to other nonnatural but noncontingent factors, such as a presumed symbolism of geometrical

14. Jauss' discussion of Charles Perrault's use of architecture as the basis for distinguishing two kinds of "beauty" in poetry—the "ideal," or ahistorical, and the "arbitrary," or historically "relative"—makes no mention of its literal source, the writings of Claude Perrault which Charles often repeats word for word (see Jauss, "Ästhetische Normen," pp. 54–56, 58–59). The direct influence of Claude on his brother is mentioned in the context of the art historical "Exkurs" on the *querelle* by M. Imdahl, which follows Jauss' "Introduction"; see Charles Perrault, *Parallèle des Anciens et des Modernes en ce qui regarde les Arts et les Sciences* (Munich: Eidos, 1964), pp. 76–79. But the influence that Claude Perrault, writing as a theoretician of architecture, exercised through Charles Perrault upon the entire course of the *literary querelle,* is not, to my knowledge, acknowledged in the critical literature. Perhaps this is because Charles does not attribute to arbitrary beauty the theoretical priority given it by his brother; yet this is the very priority shared by literary theorists such as Jauss who focus on the historical specificity of all artworks.

15. "Or j'oppose à ces sortes de beautez que j'appelle Positives & convaincantes, celles que j'appelle Arbitraires . . . & qui ne sont point rendües agreables par les raisons dont tout le monde est capable, mais seulement par l'accoûtumance, & par une liaison que l'esprit fait de deux choses de differente nature: car par cette liaison il arrive que l'estime dont l'esprit est prevenu pour les unes dont il connoist la valeur, insinue une estime pour les autres dont la valeur luy est inconnüe, & l'engage insensiblement à les estimer egalement" (Now I oppose to those sorts of beauties I call positive and convincing those that I call arbitrary . . . and which are not made agreeable on the basis of reasonings of which everyone is capable, but solely on the bases of habit and of a relation that the spirit makes between two different things: for by this relation it comes to pass that the esteem in which the spirit is predisposed to hold those whose value it knows insinuates an esteem for those others whose value is unknown, and engages the spirit insensibly to esteem them equally) (Perrault, *Ordonnance,* p. vii).

forms.[16] Making no apology for—indeed, without even commenting on—
its radical modernity, Perrault calls this thoroughly heterodox conception
of the grounds for aesthetic pleasure, simply, "aimer les choses par compagnie," loving things by the company they keep.[17]

But what kind of "modern" is this who asserts the arbitrary nature of
aesthetic pleasure and proportions in the course of translating the most authoritative source of "ancient" architectural norms, Vitruvius? Pursuing a
historical logic at odds with either party to the *querelle,* Perrault reasoned
that precisely *because* the grounds for establishing taste and proportions are
arbitrary, such establishment is shaped in part by "authority": "Le fondement que j'appelle arbitraire est la Beauté qui dépend de l'Autorité & de
l'Accoutumance [*sic*]"[18] (The foundation that I call arbitrary is beauty
which depends on authority and habit). Authority placed on a par with
habit would hardly prove reassuring to Boileau. Anticipating the critical
response to this "paradox," Perrault went further still, describing "blind
respect" for the "ancients" as a purposeful mystification, a ploy to guard
authority for oneself:

> Je scay bien que nonobstant tout ce que je puis dire, on aura de
> la peine à gouster cette proposition, qui passera pour un Paradoxe
> capable de faire élever un grand nombre de contradicteurs, & que
> parmy quelques honnestes gens qui croient de bonne foy qu'il y va
> de la gloire de l'Antiquité qu'ils ayment, d'estre reputée infaillible, in-

16. While Perrault's theory was to prove highly influential in French architectural
theory of the early eighteenth century, the paradigm of a transcendent significance of
geometrical forms—of a God geometrician—returns crystallized, in the latter half of
the century, in the works of Boullée and Ledoux. See esp. Alberto Pérez-Gómez, *Architecture and the Crisis of Modern Science* (Cambridge, Mass.: MIT Press, 1983), pp.
50–56, 130–61; Teyssot, "Clasicismo," p. 25; and Emil Kaufmann, "Three Revolutionary Architects," *American Philosophical Society Transactions* 42.3 (1952). On "geometry" as "substitut[ion] for nature" in architectural theory after Perrault, see Tafuri,
"'Architectura artificialis,'" pp. 389, 398.

17. Perrault, *Ordonnance,* p. xiii, and Perrault, *Les dix livres,* pp. 12n13, 105n7. Cf.
Herrmann, *Theory of Perrault,* pp. 32, 34, 56, 60–62; Picon, *Perrault,* p. 145; Hubert
Damisch, "La colonnade de Perrault et les fonctions de l'ordre classique," in *L'urbanisme de Paris et l'Europe 1600–1680,* ed. Pierre Francastel (Paris: Klincksieck, 1969),
p. 93. On "accoûtumance" and the mental "prejudice" or "predisposition" ("la pre-
vention") that is its effect, see also pp. vi, x–xii in the *Ordonnance* and pp. 12n13, 105n7,
106n12 in *Les dix livres.*

18. Perrault, *Les dix livres,* p. 12n13.

imitable & incomparable, peut-estre parcequ'ils [*sic*] n'y ont pas assez pensé, il s'en meslera beaucoup d'autres qui sçavent bien ce qu'ils font quand ils couvrent de ce respect aveugle pour les ouvrages Antiques, le desir qu'ils ont que les choses de leur profession paroissent avoir des mysteres dont ils sont les seuls interpretes.[19]

I know well that in spite of everything I can say it will be difficult for others to appreciate this proposition, which will pass for a paradox capable of giving rise to a great number of nay-sayers, and that mixed in among the honest people who believe in good faith that to be reputed infallible, inimitable, and incomparable is part of the glory of the antiquity they love, perhaps because they have not thought about it enough, there will be many others who know perfectly well what they are doing when they cover, with this blind respect for ancient works, their own desire that the things of their profession appear to have mysteries of which they alone are the interpreters.

The authority of Vitruvius is no mystery for Perrault, and his translation, preface, and commentary aim at making any reader his interpreter. Vitruvius' authoritative status derives from his own learning and study, not only of architecture in its accomplished Greek models but also of "all knowledge to be gained from letters and liberal arts" ("toutes les connoissances tant des belles lettres que des arts liberaux").[20] Like taste, Vitruvius' authority was "acquired," formed by making a habit of "understanding": "son esprit accoûtumé dès la naissance à comprendre les choses les plus difficiles, s'etoit acquis une facilité que les simples Artisans n'ont point de pénétrer les secrets les plus cachez & toutes les difficultez d'un art aussi vaste & aussi difficile que l'Architecture"[21] (used to understanding the most difficult things from birth, his spirit acquired a facility that simple

19. Perrault, *Ordonnance*, pp. xix–xx. See also *Les dix livres*, p. 163, "Explication de la Planche XLI" (a schematization of ancient music): "Quelques-uns croient que ce qui nous rend ces mysteres impenetrables, n'est que la trop grande opinion que nous avons des merveilles que l'on dit qu'ils renferment, parce que cette opinion fait que nous y cherchons ce qui peut-estre n'y est point" (Some believe that all that renders these mysteries impenetrable is the exaggerated opinion we have of the marvels they are said to enclose, for that opinion makes us search for something which may not be there). Cf. Herrmann, *Theory of Perrault*, pp. 44–45.

20. Perrault, Préface to *Architecture générale de Vitruve, Reduite en Abregé* (Amsterdam: Huguetan et Gallet, 1681), pp. 2–3, 8.

21. Ibid., pp. 2–3.

artisans don't have for penetrating the deepest secrets and all the difficulties of an art as vast and as difficult as architecture). The exercise of understanding confers understanding; just as architects "imitated each other's works" without assuming that the proportions used before them "possess a positive and necessary beauty," so authority has no natural origin and can offer no positive models.[22] "Blind" admiration of the ancients, on the other hand, serves only to deter understanding, to fortify one's own sacerdotal pretensions, and to discredit theoretical reasoning such as Perrault's. When François Blondel, speaking as director of the Académie Royale, rejects Perrault's theory as "too metaphysical," Perrault recognizes this "veneration" of the ancients for the interested obfuscation it is, an anti-intellectual denial of the ability to reason in others which uses the prestige of the dead as its shield. It had been his belief, Perrault writes:

> qu'on avoit de la veneration pour les ouvrages de ces grands hommes & pour les precepts qu'ils nous ont laissez, parce que c'étoient des choses toujours fondées sur la raison. . . . Cependant je voy que ce n'est point cela, & qu'il n'est point question d'examiner si tout ce que les anciens ont dit, est raisonnable ou non, mais de l'admirer, de le suivre aveuglement . . . que de s'attirer des injures en pensant exciter les sçavans à cultiver & à perfectionner un Art qui demande beaucoup d'esprit, de jugement & de raison. . . . Je ne croyois pas aussi que les Architectes de ce temps fussent incapables de raisonnement, ainsi que l'Auteur [Blondel] fait entendre quand il dit que les raisons dont je me sers pour appuyer mon opinion, *sont des choses trop metaphysiques pour eux.*[23]

that one venerated the works of these great men and the precepts they left us because these were things which were always founded in rea-

---

22. "ces proportions ont esté établies par un consentement des Architectes, qui, ainsi que Vitruve témoigne lui-mesme, ont imité les ouvrages les uns des autres, & qui ont suivi les proportions que les premiers avoient choisies, non point comme ayant une beauté positive, necessaire & convainquante, & qui surpassast la beauté des autres proportions, comme la beauté d'un diamant surpasse celle d'un caillou" (these proportions were established by the consent of architects who, as Vitruvius himself testifies, imitated each other's works and followed the proportions that earlier architects chose not because these were thought to have a positive, necessary, and convincing beauty which surpassed that of other proportions as the beauty of a diamond surpasses that of a stone) (Perrault, *Les dix livres*, p. 105n7).

23. Ibid., p. 206n3.

son. . . . Now, however, I see that this is not the case, and that it is not a question of examining if everything that the ancients said is reasonable or not, but of admiring it and following it blindly . . . rather than attracting insults in thinking of exciting the learned to cultivate and perfect an art which demands a great deal of spirit, judgment, and reason. . . . I also didn't think that the architects of today were incapable of reasoning, as the author [Blondel] has us understand when he says that the reasons I use to support my opinion *are things which are things which are too metaphysical for them.*

"Too metaphysical"—it is as if Descartes were turned on his head, his negative grounds for seeking a method confused with his goal. As Descartes rejected the "philosophy" without foundation he was taught, so Perrault seeks to replace a false metaphysics of architecture, a fictive account of its origin and meaning extending, by way of ancient demi-gods and contemporary priests, from the harmony of the heavens to nature on earth. That metaphysical, all too metaphysical version of the imitative and divine nature of proportional relations is the powerful, empirically irrefutable myth to which Perrault opposed the power to reason, a power which depends, by contrast, on the recognition that the foundation of proportions is arbitrary.[24] If, in rejecting a metaphysics of "blind veneration" and imita-

---

24. The tenacity of the myth of a transcendent origin of pleasing proportions extends beyond participants in the *querelle*. At the close of the Préface to his *Ordonnance,* Perrault recommends to the public Antoine Desgodet's recently published *Edifices antiques de Rome* (Paris: Jean Baptiste Coignard, 1682), which documented the extremely wide variability of the proportions employed in Roman monuments. Although Desgodet's exact measurements of the most admired Roman buildings, made by order of Colbert, found absolutely no consistent ratio among them, works like Réné Ouvrard's *Architecture harmonique ou application de la doctrine des proportions de la musique à l'architecture* (Paris: J. B. De La Caille, 1679) and Philibert De L'Orme's *Architecture* (Rouen: Daniel Ferrand, 1648) continued to be cited as evidence of a priori rules of proportion by Blondel and the Academy. On the academic reception of Ouvrard and De L'Orme, see Kaufmann, "Die Architekturtheorie," pp. 207, 230. On Blondel and the "transcendental" nature of proportions, see Pérez-Gómez, *Architecture,* pp. 44–47: "Blondel realized that Perrault's theory questioned the fundamental metaphysical justification of architecture" (p. 47). That question seems no less, if indeed not more, pressing today. Pérez-Gómez, who recognizes that the "metaphysical" position defended is in fact Blondel's, regrets the advent of "modern"—functional, or *non*-metaphysical—architecture and rejoins the controversy on the side of Blondel: "In Claude Perrault's theory, architectural proportion lost for the first time, in an ex-

tion in favor of the exercise of reason, Perrault is a "modern" and a "Cartesian," this critical tendency is not entirely historically determined.[25] According to Perrault, Vitruvius and the "ancients" were "moderns" as well.

The ancient models we take as our measure were themselves "inventions," Perrault argues, modern products of reason founded in "fantaisie." The objection to architectural innovation as a departure from the imitation of ancients is "founded" instead on "a prejudice," "the false supposition" that such nonimitative works must be "bizarre and capricious."[26] The illogic of that founding mystification works itself out in two ways. First, there can be no reason to fear the adverse effects of "deregulation in the arts" ("déreglement dans tous les arts"): those innovations which are indeed "ridiculous" will necessarily "destroy themselves" ("se doivent détruire d'elles-mêmes").[27] Second, if the "law" of imitation had ruled the "ancients," we would not now have models to follow: "Si cette Loy avoit eu lieu, l'Architecture ne seroit jamais parvenuë au point où l'ont mise *les inventions des Anciens, qui ont esté nouvelles en leur temps*"[28] (If this law

---

plicit way, its character as a transcendental link between microcosm and macrocosm [based on the notion of celestial and proportional harmony]"; "truly meaningful architecture has been, by necessity, the exception rather than the rule over the last two centuries. . . . symbolic intentions are thoroughly rejected in a prosaic world" (pp. 32, 323).

25. On Perrault as "modern" in relationship to Descartes, see Pérez-Gómez, *Architecture*, p. 34: "Perrault's theory of architecture is the first in which the distance between a visible form and an invisible content becomes problematical. Such a disparity could only exist after the inception of Cartesianism." See also Emile Kranz, *Essai sur l'esthétique de Descartes* (Paris: Baillière et Cie, 1882), pp. 59ff.; Hautecoeur, *Histoire de l'architecture classique*, pp. 468–69; Herrmann, *Theory of Perrault*, pp. 35–36, 42–45, 56; Picon, *Perrault*, pp. 103–14.

26. "La principale objection . . . est fondée sur un prejugé & sur la fausse supposition qu'il n'est pas permis de se départir des usages des Anciens; que tout ce qui n'imite pas leurs manieres doit passer pour bizarre & pour capricieux" (Perrault, *Les dix livres*, p. 79n16).

27. Ibid.

28. Ibid. (my emphasis). In this respect, the "moderns" who have written new orders of architecture are described in the *Ordonnance* as following "the example of the ancients themselves": "ces Ecrivains qui hors Vitruve sont tous modernes, l'ont fait à l'exemple des Anciens mesmes, qui au lieu de Livres ont laissé des ouvrages d'Architecture, dans lesquels chacun a mis quelque chose de son invention: Or ces nouveautez ont toûjours esté considerées comme le fruit du travail de l'étude & la recherche que des genies inventifs ont fait pour perfectionner les choses dans lesquelles les Anciens avoient laissé quelque defectuosité" (these writers who, aside from Vitruvius, are all moderns, fol-

had existed, architecture would never have arrived at the point at which
the inventions of the ancients left it, inventions which were new in their day).
This view of the ancients *as* moderns upsets the "ancient" as well as "modern" evaluation of art history, based on positive notions of origins and of
progress, respectively. No less controversial when proposed one and a half
centuries later by Stendhal, during the debate over "romanticism" which
that romantic subversively entitled *Racine* et *Shakespeare* (1823), Perrault's
"modern" understanding of classical models as "new in their day" offers no
normative criteria for judging—or, more precisely, prejudging—either ancient or modern works.[29] Founding beauty and proportion in "fantaisie,"
basing aesthetic pleasure on habit, association, and authority, and deriving authority from knowledge confirmed by reason, Perrault's is a radical
humanism which both "ancients" and "moderns" must find distasteful, as
it argues that the aesthetic hierarchies espoused by either camp are fundamentally "arbitrary," nonintrinsic, and thus transformable in nature. This
is not to say that aesthetic judgments cannot or should not be made, but,
quite the contrary, that they are made, by means and measures that we
only partly control.

It is Perrault who seeks to increase that control by inventing a new
means of proportional measurement, one whose wholly artificial and arbi-

---

lowed the example of the ancients themselves, who, instead of books, left works of
architecture in which each one put something of his own invention: for these novelties
have always been considered as the fruit of the labor of study and research that these
inventive geniuses undertook in order to perfect things in which the ancients had left
some defect) (*Ordonnance*, p. xxv).

29. See Stendhal, *Racine et Shakespeare* (Paris: Garnier-Flammarion, 1970). On Stendhal's updating and upsetting of the opposing terms of the *querelle* ("Racine was
romantic"; "ALL GREAT WRITERS WERE ROMANTIC IN THEIR TIME" [p. 106]), see my
"Temporality of Convention: Convention Theory and Romanticism," in *Rules and
Conventions: Literature, Philosophy, Social Theory*, ed. Mette Hjort (Baltimore: Johns
Hopkins University Press, 1992), pp. 274–93. On Perrault's analogous conception of
the modern, see Kambartel's important distinction between its transhistorical foundation in "fantaisie" and the "positive beauties" of modern art advocated by Charles Perrault: "And while Claude Perrault aimed at granting the moderns the same chance at
the free unfolding of artistic imagination [*Phantasie*] which the ancients once allowed
themselves, Charles Perrault, by contrast, endeavored to prove that in architecture as
in all other arts the ancients had been surpassed by the considerable increase and im-
provement of positive beauties on the part of the moderns" (Kambartel, *Symmetrie
und Schönheit*, p. 105).

trary basis will make it adaptable to problems of establishing proportions
in any context while making the relations between parts of architectural
orders easier to memorize. Commonly referred to as his "method,"[30] Perrault's procedure for establishing a universal working order within the five
historical orders follows Descartes; its technique and meaning break with
the accumulation of diverse architectural patterns just as Descartes' rules
of procedure break with the labyrinth of scholastic logic. Its closest model
is Descartes' *Géométrie*.[31] Like Descartes, Perrault proposed to base his
method on a unit measure which, freed from any specific physical manifestation, could be set to suit the purpose of generating proportions. Departing from Vitruvius and tradition, Perrault chose one-third of the diameter
of a column as his unit so as to ensure that the proportional relations between parts and orders of columns could be represented by the simplest
means, whole numbers.[32] Although Perrault claimed to take as his measure
the average of ancient "examples,"[33] what mattered most to his method —
as to Descartes' — was the concept of the "mean" ("moyenne") itself: corre-
sponding to the measurement of no particular body, this arbitrary measure
determined the relations composing the whole.[34] Like the proportional
"relations" represented by mathematical orders in the new notation of
Descartes' equations,[35] proportions in Perrault's theory of architecture are
arbitrary intellectual constructions first and linear configurations second.
Indeed, Perrault refused to "correct" these relations for the senses, contra-
dicting, in this most Cartesian principle, the entire visual tradition which

30. Cf. Damisch, "La colonnade," pp. 86–87, 93; Herrmann, *Theory of Perrault,* pp.
168; Pérez-Gómez, *Architecture,* pp. 17–47; Picon, *Perrault,* pp. 151–56.

31. The striking identity of the techniques of proportional abstraction described in
the *Géométrie* (Book One), the *Discours* (Part Two), the *Regulae* (Rules VI, XIV, XVI,
XVIII), and Perrault's *Ordonnance* has not, to my knowledge, been noted, although
generic references to Perrault's "rationalism" and "method" mark him, explicitly or implicitly, as a Cartesian theorist.

32. Perrault, *Ordonnance,* pp. xiv–xvii, xxi–xxiii, xxvi–xxvii. Cf. Herrmann, *Theory of
Perrault,* pp. 95–129; Pérez-Gómez, *Architecture,* pp. 28–31; Picon, *Perrault,* p. 145.

33. Perrault, *Ordonnance,* p. xxii.

34. On Perrault's use of the mean, see Philippe Gresset, "Le classicisme — un style? Architecture et pensée visuelle: Les architectes classiques à l'épreuve de leur fondement,"
Les cahiers de la recherche architecturale 18 (1985): 9, 14. Cf. Descartes, *Regulae,* Rule VI,
on the representational relationship between orders of equations and "proportional
means" ("moyennes proportionelles") (*OP,* 1:106–7).

35. See chap. 5, notes 30, 31, 32, and 33.

holds that architecture must include an adjustment for the natural optical deformations experienced by the viewing body; that proportions must themselves be deformed so as to create the sensory impression of regularity.[36]

Finally, such an ordering of proportions would make them "easy to retain" ("donne . . . la facilité de les retenir"): Perrault, like Descartes, wished to substitute rapid memorization for the circular, time-consuming effort of remembering, clearing the mind of the strictures of apparent matter, whether a line segment or building.[37] Architecture, defined by Perrault as the "practice" of "executing plans" (*desseins*) and the "theory" of "appropriate proportions," would be a single activity in which drawing manifests thought and nothing else.[38] Activating an arbitrary system retained by simple memorization, the hand produces lines determined only by the mind. These lines would not be the geometrical representation of axioms, for they delineate a new "thing" to be built; nor would they represent any thing or set of relations in nature. Architecture would be as Descartes

36. See Herrmann, *Theory of Perrault*, pp. 70–94; and Picon, *Perrault*, pp. 150–51, esp. 155: ". . . the notion of scale disappears for the sake of purely arithmetic considerations. In more general terms, the theory of Perrault denounces the links which are meant to join mathematical and optical laws to the perceptions of the spectator. . . . In subordinating, without nuances, the sensory to the rational, the *Ordonnance* actually performs a displacement: it transfers the center of gravity of the discipline of architecture from the building to its conception, an essentially abstract conception which no longer knows how to negotiate with naive perception, but knows very well how to submit it to its own demands."

37. Perrault, *Ordonnance*, p. xxvi. On the facility of memorization established by his proportional system, see also p. xvii: "pour trouver, retenir, & imprimer dans la memoire la proportion qu'il doit avoir, il n'y a rien de plus facile" (to find, retain, and print in memory the proportion one must have, there is no more easy way), and p. xxiii. Cf. Picon, *Perrault*, p. 151.

38. Perrault, *Les dix livres*, chap. 1, "Ce que c'est que l'Architecture" (What Architecture Is), p. 2: "Cette Science s'acquiert par la *Pratique* [*Fabrica*] & par la *Théorie* [*Ratiocinatio*]. La Pratique consiste dans une application continuelle à l'execution des desseins que l'on s'est proposé, suivant lesquels la forme convenable est donnée à la matiere dont toutes sortes d'ouvrages se font. La Theorie [*sic*] explique & demontre la convenance des proportions que doivent avoir les choses que l'on veut fabriquer" (This science is acquired through *practice* and *theory*. Practice consists of applying oneself continually to the execution of drawings that one has planned, according to which the appropriate form is given to the matter from which all kinds of works are made. Theory explains and demonstrates the appropriateness of the proportions which the things one wants to construct must have).

imaged it in "thought": a materialization of method, thinking ordered by thought itself, not imperceptibly, but in lines—which is to say, by thought which is not itself when it orders thinking.

Whether or not this is conceived as a step forward for architectural aesthetics and aesthetics in general will depend on what one affirms or negates in aesthetics.[39] Manfredo Tafuri has argued that the threat to the possibility of aesthetic order posed by the "dangerous Blondel-Perrault polemic" prompted the Académie Royale to generate a kind of *grammaire générale et raisonnée* of architecture, a "combinatory elaboration" of the parts of architectonic "discourse" by which "the arbitrariness of the system" would gain "a logical justification."[40] At the same time, Tafuri concludes, Perrault's "reduction to zero of [the] symbolic functions" of architecture brought about a "superhistorical alliance" between Boullée and Blondel and the reintroduction and reinstitutionalization of symbolic

39. Evaluations of Perrault instructively reveal the underlying aesthetic values upon which they draw. The loss of a *symbolic* aesthetic function, dated from Perrault, may be lamented in an apparently unconscious imitation of Hegel's symbolic-classic historical progression; see Pérez-Gómez' thesis that, due to the rise of "functionalism" prepared by Perrault, "symbolic intentions are thoroughly rejected in a prosaic world" (*Architecture*, p. 323). Or, that loss may be viewed as a gain in systematic signification, the possibility of a rational *semiotic* aesthetics; see Damisch, "La colonnade," p. 93: "With Claude Perrault, a conception of the classical order and its functions which is no longer picturesque and symbolic but systematic and truly *signifying* is affirmed in an explicit manner for the first time" (emphasis in text). Aesthetics may be viewed instead traditionally as the domain of object-related sense perception, improperly submitted to systematic reason; see Picon, *Perrault,* pp. 155–56: "Conceived by Blondel as the reflection of a natural order of the world which surpasses it, architecture derives for Perrault from the autonomy of human reason. . . . Where the *Cours d'architecture* [of Blondel] reasons by way of multiple figures and examples, the *Ordonnance* proposes a method. This method does not relate to buildings but to the faculties of reason of man." Or, aesthetics may mean the rejection of traditional definitions and examples of "the aesthetic," the domain of an historically "variable," "anti-normative" conception of beauty and of art; see Kambartel, *Symmetrie und Schönheit,* p. 144, on modern abstract, "non-relational" art, whose "indifferent structure of repetition" he traces back to Perrault's "arbitrary beauty": "[non-relational art] understands itself as . . . antinormative and even anormative in that, in absolutizing modern symmetry in the form of an iterative structure, it holds all art to be variable in an historically determined way and thus raises the possibility that its own artistic direction may be dissolved by other ones, which are necessarily codetermined by that direction in their own history of development."

40. Tafuri, " 'Architectura artificialis,' " pp. 379, 384.

functions, now understood as "rhetorical" rather than "natural" in origin, by the bourgeoisie of the next century.[41]

Such countervailing tendencies—toward a self-conscious grammatization of architectonics on the one hand and its equally self-conscious rhetorization on the other[42]—indicate that the formal identity of aesthetics will remain in question insofar as the identification of beauty is made on the basis of association and habit. For this very reason Perrault offers a systematization of proportions based not on aesthetic impressions but on authoritative knowledge of past inventions. His theory and method make no claim to define, in a positive sense, a quality founded in "fantaisie." In that sense, Perrault, who did not question the experience of pleasure in the beautiful, may be considered to be anti-aesthetic, or, at the very least, even though his theoretical writings focus on the question of beauty in architecture, as unconcerned as the modern antisensualist, Descartes, with defining *an* aesthetics.

If Perrault, like Descartes, did not offer a positive theory of sense perception, an aesthetics, he did identify, as did Descartes, another way of understanding the relation of architectural form to reason, by comparing the rules of Vitruvius to linguistic rules and written signs. Neither imitative nor inherently pleasing in the aesthetic sense, "language" and written "characters" institute an order where the ground of sensory identification is displaced by "fantaisie." Not by any theory of the beautiful to which they subscribe, but "by the great authority they have always had," Vitru-

41. Ibid., pp. 379n6, 397–98.

42. On the systematic, if *un*conscious, tendency to view artifactual activity *either* in grammatical *or* rhetorical terms, an observation—based on literal discourse—which is shared by Tafuri's analysis of the historical conceptualization of architectonic "discourse," see Paul de Man's seminal analyses, "Semiology and Rhetoric," in *Allegories of Reading: Figural Language in Rousseau, Nietzsche, Rilke, and Proust* (New Haven: Yale University Press, 1979), pp. 3–19, and "The Resistance to Theory," in *The Resistance to Theory* (Minneapolis: University of Minnesota Press, 1986), pp. 3–20. See also Roman Jakobson's analysis of the technical coextensivity of rhetoric and grammar: "Linguistics and Poetics," in *The Structuralists from Marx to Lévi-Strauss*, ed. Richard and Fernande DeGeorge (New York: Anchor Doubleday, 1972), pp. 85–122 ("poeticalness is not a supplementation of discourse with rhetorical adornment but a total re-evaluation of the discourse and of all its components whatsoever" [p. 119]). See also Jakobson, "The Metaphoric and Metonymic Poles," in Jakobson, *Selected Writings* (The Hague: Mouton, 1981), 3:76–82.

vius' writings "establish the true rules of the beautiful and the perfected in buildings":

> *car la Beauté n'ayant guère d'autre fondement que la fantaisie,* qui fait que les choses plaisent selon qu'elles sont conformes à l'idée que chacun a de leur perfection, on a besoin des regles qui forment & qui rectifient cette Idée: & il est certain que ces regles sont tellement necessaires en toutes choses, que si la Nature les refuse à quelques-unes, ainsi qu'elle a fait au langage, aux caractères de l'écriture, aux habits & à tout ce qui depend du hazard, de la volonté, & de l'accoutumance; il faut que l'institution des hommes en fournisse, & que pour cela on convienne d'une certaine autorité qui tienne lieu de raison positive.[43]

> *for, since beauty has hardly any foundation other than free imagination,* so that things please according to their conformity to the idea that we each have of their perfection, we need rules that form and rectify this idea: and it is certain that these rules are so necessary in all things that if nature refuses them to some, as she had done to language, to the characters of writing, to clothing, and to all that depends on chance, on will, and on habit, then human institution must furnish them, and, to that end, agree by convention to a certain authority which takes the place of positive reasoning.

Perrault does not say that architecture is "a language" or that it does what language does.[44] He says that beauty (in architecture) conforms to

---

43. Perrault, *Les dix livres,* fifth page of unnumbered Préface (my emphasis). On this important passage, cf. Herrmann, *Theory of Perrault,* p. 31; Picon, *Perrault,* p. 154; and Damisch, "La colonnade," p. 93.

44. A similar point is stressed by Alain Guiheux and Dominique Rouillard in "Echanges entre les mots et l'architecture dans la seconde moitié du XVIIe siècle à travers les traités de l'art de parler," *Les cahiers de la recherche architecturale* 18 (1985): 18: "It is not because Perrault, in writing on architecture, also speaks of language that architecture is a language, and apparently they are only linked by a single common point, obedience to rules." Guiheux and Rouillard are less interested, however, in the theoretical reasons for Perrault's reference to language, letters, and fashion, than in demonstrating its origins in a reversal of the comparison: the commonplace use of architectural metaphors in treatises of rhetoric to indicate proper construction and ornamentation. This seems to me to sidestep or to overlook the highly unconventional point Perrault makes in dealing with a nonverbal issue of aesthetics from a nonornamental understanding of language. Cf. Tafuri's emphasis on the "arbitrary" rather

an "idea," like other "things" that are not ruled by nature, such as language, written signs, and garments. Language functions to name, refer, and posit; to represent or describe, define, and qualify; to coordinate, compare, predicate, and question; and from these activities it not only makes information but forms discourse, fiction. Yet these meaning-bearing characteristics of language are not the aspect of language that is meaningful for Perrault. What he appreciates in language in this central comparison—what makes the references to "language," written "characters," and "clothes" follow each other without further discrimination, as in a list—is its essential superficiality, the superficial nature of rules and visible forms that could be otherwise, no matter how "deep" their grammar appears to be, no matter how much like second nature their usage is.[45]

As in his discussions of aesthetic pleasure, Perrault makes no value judgment on the linguistic phenomena he describes. Just as pleasure in the beautiful is experienced without reflection upon its arbitrary foundation,

---

than grammatical or symbolic identity of "classical language" ("'Architectura artificialis,'" pp. 377–78). Teyssot, by contrast, emphasizes the analogy between linguistic order and architectonic "beauty" in Perrault's theory—"that is to say, the proper organization of the plan and the figured and constructed space"—from the perspective of classical epistemology as described by Port Royal grammarians and, recently, Foucault. On this view of "classical thought," "the world is an *analogon* of language," and "the perception of space regulated by practice and discursive reflection on the part of the academic tend to blend into one another" (Teyssot, "Clasicismo," pp. 22–23; cf. Michel Foucault, *Les mots et les choses* [Paris: Seuil, 1966], and Foucault, Préface to Antoine Arnauld and Claude Lancelot, *Grammaire générale et raisonée* [Paris: Republications Paulet, 1969], pp. iii–xxvii). The present analysis points to the linear visibility, rather than rational transparency, of *fantaisie* in Perrault's analogy between arbitrary, architectonic beauty and "writing."

45. In this view of architecture as conformable to rules yet not wholly semiotic, as a conventional, visible order ("writing") which, however, is not identifiable with the production of meaning, Perrault makes a distinction remarkably similar to Lefebvre's: "Semiology is . . . the source of the claim that space is susceptible of a 'reading,' and hence the legitimate object of a practice (reading/writing). The space of the city is said to embody a discourse, a language. Does it make sense to speak of a 'reading' of space? Yes and no. Yes, inasmuch as it is possible to envisage a 'reader' who deciphers or decodes and a 'speaker' who expresses himself by translating his progression into a discourse. But no, in that social space can in no way be compared to a blank page upon which a specific message has been inscribed. . . . If there is indeed text, inscription or writing to be found here, it is in a context of conventions, intentions and order (in the sense of social order *versus* social disorder)" (Lefebvre, *Production of Space*, p. 142).

so the rules that determine language, letters, and clothes are "necessary"—not intrinsically, but to the arbitrary existence of their artificial, meaning-bearing systems. In a passage in the *Ordonnance* in which he directly compares the drawing of buildings with writing, Perrault additionally distinguishes the necessity of characters themselves from the contingent, historical style in which they are written. The "order" of architecture by this description would have the specificity and superficiality of temporally "perfected" script:

> quand il s'agit de dessiner un Ordre pour un Edifice que l'on bas-tit aujourd'huy, je ne croy pas que cette imitation si scrupuleuse de l'Antique soit necessaire, & comme l'on ne pourroit pas approuver le dessein d'un ouvrier qui voudroit faire l'écriture d'une medaille du Roy, ou d'une inscription dattée de l'an mil six cens quatre-vingt trois, avec des caracteres semblables à ceux qui se voyent dans les medailles Romaines Antiques, qui sont differens & n'ont point la beauté des caracteres Romains dont nous nous servons, & que nous avons perfectionnez; je ne croy pas aussi qu'on dût blasmer un Archi-tecte qui observeroit & suivroit curieusement les changemens que les habiles dans son Art ont introduit avec raison & jugement, & mesme avec approbation.[46]

> in drawing an order for a building that one builds today, I don't believe that such a scrupulous imitation of the ancient order is nec-essary; and as one could not approve the design [*dessein*] of a worker who wished to effect the writing on a medal of the King, or of an in-scription dated 1643, with characters resembling those one sees on an-cient Roman medals, which are different and do not have the beauty of the Roman characters which we use, and which we have perfected, so I don't believe that one should blame an architect who observes and follows with curiosity the changes that the skillful in his art have introduced with reason and judgment, and even with approbation.

Viewed as typeface or style of script—the visible form of the visible form of language—"writing" changes, like the shapes of buildings or shoes. The "characters" once used by Romans have since been replaced by "Roman characters," their more "perfect" descendents that bear them little resemblance even as they borrow their name. Not in spite of this histori-

46. Perrault, *Ordonnance,* pp. xxiv–xxv.

cal mutability but rather because of it, conventional forms are available to the work of "reason and judgment." In this sense, then, Perrault associates "language" with the "characters of writing." Working theoretically in a thoroughly material fashion, from the (perceptual) outside in, Perrault views the lines that compose letters, the most external aspect of language, as the avenue of reason—not because they embody an inherent, symbolic, or mystical unity of thought and matter, but because, on the contrary, they are united to and predetermined by nothing at all.

Understood neither to represent things nor to signify innate ideas, "language," by this account, bears no resemblance to the ruled articulation of the corporeal world and of reason studied contemporaneously by such Port Royal grammarians as the Cartesian Arnauld.[47] In arguing that perception is governed by ideas, rather than any kind of intermediary representation, and that "signs"—whether of the "institutional" and "arbitrary" kind, which "depend on our 'fantaisie,' "[48] or of the "natural," "mirror"-like kind, which are "as an image" of "what they represent"[49]—are not necessary to thought, Arnauld paradoxically hypothesizes a greater proximity of "sound" to thinking. In order to isolate sound from its own materiality, he then further distinguishes between the "idea" of a sound and its "image," the former, most remarkable abstraction of matter *from matter* defined as alone evoking thought, in direct contrast to Perrault's increasingly material distinction between characters and script.[50] Perrault's

---

47. Arnauld's *Grammaire générale et raisonée* (1660), written with Lancelot, and the *Logique, ou l'art de penser* (1662), written with Nicole, were republished continuously throughout the seventeenth and into the nineteenth century.

48. Antoine Arnauld and Pierre Nicole, *Logique, ou l'art de penser*, 5th ed. rev. (Paris: Vrin, 1981), Part One, chap. 1, p. 43; chap. 4, p. 54.

49. Ibid., chap. 4, p. 54.

50. Ibid., Part One, chap. 1, p. 46: "this image of the sound of thought that we imagine is not the image of the thought itself but only of a sound"; and Part Two, chap. 1, p. 103: "it is certainly useful for the aim of logic, which is *to think well*, to understand the diverse usages of the sounds that are meant to signify ideas, and that the spirit had the habit of linking so narrowly that one can hardly be conceived without the other, so that the idea of the thing excites the idea of the sound, and the idea of the sound that of the thing." On the independence of thought from its "clothing" in "external signs" and the use of language as a "habit" formed in communicating thought with others, see the Préambule, p. 38. See also Roland Douzé, *La grammaire générale et raisonnée de Port-Royal: Contribution à l'histoire des idées grammaticales en France*, 2nd ed. (Bern: Francke, 1971), chap. 1, "Descartes et la grammaire générale et raisonnée," pp.

interest in "language" as a system of writing available to reason *because* its order is on its surface—a superficies one can see for itself, founded in "fantaisie" solidified by habit—is far from the identification of language use with the art of logic by Cartesian universal grammarians,[51] but it may, in a practical way, be closer to Descartes.

For, Descartes' "method" used an arbitrary, linear unit of measure—the institution of a conventional basis for ordering proportions repeated by Perrault—and a sign system that despatialized proportions, making them legible. Without their designation by the arbitrary signs that represent them in equations, these proportions could neither be represented as an "intuition" nor plotted as a line. Lines and letters do not represent independent ideas in the method; they represent each other. The order produced between them may be seen as an arbitrary representation of Descartes' "design" in the *Discours de la méthode*. For a method that requires discourse can be grounded neither in given things nor in autonomous thought. Like Perrault, the example Descartes gives of the procedure of such a method is the order followed in script. But to the artificial, visible regularity of the written Descartes adds the fact of immediate, material unintelligibility. The order of method, he suggests, is like the order we produce when attempting to read script that is at once distinct and illegible, "writing disguised beneath unknown characters":

> la méthode . . . n'est le plus souvent rien d'autre que l'observation scrupuleuse d'un ordre, que cet ordre existe dans la chose même, ou bien qu'on l'ait ingénieusement introduit par la pensée: par exemple, si nous voulons lire une écriture déguisée sous des caractères inconnus, *nous ne voyons aucun ordre s'y manifester clairement, mais nous en forgeons un pourtant*, tant pour examiner toutes les présomptions que l'on peut faire sur chaque signe, chaque mot ou chaque phrase, que

---

25–44; André Robinet, *Le langage à l'âge classique* (Paris: Klincksieck, 1978), pp. 21–34, 79–82; and Stephen Gaukroger's excellent Introduction to *On True and False Ideas*, by Antoine Arnauld, pp. 1–41.

51. In the *Logique* Arnauld and Nicole add a fourth and final section "on method" to the tripartite division of "perception," "judgment," and "reasoning" found in the *Grammaire*. Consistent with their identification of specific knowledge with proper language use, the eight "rules" of method they propose are based, unlike those in the *Regulae* and the *Discours*, on principles of definition. See Arnauld and Nicole, *Logique*, Part Four, chap. 11, pp. 333–35, "La méthode des sciences reduite à huit regles principales [*sic*]."

> pour ordonner ces présomptions de manière à connaître par énumé-
> ration tout ce que l'on peut en déduire.[52]

> method is most often nothing other than the scrupulous observa-
> tion of an order, whether this order exists in the thing itself or one
> has ingeniously introduced it in thought: for example, if we want to
> read writing concealed beneath unknown characters, *we see no order
> manifest itself clearly, but we forge one nonetheless,* as much to examine
> the assumptions one can make about each sign, each word or each
> phrase, as to order these assumptions in such a way as to find out by
> enumeration everything that can be deduced from them.

What we do with unfamiliar script cannot be identified as "method"
apart from the assumed but thoroughly abstract discourse ("each sign,
each word or each phrase") and the comparative process of understanding the parts of that discourse ("everything that can be deduced from
them") upon which we work, "forging" "order" where "we see no order
manifest itself clearly." The ability to read such script must be deduced
from its linear visibility; "unknown characters" convey no meaning which
would make order manifest, making those characters, in effect, disappear,
by revealing itself as that which they "conceal." In such a verbal context, without the mediation of recognizable, linguistic representation, the
order we "observe" may either "exist in the thing itself" or be brought
into existence "ingeniously," by "thought." Rather than trouble method,
such uncertainty ensures the certainty of a method which instead seeks no
extra-discursive source. If "method," Descartes informs us, "is often nothing other than the scrupulous observation of an order" derived in the act
of comparing signs, the only deductions of which we can be certain must
be grounded in signs without apparent content. Recalling Perrault's view
that building resembles language not as discursive semiosis but as writing,
we may reason that building considered apart from the historical lexi-
con of habit, association, and authority—building opposed to Descartes'
"book of the world"—would pose such a script to the eye. The order (and
beauty) of architecture to be "forged" out of discourse would be entirely
the work of the mind. But this is another way of stating Descartes' image
of thinking, the drawing of his architect, his "I."

---

52. Descartes, *Regulae*, Rule X, *OP,* 1:127 (my emphasis).

Epilogue: The Line between Aesthetics and Knowledge

Perrault's analysis of architectonic beauty based on *fantaisie* and convention introduces reason, human history, and accident into the field of aesthetic theory. Following Descartes, Perrault opposes and subordinates natural forms to those which are arbitrarily composed, identifying the latter with the peculiar matter of drawing and writing. In order to underscore the fundamentally different conceptions of aesthetics, philosophy, and their intersection that arise from a modern, Cartesian conception of the line, it would be helpful, in concluding, to situate that conception in the context of modern and explicitly "post"-modern philosophies whose descriptions of exclusively aesthetic and rationalist thinking are disputed by Descartes' *Discours*.

In *L'oeil et l'esprit* Merleau-Ponty criticizes a Descartes who fails to join vision to spirit, soul, or intellect, a Descartes who refuses to position thought within a body that grasps things in space corporeally, according to the perspective of the (bodily) eye: "Descartes was right in setting space free. His mistake was to erect it into a positive being, outside all points of view, beyond all latency and all depth, having no true thickness."[1] This Descartes *sans profondeur*,[2] or aesthetic point of view, saw no difference between engraving and painting, and, predictably, took "line drawings" (*le dessin*) as "typical" of "pictures," ignoring "that other deeper opening

---

1. "Descartes avait raison de délivrer l'espace. Son tort était de l'ériger en un être tout positif, au-delà de tout point de vue, de toute latence, de toute profondeur, sans aucune épaisseur vraie." Merleau-Ponty, *L'oeil et l'esprit* (Paris: Gallimard, 1964), p. 48; "Eye and Mind," trans. Carleton Dallery, in Merleau-Ponty, *The Primacy of Perception*, ed. and intro. James M. Edie (Evanston, Ill.: Northwestern University Press, 1964), p. 174; English trans. hereafter cited as "Eye and Mind."
2. Cf. "Eye and Mind," pp. 177, 179; *L'oeil et l'esprit*, pp. 55–56, 64.

upon things given us by secondary qualities, especially color."[3] "The real power of painting" for Descartes, Merleau-Ponty concludes accurately, "lies in design [*dessin*]."[4]

But just as Merleau-Ponty implicitly makes the conflation between "drawing" and "design" suggested by contemporary usage of the term *dessin*,[5] he identifies the act of line drawing—as Descartes does not—with the imitation of preexisting things: "for Descartes it is unarguably evident that one can paint only existing things, that their existence consists in being extended, and that design, or line drawing [*le dessin*], alone makes painting possible by making the representation of extension possible."[6] In a similar vein he criticizes "a prosaic conception of the line" which understands it "as a positive attribute and a property of the object in itself," stating further:

> this line has been contested by all modern painting, and probably by
> all painting, as we are led to think by da Vinci's comment in his *Trea-*
> *tise of Painting:* "The secret of the art of drawing is to discover in each

3. "Eye and Mind," pp. 171–72; *L'oeil et l'esprit*, pp. 42–43: "Il est significatif qu'ayant à parler des 'tableaux' il prenne pour typique le dessin. . . . S'il avait examiné cette autre et plus profonde ouverture aux choses que nous donnent les qualités secondes, notamment la couleur." Here and throughout his comments on Descartes—as in his observation that "le modèle cartesian de la vision, c'est toucher" (p. 37) (the Cartesian concept of vision is modeled after the sense of touch [p. 170])—Merleau-Ponty follows Wölfflin's now canonical distinction between "linear" and "painterly" painting, the former defined as a delineation of real, tangible objects that makes the experience of painting "similar to" tactile experience; the latter, as the introduction of a purely optical "appearance" into painting: "A more developed art has learned to surrender itself to mere appearance. With that, the whole notion of the pictorial has shifted. The tactile picture has become the visual picture—the most decisive revolution in orientation which art history knows" (see Wölfflin, *Kunstgeschichtliche Grundbegriffe*, chap. 1, "Das Lineare und das Malerische," 23–24).

4. "Eye and Mind," p. 172; *L'oeil et l'esprit*, p. 43: "pour lui . . . toute la puissance de la peinture repose sur celle du dessin." It is of course Merleau-Ponty's English language translator who in this case astutely translates *dessin* as, alternately, "line drawing" and "design," a necessary, contextual distinction based on Merleau-Ponty's own argument that the power of painting cannot be identified with line drawing.

5. See chap. 3, n. 10.

6. "Eye and Mind," p. 172; *L'oeil et l'esprit*, p. 44: "c'est pour Descartes une évidence qu'on ne peut peindre que des choses existantes, que leur existence est d'être étendues, et que le dessin rend possible la peinture en rendant possible la représentation de l'étendue."

object the particular way in which a certain flexuous line, which is, so to speak, its generating axis, is directed through its whole extent."[7]

If, on the one hand, according to Merleau-Ponty, Descartes appreciates line drawing as the "representation of extension," on the other hand, he is said to reject the "*de facto* vision" of "thought united with a body" that Merleau-Ponty locates in painting: for Descartes, Merleau-Ponty argues (again accurately), "one can draw nothing from [such a vision] which deserves to be called true."[8] Descartes is thus simultaneously guilty of stressing and neglecting a "*de facto* vision" of things: his formalist view of drawing, in contrast to da Vinci's axiological one, is said to border on the "prosaic" notion of a linear representation of "existing things," while at the same time restricting that notion to the status of a false representation. For Merleau-Ponty, in other words, Descartes fails to arrive at a notion of transcendent corporeality, a truth of phenomenological reality, which the "vision" represented in painting represents better than lines (let alone words). Descartes' shortcoming was not to have achieved the synthesis of bodily being and truth that Merleau-Ponty himself attempted to achieve—in writing—for phenomenology, and that "modern" painting, or perhaps all painting, but principally Cézanne's painting, according to Merleau-Ponty, does.[9]

As the preceding study has attempted to demonstrate, however, Descartes' abstraction from the perception of things and production of *the things of the line and the self* go deeper—to use Merleau-Ponty's literalization of the illusion of a "third dimension" in painting[10]—than the

7. Ibid., pp. 182–83; *L'oeil et l'esprit*, p. 72: "Il y a eu par exemple une conception prosaïque de la ligne comme attribut positif et propriété de l'object en soi. . . . Cette ligne-là est contestée par toute la peinture moderne, probablement par toute peinture, puisque Vinci dans le *Traité de la Peinture* parlait de 'découvrir dans chaque objet . . . la manière particulière dont se dirige à travers toute son étendue . . . une certaine ligne flexueuse qui est comme son axe générateur.' "

8. Ibid., p. 176; *L'oeil et l'esprit*, pp. 54–55: "cette vision de fait . . . pensée unie à un corps . . . on ne peut rien en tirer qui mérite d'être dit vrai."

9. On Cézanne's reported ability to "think in painting" ("il 'pense en peinture' "), see "Eye and Mind," 178–81 (*L'oeil et l'esprit*, pp. 60–66). See also Merleau-Ponty's classic essay, "Le doute de Cézanne" (chap. 1 of *Sens et non-sens* [Paris: Nagel, 1948], pp. 15–49; "Cézanne's Doubt," trans. Hubert L. and Patricia Allen Dreyfus, *Sense and Non-Sense* [Evanston, Ill.: Northwestern University Press, 1964], pp. 9–25).

10. "Eye and Mind," pp. 172, 174; *L'oeil et l'esprit*, pp. 45, 48.

ultimately superficial dichotomies between drawing and painting and true and false visions of being. For Descartes, the self who sees truly *must itself first be made known as a thing*, and that knowledge cannot be arrived at through the sight, or any other perception, of an object. The self who recognizes linear extension as the only indubitable substance must also make itself into such a substance. Beyond or before vision, and any form of its representation, both self and line "are" in Descartes a projection of thought. When Merleau-Ponty argues that in modern painting, "figurative or not, the line is no longer a thing or an imitation of a thing," he demonstrates his adherence to an understanding of line that remains far more traditional than Descartes' radical notion of things made knowable to begin with as "étendue."[11]

In the modern philosophy of Descartes, line *is* itself a thing in the world *because* it is not an imitation of a thing. When, quoting Klee's turn on da Vinci's definition of an axiological line, Merleau-Ponty states that it would be impossible to "give the generating axis of a man" — "the painter 'would have to have a network of lines so entangled that it could no longer be a question of a truly elementary representation' " — he falls short of Descartes' modern conception of a simple, arbitrary unit, "I" ("je"), that, extended along the double axes of thinking and being, traces the line, or *cogito,* between them.[12] What this study has named Descartes' "line of thought" produces, rather than reproduces, the drawing subject. It constitutes "man," the very agent of aesthetic "representation." It does this by abstracting from a demonstrable self ("ce moi"), and all other "existing things," a grammatical subject arbitrarily represented by the notational sign, "I." The temporality of the act of thinking ("pendant que je voulais ainsi penser") extends and translates "I" into being, making a notational sign into a self-reflexive *and* material subject, "something" ("quelque chose"), *for as long as thinking lasts.* The model for this deduction of the being of the subject is the comparative, notational method explained and implemented in the *Géométrie,* a method for drawing lines that do not derive from preexisting figures.

In this sense, which in no way corresponds to Merleau-Ponty's bodily

---

11. Ibid., p. 184; *L'oeil et l'esprit,* p. 76: "Figurative ou non, la ligne en tout cas n'est plus imitation des choses ni chose."

12. Ibid., p. 184; *L'oeil et l'esprit,* p. 75: "pour donner l'axe générateur d'un homme, le peintre, dit Klee, 'aurait besoin d'un lacis de lignes à ce point embrouillé qu'il ne saurait plus être question d'une représentation véritablement élémentaire.' "

sense of "vision," Descartes does not imitate being but draws it from thought. But in this sense, too, and more profoundly, possibly, than Merleau-Ponty desired, Descartes joins body indissolubly to thinking, as its (temporary) result. More modern than the most modern painter Merleau-Ponty describes, Descartes produces a truth of material being, just as his *Géométrie* produces a necessary, and previously unknown, "étendue."

But just as Descartes does not arrive at this truth on the bases of existing beings or of aesthetic "vision," he also does not depart from the intellect alone, whatever that might be. He posits a sign which acquires the content of "something" in the course of its translation by thinking, while recognizing after the fact that, during the course of that translation, "I" had to reside somewhere. As his *Géométrie* introduces the use of notation, composing the written "representation" (or "intuition") of previously unknown substance from the rapid comparison of signs in multiple equations, Descartes' founding of "the first principle of the philosophy [he] sought," his method for drawing substance into being, requires the context of his "talking about it," discourse. And since the particular thing sought here is the subject itself—since the "foundation" on which Descartes would "build" must be his own ("à moi")—the discourse which makes method possible must also be autobiographical. Words must be the medium of Descartes' narrative "tableau," the context of his "thought" of freely drawn lines in the *Discours*. And words—the *cogito*—must produce him, during the act of thinking, as "something" he can know.

Yet this is not to say that words equal thought itself. That equation is most familiar to us now from the description of seventeenth-century rationalism presented from the "post"-modern perspective offered by Foucault.[13] Having hypothesized a sixteenth century in which language is believed to "resemble" the world, to be itself "like a thing of nature," "a thing written in the world," Foucault describes a seventeenth and an early eighteenth century in which words become unsubstantial "discourse,"

---

13. "Le langage classique est beaucoup plus proche qu'on ne croit de la pensée qu'il est chargé de manifester. . . . Non pas effect extérieur de la pensée, mais pensée elle-même" (The language of the classical age is much closer to the thought it is charged with expressing than is generally supposed. . . . It is not an exterior effect of thought, but thought itself). Foucault, *Les mots et les choses* (Paris: Seuil, 1966), pp. 92–93 (*The Order of Things* [New York: Random House, 1971], p. 78; English trans. hereafter cited as *The Order of Things*).

signs without "being" formed for analytic purposes alone.[14] According to Foucault, who sees no paradox in this description, the language of rational analysis is a "*transparent*" "representation."[15] Inexplicably, fatalistically, such transparency, however, meets its historical limit. The "classical age" is replaced in Foucault's "archaeology" by the "modern age" in which language makes its reappearance, in the "counterdiscourse" of literature, as itself, "the raw being forgotten since the sixteenth century."[16] And as the "being" of language reappears, man, the finite object of inquiry created at the end of the eighteenth century, disappears.[17]

The dramatic, indeed melodramatic, structure of this history exercises a certain appeal: there is a perverse pleasure to be had in a spectacle which promises not the "sovereignty" but the demise of the viewer.[18] But Foucault's prognosis of the end of man merely repeats the fate he had initially assigned to things, at the moment when they were "separated" from the words with which they were said to have been united.[19] What is ultimately described, then, in *Les mots et les choses,* is a history in which words and things *exclude* one another: before the classical age the category of things subsumes the category of words, which supposedly resemble them and are themselves like them; in the classical age, words subsume things by referring solely to themselves and each other. For, the putative transparency of the classical word, its eclipse of things, also leads to a concept of representation which must, by Foucault's description, double back on itself, making the representation and the represented one.[20] Foucault's recourse

---

14. *The Order of Things,* pp. 34–35, 43; *Les mots et les choses,* pp. 49–50, 58.

15. Ibid., pp. 56, 64, 75 (my emphasis); *Les mots et les choses,* pp. 70, 78, 91.

16. Ibid., p. 44, also p. 300; *Les mots et les choses,* p. 59, also p. 313.

17. Ibid., pp. 303–87; *Les mots et les choses,* chaps. 9 and 10, pp. 314–98.

18. I refer here to Foucault's model of self-identical "modern" "man" replacing the absent, finite, reflected "king" of the classical age represented in Velasquez's *Las Meninas;* see ibid., pp. 308–12, 385–87; *Les mots et les choses,* pp. 318–23, 397–98.

19. "[A l'âge classique] la profonde appartenance du language et du monde se trouve défaite. . . . Les choses et les mots vont se séparer. L'oeil sera destiné à voir, et à voir seulement. . . . Le discours aura bien pour tâche de dire ce qui est, mais il ne sera rien de plus que ce qu'il dit" ([In the classical age] the profound kinship of language with the world was thus dissolved. . . . Things and words were to be separated from one another. The eye was thenceforth destined to see and only to see. . . . Discourse was still to have the task of speaking that which is, but it was no longer to be anything more than what it said). *Les mots et les choses,* p. 58 (*The Order of Things,* p. 43).

20. "Il faut que [le signe] représente, mais que cette représentation, à son tour, se

to the authority of Port Royal on this matter is, in fact, ungrounded in the grammarians' text.[21] But even without the purported support of Arnauld

---

trouve représentée en lui" ([The sign] must represent; but that representation, in turn, must also be represented within it). Ibid., p. 78 (*The Order of Things*, p. 64).

21. In support of his claim of a total occlusion of things by unsubstantial words in the classical age, Foucault cites two sentences from Part One, chap. 4 of the Port Royal *Logique*. First: "*La Logique de Port-Royal* le dit: 'le signe enferme deux idées, l'une de la chose qui représente, l'autre de la chose représentée; et sa nature consiste à exciter la première par la seconde" (ibid., p. 78) (*The Logic of Port Royal* states this as follows: 'The sign encloses two ideas, one of the thing representing, the other of the thing represented; and its nature consists in exciting the first by the second [*The Order of Things*, pp. 63–64]). Making the thing represented into the representation of what represents it, this sentence should seem at face value nonsensical, and with good reason: Foucault has directly reversed the causal sequence that appears in the Port Royal text, which instead reads as follows: "Le signe enferme deux idées, l'une de la chose qui représente, l'autre de la chose représentée; & sa nature consiste à exciter *la seconde par la premiere*" (Arnauld and Nicole, *Logique*, p. 53 [my emphasis]). The second sentence from the *Logique* is cited correctly, but only in part. Directly following the signal pronouncement given in the previous note ("Il faut que . . . cette représentation . . . se trouve représentée en lui"), Foucault writes: "Condition indispensable à l'organisation binaire du signe, et que la *Logique de Port-Royal* énonce avant même de dire ce que c'est qu'un signe: 'Quand on ne regarde un certain objet que comme en représentant un autre, l'idée qu'on en a est une idée de signe, et ce premier objet s'appelle signe'" (ibid., p. 78) (This is a condition indispensable to the binary organization of the sign, and one that the *Logique of Port-Royal* sets forth even before telling us what a sign is: "When one looks at a certain object only in so far as it represents another, the idea one has of it is the idea of a sign, and that first object is called a sign" [*The Order of Things*, p. 64]). What Foucault has deleted from this sentence is its first word, "*Mais* quand on . . ." (*But* when one . . .) (my emphasis). That contrastive "but" occurs because this sentence is placed in the *Logique* between two sentences that state opposing ideas of objects. First: "When one considers an object in itself and in its proper being, without turning the mind's eye to what it could represent, the idea one has of it is an idea of a thing, like the idea of the earth, of the sun" (*Logique*, pp. 52–53 [my translation]). The sentence from which Foucault deletes the contrastive conjunction, "but," follows next. Immediately thereafter follows a brief third sentence which explains the category of object introduced by "but": "C'est ainsi qu'on regard d'ordinaire les cartes & les tableaux" (*Logique*, p. 53) (This is how one normally views playing cards and pictures [my translation]). Arnauld and Nicole are here opposing natural objects, the earth and the sun, to artificial, pictorial objects made for the sole purpose of representation. By leaving out this rather obvious opposition (which the very title of this chapter of the *Logique*, "Des idées des choses, & des idées des signes," openly states)— along with the distinctions drawn among signs by Arnauld and Nicole which follow

and Nicole, Foucault's paradigm of words *or* things misses—and must miss—the modernity of the "classical" rationalist, Descartes.

Although Descartes is inevitably ascribed a major role in Foucault's dramatic narrative, the dematerialization of discourse *and* things said to characterize the pursuit of knowledge in the "classical age" is directly contradicted by the autobiographical narrative of that pursuit in Descartes' *Discours,* a narrative "fable" which Descartes describes as "like a tableau," and which, like that description itself, is, at all moments, anything but transparent. Limited to a few pages, Foucault's actual discussion of Descartes focuses solely on the notion of comparison introduced in the *Regulae,* interpreting comparison as a means of instituting the purely differential "order" of "rationalism" that Foucault figures in spatial terms as a kind of a priori compartmentalization of things, or taxonomic "grid." [22] The fact that the *Discours* itself defied disciplinary compartmentalization, and that Descartes' comparative method explicitly requires the introduction of visible, legible notation—that such notation does not somehow represent itself but rather known and unknown quantities, and that, unlike purportedly "transparent" signs, Cartesian notation *must be written*— none of this is considered by Foucault. Nor is the fact that "order" for Descartes is not a reified grouping or static "configuration" of things, but a temporary means of reading signs so as first to produce things. The "rationale" of Cartesian "rationalism" is to produce substance, not self-referential reason; to bring things into being, rather than survey preexisting things that it has arranged in space for the pleasure of overseeing them. Discourse in Descartes is not taxonomic, and cognition is anything but

---

it—Foucault leads us to think that the "indispensable" "condition" of all signs for Port Royal is a (still nonsensical) tautology of semiotic "transparency," the "idea" of the sign and the sign as "object" being one. In addition, this deformation of the *Logique* is taken from the very chapter, cited in the discussion of Perrault above, in which Arnauld and Nicole distinguish between natural and institutional signs, defining the latter as "words" and the "letters of words" that depend for their existence on "the free imagination [*fantaisie*] of men" (see chap. 9, n.48).

22. On Descartes, see *The Order of Things,* pp. 52–54; *Les mots et les choses,* pp. 66–68. On the grid-like order of linguistic knowledge, see, for example, ibid., pp. xx–xxiii; *Les mots et les choses,* pp. 12–15. I have discussed the issue of Foucault's spatialization of discourse elsewhere; see " 'Is that Helen?' Contemporary Pictorialism, Lessing, and Kant," *Comparative Literature* 45 (1993): 230–57, esp. pp. 234–36.

compartmentalizing vision; his "architect" can be called an "engineer," but not an archivist, genericist, or interior decorator.

Finally, when the *cogito* appears toward the close of *Les mots et les choses* as a kind of shorthand for rationalism, it is opposed by Foucault to "the unthought," "the Other" "which has accompanied man . . . since the nineteenth century," when "man," taking himself as an object, lost the (Cartesian) "privilege of reflexive knowledge, thought thinking itself."[23] Yet in proposing the possibility of "a modern *cogito*" in which thought would think not itself but "the forms of nonthinking," Foucault describes what is already modern in the philosophy of Descartes.[24] Just as signs for Descartes are not transparencies, his *cogito* is not an act of pure self-reflexivity. It is the production of "something" that, as a thing, is precisely not identical with thought: thinking and being are never conflated by Descartes into a single moment or (as Jaspers suggested) a single point. In the *Discours* and in the *Géométrie*, thinking thinks into being what is not itself—a thing, or a line—and that thinking already recognizes its own historicity: it is limited, not by an epistemic age to come, but by its own acknowledged occurrence "pendant le temps."

Knowledge in Descartes takes material form, or it does not occur at all, and that form is not a "similitude,"[25] "tableau," or any other aesthetic representation. Between aesthetics and knowledge Descartes projects modern thinking, in which thought—necessarily including the thinking of "I"—only attains to being by way of what is not thinking, discursive representation. It does this by abstracting from discourse—whether notational or autobiographical—that which alone is proper to it in the first place, the "thing" without which there would be neither things nor signs. Line, a "thing" like nothing else, the thing both aesthetics and knowledge require, becomes the sole property of the thinking subject seeking a foundation entirely its own. The discourse that, seeking a foundation in the self, founds the self as "thinking thing," first finds, by discursive detour, the "thing" of thinking, line.

23. See ibid., pp. 326–27; *Les Mots et les choses*, p. 337. Indeed, for Foucault, perhaps alone among all Descartes' interpreters to this day, the *cogito* is precisely anything but a statement *requiring* reflection in that it represents for him the transparent "relationship between representation and being" by which he characterizes the "classical age" (see ibid., p. 312; *Les mots et les choses*, p. 323).

24. Ibid., p. 324; *Les mots et les choses*, p. 335.

25. Ibid., pp. 17–25; *Les mots et les choses*, pp. 32–40.

BIBLIOGRAPHY

Primary Texts

Arnauld, Antoine and Pierre Nicole. *Logique ou l'art de penser.* 5th ed. rev. Paris: Vrin, 1981 [Paris: Guillaume Des Prez, 1683].

———— and Claude Lancelot. *Grammarie générale et raisonnée de Port Royal.* Reprint of 1st ed. Menston, England: Scholar Press, 1969 [Paris: Le Petit, 1660].

Cahné, Pierre-Alain. *Index du Discours de la Méthode de René Descartes,* Rome: Edizioni dell'Ateneo, 1977.

De L'Orme, Philibert. *Architecture.* Rouen: Daniel Ferrand, 1648.

Descartes, René. *Correspondance.* Ed. Charles Adam and Gérard Milhaud. 8 vols. Paris: Félix Alcan, 1936–63. [*AM*]

————. *Discours de la méthode.* Ed. Étienne Gilson. Paris: Vrin, 1925.

————. *Discours de la méthode, avec introduction et remarques de Gilbert Gadoffre.* Manchester: University of Manchester Press, 1941.

————. *The Geometry of René Descartes.* Facsimile of the first edition (1637), with notes and translation from the French and Latin by David Eugene Smith and Marcia L. Latham. Chicago: Open Court, 1925.

————. *Oeuvres.* Ed. Charles Adam and Paul Tannery. 12 vols. Paris: Léopold Cerf, 1897–1913. [*AT*]

————. *Oeuvres philosophiques* [*OP*]. Ed. Ferdinand Alquié. 3 vols. Paris: Garnier, 1963. Vol. 1: *Discours de la méthode* and *Regulae* [*Rules*]. Vol 2: *Méditations* and *Recherche de la vérité.*

Desgodet, Antoine. *Edifices antiques de Rome.* Paris: Jean Baptiste Coignard, 1682.

Hamilton, Edith, and Huntington Cairns. *The Complete Dialogues of Plato.* Princeton: Princeton University Press, 1973.

Hegel, G. W. F. *Enzyklopädie der philosophischen Wissenschaften im Grundrisse.* Ed. Friedhelm Nicolin and Otto Pöggeler. Hamburg: Felix Meiner, 1969 [1830].

————. *Vorlesungen über die Geschichte der Philosophie.* 3 vols. Frankfurt: Suhrkamp, 1971.

Husserl, Edmund. "Der Ursprung der Geometrie als intentional-historisches Problem." Ed. Eugen Fink. *Revue internationale de philosophie* 1 (1939): 203–25.

———. *The Crisis of European Sciences and Transcendental Philosophy.* Trans. and with an introduction by David Carr, pp. 353–78. Evanston, Ill.: Northwestern University Press, 1970.

———. *L'origine de la géometrie,* trans. and introduction by Jacques Derrida. Paris: Presses Universitaires de France, 1962.

Jaspers, Karl. *Descartes und die Philosophie.* Berlin: de Gruyter, 1937.

Kant, Immanuel. *Werkausgabe.* 12 vols. Ed. Wilhelm Weischedel. Frankfurt: Suhrkamp, 1977.

Kleist, Heinrich von. *Sämtliche Werke und Briefe.* 2 vols. 7th ed. rev. Ed. Helmut Sembdner. Munich: dtv, 1987 [Munich: Carl Hanser, 1961].

McKeon, Richard, ed. *The Basic Works of Aristotle.* New York: Random House, 1941.

Ouvrard, Réné. *Architecture harmonique ou application de la doctrine des proportions de la musique à l'architecture.* Paris: J. B. De La Caille, 1679.

Perrault, Charles. *Parallèle des anciens et des modernes en ce qui regarde les arts et les sciences.* Facsimile edition. Munich: Eidos, 1964. [orig. 4 vols. 1688–97.]

Perrault, Claude, trans. *Architecture générale de Vitruve, Reduite en Abrégé. Avec préface par Mr. Perrault de l'Académie des Sciences à Paris.* Amsterdam: Huguetan et Gallet, 1681.

———, trans. *Les dix livres d'architecture de Vitruve corrigez et traduits nouvellement en François, avec des notes et des figures.* 2nd ed. rev., corr., and expanded. Paris: Jean Baptiste Coignard, 1674.

———. *Ordonnance des cinq espèces de colonnes selon la méthode des anciens.* Paris: Jean Baptiste Coignard, 1683.

Stendhal. *Racine et Shakespeare.* Paris: Garnier-Flammarion, 1970 [1823].

Secondary Literature

Allard, Jean-Louis. *Le mathématisme de Descartes.* Ottawa: Editions de l'Université d'Ottawa, 1963.

Alquié, Ferdinand. "Introduction," *Le Discours de la Méthode et les Essais.* In *Oeuvres philosophiques.* Ed. Ferdinand Alquié. 3 vols. Paris: Garnier, 1963.

Auerbach, Erich. "Figura." In *Scenes from the Drama of European Literature,* pp. 11–76. Minneapolis: University of Minnesota Press, 1984 [New York, 1959; originally published in *Neue Dantestudien* (Istanbul, 1944), pp. 11–71].

Ayer, A. J. "'I think, therefore I am.'" In *Descartes: A Collection of Critical Essays,* ed. Willis Doney, pp. 80–87. Notre Dame, Ind.: University of Notre Dame Press, 1968 [New York: Doubleday, 1967].

Baillet, Adrien. *La vie de Monsieur Des Cartes.* 2 vols. Reprint. New York: Garland, 1987 [Paris: Daniel Horthemels, 1691].

Beck, Lewis J. *The Method of Descartes: A Study of the Regulae.* Oxford: Clarendon, 1952.

Belaval, Yvon. *Leibniz critique de Descartes.* Paris: Gallimard, 1960.

Benjamin, Andrew. "Deconstruction, Architecture, and Philosophy." In *Deconstruction: Omnibus Volume,* ed. Andreas Papadakis, Catherine Cooke, and Andrew Benjamin, pp. 80–84. London: Academy Editions, 1989.

Berman, Marshall. *All That Is Solid Melts into Air: The Experience of Modernity.* London: Penguin, 1988 [New York: Simon & Schuster, 1982].

Beth, M. E. W. "Le savoir déductif dans la pensée cartésienne." In *Descartes: Cahiers de Royaumont. Philosophie No. II,* pp. 141–65. London: Garland, 1987.

Beyssade, Jean-Marie. *La philosophie première de Descartes: Le temps et la cohérence de la métaphysique.* Paris: Flammarion, 1979.

Blunt, Anthony. *Art and Architecture in France 1500–1700.* London: Penguin, 1953.

Bochner, Salomon. *The Collected Papers of Salomon Bochner.* Ed. Robert C. Gunning. 4 vols. Providence, R.I.: American Mathematical Society, 1992.

Bohm, David. *Quantum Theory.* New York: Dover, 1989 [1951].

Boutroux, Pierre. *L'imagination et les mathématiques selon Descartes.* Paris: Félix Alcan, 1900.

Boyer, Carl B. *The History of the Calculus and Its Conceptual Development.* New York: Dover, 1949.

———. "Descartes and the Geometrization of Algebra." *American Mathematical Monthly* 66 (1959): 390–93.

———. *History of Analytic Geometry.* Princeton Junction: Scholar's Bookshelf, 1988 [*Scripta Mathematical Studies* no. 6–7, 1956].

———. *A History of Mathematics.* New York: Wiley, 1968.

Brands, Helmut. *Cogito Ergo Sum. Interpretationen von Kant bis Nietzsche.* Freiburg: Karl Alber, 1982.

Brodsky, Claudia. "Architecture and Architectonics: 'The Art of Reason' in Kant's *Critique*." In *Canon.* Vol. 3 of *The Princeton Journal: Thematic Studies in Architecture,* ed. Taisto Mäkelä, pp. 103–17. New York: Princeton Architectural Press, 1988.

———. " 'The Impression of Movement': Jean Racine, Architecte." *Yale French Studies* 76 (1989): 162–81.

Brodsky Lacour, Claudia. " 'Is that Helen?' Contemporary Pictorialism, Lessing, and Kant." *Comparative Literature* 45 (1993): 230–57.

———. "The Temporality of Convention: Convention Theory and Romanticism." In *Rules and Conventions: Literature, Philosophy, Social Theory,* ed. Mette Hjort, pp. 274–93. Baltimore: Johns Hopkins University Press, 1992.

———. "Whatever Moves You: 'Experimental Philosophy' and the Literature of Experience in Diderot and Kleist." In *Traditions of Experiment from the Enlightenment to the Present: Essays in Honor of Peter Demetz,* ed. Nancy Kaiser and David E. Wellbery, pp. 17–43. Ann Arbor: University of Michigan Press, 1993.

Brunschvig, Léon. *Descartes et Pascal, lecteurs de Montaigne.* Neuchâtel: Baconnière, 1942.

———. "Mathématiques et métaphysique chez Descartes." *Revue de métaphysique et de morale* 34 (1927): 277–324.

Cahné, Pierre-Alain. *Un autre Descartes: Le philosophe et son langage.* Paris: Vrin, 1980.

Cajori, Florian. *A History of Mathematics.* 3rd ed. New York: Chelsea, 1980 [1895].

————. "History of Zeno's Arguments on Motion." *American Mathematical Monthly* 22 (1915): 1–297.

————. "The Purpose of Zeno's Arguments on Motion." *Isis* 3 (1920): 7–20.

Carr, Thomas M. *Descartes and the Resilience of Rhetoric: Varieties of Cartesian Rhetorical Theory.* Carbondale: Southern Illinois University Press, 1990.

Caton, Hiram. *The Origin of Subjectivity: An Essay on Descartes.* New Haven: Yale University Press, 1973.

Coolidge, Julian. "The Origin of Analytic Geometry," *Osiris* 1 (1936): 231–50.

Costabel, Pierre. "Les *Essais de la Méthode* et la réforme mathématique." In *Le discours et sa méthode,* ed. Nicolas Grimaldi and Jean-Luc Marion, pp. 213–26. Paris: Presses Universitaires de France, 1987.

Cottingham, John. *Descartes.* Oxford: Basil Blackwell, 1986.

————. "Descartes on Thought." *Philosophical Quarterly* 28 (1978): 208–14.

Cress, Donald A., trans. *Discourse on Method and Meditations on First Philosophy,* by René Descartes. Indianapolis: Hackett, 1980.

Curley, Edwin M. "Cohérence ou incohérence du *Discours.*" In *Le discours et sa méthode,* ed. Nicolas Grimaldi and Jean-Luc Marion, pp. 41–64. Paris: Presses Universitaires de France, 1987.

Damisch, Hubert. "La colonnade de Perrault et les fonctions de l'ordre classique." In *L'urbanisme de Paris et l'Europe 1600–1680,* ed. Pierre Francastel, pp. 85–93. Paris: Klincksieck, 1969.

————. *L'origine de la perspective.* 2nd ed. rev. Paris: Flammarion, 1993 [1987].

Deleuze, Gilles. *Le pli: Leibniz et le baroque.* Paris: Minuit, 1988.

———— and Félix Guattari. *Mille plateaux.* Vol. 2 of *Capitalisme et schizophrénie.* Paris: Minuit, 1980.

de Man, Paul. "Hegel on the Sublime." In *Displacement: Derrida and After,* ed. Mark Krupnik, pp. 139–53. Bloomington: Indiana University Press, 1983.

————. "The Resistance to Theory." In *The Resistance to Theory,* pp. 3–20. Minneapolis: University of Minnesota Press, 1986.

————. "Semiology and Rhetoric." In *Allegories of Reading: Figural Language in Rousseau, Nietzsche, Rilke and Proust,* pp. 3–19. New Haven: Yale University Press, 1979.

————. "Sign and Symbol in Hegel's *Aesthetic.*" *Critical Inquiry* 8 (1982): 761–75.

Derrida, Jacques. "Architettura ove il desiderio può abitare." *Domus* 671 (1986): 17–24.

————. "Cinquante-deux aphorismes pour an avant-propos." In *Psyche,* pp. 509–518. Paris: Galilée, 1987.

————. *De la grammatologie.* Paris: Minuit, 1967.

————. *L'écriture et la différence.* Paris: Seuil, 1967.

————. "Jacques Derrida in Discussion with Christopher Norris." In *Architectural Design* 59 (1989): 7–11.

————. "La philosophie dans sa langue nationale." In *Du droit à la philosophie,* pp. 283–309. Paris: Galilée, 1990.

————. "Point de folie—Maintenant l'architecture." In *Psyché,* pp. 477–93. Paris: Galilée, 1987.

————. "Pourquoi Peter Eisenman écrit de si bons livres." In *Psyché*, pp. 495–508. Paris: Galilée, 1987.

————. *Le problème de la genèse dans la philosophie de Husserl.* Paris: Presses Universitaires de France, 1990 [written 1953–54].

————. "Les romans de Descartes ou l'économie des mots." In *Du droit à la philosophie*, pp. 311–41. Paris: Galilée, 1990.

————. *La voix et le phénomène.* Paris: Presses Universitaires de France, 1967.

Donagan, Alan. "Descartes' Treatment of Mind and Body." In *Descartes: Critical and Interpretive Essays,* ed. Michael Hooker, pp. 186–96. Baltimore: Johns Hopkins University Press, 1978.

Douzé, Roland. *La grammaire générale et raisonné de Port-Royal: Contribution à l'histoire des idées grammaticales en France.* 2nd ed. Berne: Francke, 1971 [1967].

Eves, Howard. *An Introduction to the History of Mathematics.* 3rd ed. New York: Holt, Rinehart and Winston, 1976 [1964].

"Eye and Mind" [*L'oeil et l'esprit*]. By Maurice Merleau-Ponty. Trans. Carleton Dallery. In *The Primacy of Perception,* ed. and intro. James M. Edie. Evanston, Ill.: Northwestern University Press, 1964.

The Fold: Leibniz and the Baroque [*Le pli: Leibniz et le baroque*]. By Gilles Deleuze. Trans. Tom Conley. Minneapolis: University of Minnesota Press, 1993.

Foucault, Michel. *Les mots et les choses.* Paris: Seuil, 1966.

————. *The Order of Things* [Eng. trans. of *Les mots et les choses*]. New York: Random House, 1971.

————. Préface to *Grammaire générale et raisonnée,* by Antoine Arnauld and Claude Lancelot, pp. iii–xxvii. Paris: Republications Paulet, 1969.

Friedrich, Hugo, *Descartes und der französische Geist.* Leipzig: Felix Meiner, 1937.

Gadoffre, Gilbert. "Le *Discours de la Méthode* et l'histoire littéraire." *French Studies* 2 (1948): 301–14.

————. "Le *Discours de la Méthode* et la Querelle des Anciens. In *Modern Miscellany: Presented to Eugène Vinaver,* ed. T. E. Lawrenson, F. E. Sutcliffe, and G. F. A. Gadoffre, pp. 79–84. Manchester: University of Manchester Press, 1969.

————. *Introduction au Discours de la Méthode.* Manchester: University of Manchester Press, 1947.

————. "Réflexions sur la genèse du *Discours de la Méthode.*" *Revue de Sythèse* 22 (1948): 11–27.

————. "Sur la chronologie du *Discours de la Méthode. Revue d'histoire de la philosophie et d'histoire générale de la civilisation.* Jan.–Mar. (1943): 45–70.

Garber, Daniel. "Descartes et la méthode en 1637." In *Le discours et sa méthode,* ed. Nicolas Grimaldi and Jean-Luc Marion, pp. 65–87. Paris: Presses Universitaires de France, 1987.

————. "Science and Certainty in Descartes." In *Descartes: Critical and Interpretive Essays,* ed. Michael Hooker, pp. 74–88. Baltimore: Johns Hopkins University Press, 1978.

Gaukroger, Stephen. "Descartes' Project for a Mathematical Physics." In *Descartes:*

Philosophy, Mathematics and Physics, ed. Stephen Gaukroger, pp. 97–140. Sussex: Harvester, 1992.

———. "The Nature of Abstract Reasoning: Philosophical Aspects of Descartes' Work in Algebra." In *The Cambridge Companion to Descartes,* ed. John Cottingham, pp. 91–114. Cambridge: Cambridge University Press, 1992.

———. Introduction to *On True and False Ideas,* by Antoine Arnauld. Intro. and trans. Stephen Gaukroger, pp. 1–41. Manchester: University of Manchester Press, 1990.

Gilson, Étienne, ed. *Discours de la méthode.* By René Descartes. Paris: Vrin, 1925.

Goodkin, Richard E. *Around Proust.* Princeton: Princeton University Press, 1991.

———. *The Tragic Middle: Racine, Aristotle, Euripides.* Madison: University of Wisconsin Press, 1991.

Gouhier, Henri. *La pensée métaphysique de Descartes.* Paris: Vrin, 1962.

Gray, Jeremy. *Ideas of Space: Euclidean, Non-Euclidean, and Relativistic.* Oxford: Clarendon, 1989.

Gresset, Philippe. "Le classicisme — un style? Architecture et pensée visuelle: Les architectes classiques à l'épreuve de leur fondement." *Les cahiers de la recherche architecturale* 18 (1985): 6–17.

Grosholz, Emily. "Descartes' Unification of Algebra and Geometry." In *Descartes: Philosophy, Mathematics and Physics,* ed. Stephen Gaukroger, pp. 156–68. Sussex: Harvester, 1992.

Guiheux, Alain and Dominique Rouillard. "Echanges entre les mots et l'architecture dans la seconde moitié du XVIIème siècle à travers les traités de l'art de parler." *Les cahiers de la recherche architecturale* 18 (1985): 18–27.

Hacking, Ian. "Proof and Eternal Truths: Descartes and Leibniz." In *Descartes: Philosophy, Mathematics and Physics,* ed. Stephen Gaukroger, pp. 169–80. Sussex: Harvester Press, 1992.

Hamelin, O. *Le système de Descartes.* Préface by Emile Durkheim. Paris: Félix Alcan, 1921.

Hamon, Philippe. *Expositions: Littérature et architecture au XIXème siècle.* Paris: José Corti, 1989.

Hautecoeur, Louis. *Histoire de l'architecture classique en France.* 7 vols. Paris: Picard, 1944–57.

Herrmann, Wolfgang. *The Theory of Claude Perrault.* London: A. Zwemmer, 1973.

Hintikka, Jaako. "*Cogito Ergo Sum:* Inference or Performance?" In *Descartes: A Collection of Critical Essays,* ed. Willis Doney, pp. 108–39. Notre Dame, Ind.: University of Notre Dame Press, 1968 [New York: Doubleday, 1967].

———. "A Discourse on Descartes's Method." In *Descartes: Critical and Interpretive Essays,* ed. Michael Hooker, pp. 74–88. Baltimore: Johns Hopkins University Press, 1978.

Hollier, Denis. *La prise de la Concorde: Essais sur Georges Bataille.* Paris: Gallimard, 1972.

Hooker, Michael. "Denial of Mind-Body Identity." In *Descartes: Critical and Interpre-*

tive Essays, ed. Michael Hooker, pp. 170–85. Baltimore: Johns Hopkins University Press, 1978.

Imdahl, M. "Exkurs." In *Parallèle des Anciens et des Modernes,* by Charles Perrault, pp. 76–79. 4 vols. 1688–1697. Facsimile ed. Munich: Eidos, 1964.

Jakobson, Roman. "Linguistics and Poetics." In *The Structuralists from Marx to Lévi-Strauss,* ed. Richard and Fernande DeGeorge, pp. 85–122. New York: Anchor Doubleday, 1972. [Orig. pub. in *Style in Language,* ed. Thomas A. Sebeok, pp. 350–77 (Cambridge, Mass: MIT Press, 1960)].

———. "The Metaphoric and Metonymic Poles." In *Selected Writings,* 3: 76–82. The Hague: Mouten, 1981. [Orig. pub. in *Fundamentals of Language,* by Roman Jakobson and Morris Halle, pp. 76–82. The Hague: Mouton, 1956].

Jauss, Hans Robert. "Asthetische Normen und geschichtliche Reflexion in der 'Querelle des Anciens et des Modernes.' " "Introduction" to *Parallèle des Anciens et des Modernes,* by Charles Perrault, pp. 8–64. 4 vols. 1688–1697. Facsimile ed. Munich: Eidos, 1964.

Judovitz, Dalia. *Subjectivity and Representation in Descartes: The Origin of Modernity.* Cambridge: Cambridge University Press, 1988.

Kambartel, Walter. *Symmetrie und Schönheit: Über mögliche Voraussetzungen des neueren Kunstbewusstseins in der Architekturtheorie Claude Perraults.* Munich: Wilhelm Fink, 1972.

Kaufmann, Emil. "Three Revolutionary Architects." *American Philosophical Society Transactions* 42.3 (1952).

———. "Die Architekturtheorie der französischen Klassik und des Klassizismus." *Repertorium für Kunstwissenschaft* 44 (1924): 197–237.

Kenny, Anthony. "Descartes on Ideas." In *Descartes: A Collection of Critical Essays,* ed. Willis Doney, pp. 227–49. Notre Dame, Ind.: University of Notre Dame Press, 1968 [New York: Doubleday, 1967].

Klein, Jacob. *Greek Mathematical Thought and the Origin of Algebra.* Cambridge, Mass.: MIT Press, 1968 [Berlin, 1934–36].

Kranz, Emile. *Essai sur l'esthétique de Descartes.* Paris: Baillière et Cie, 1882.

Lang, Berel. *The Anatomy of Philosophical Style: Literary Philosophy and the Philosophy of Literature.* Oxford: Basil Blackwell, 1990.

Lefebvre, Henri. *The Production of Space.* Trans. Donald Nicholson-Smith. Oxford: Basil Blackwell, 1991 [Paris: Anthropos, 1974].

Lukács, Georg. *The Theory of the Novel: A Historico-Philosophical Essay on the Forms of Great Epic Literature* [*Die Theorie des Romans: Ein geschichtsphilosophischer Versuch über die Formen der grossen Epik*]. Trans. Anna Bostock. Special edition with 1962 preface by the author. Cambridge, Mass.: MIT Press, 1971 [Berlin: B. Cassirer, 1920; reprint, Berlin: Luchterhand, 1971].

Lyons, John D. "Subjectivity and Imitation in the *Discours de la Méthode.*" *Neophilologus* 66 (1982): 508–24.

Mahoney, Michael S. "The Beginnings of Algebraic Thought in the Seventeenth Century." In *Descartes: Philosophy, Mathematics, and Physics,* ed. Stephen Gaukroger, pp. 141–55. Sussex: Harvester, 1992.

Marion, Jean-Luc. "Ouverture." In *Problématique et réception du Discours de la Méthode et des Essais*, ed. Henry Méchoulan, pp. 9–21. Paris: Vrin, 1988.

Merleau-Ponty, Maurice. *L'oeil et l'esprit*. Paris: Gallimard, 1964.

———. *Phénoménologie de la perception*. Paris: Gallimard, 1945.

———. *The Primacy of Perception*. Ed. and intro. by James M. Edie. Evanston, Ill.: Northwestern University Press, 1964.

———. *Sens et non-sens*. Paris: Nagel, 1948.

Meschkowski, Herbert. *Probleme der Mathematikgeschichte*. 2 vols. Zurich: Bibliographisches Institut Wissenschaftsverlag, 1979.

Nancy, Jean-Luc. *Ego Sum*. Paris: Flammarion, 1979.

Norris, Christopher and Andrew Benjamin. *What Is Deconstruction?* London: Academy Editions, 1988.

Pais, Abraham. *Inward Bound*. Oxford: Oxford University Press, 1986.

———. *Neils Bohr's Times, in Physics, Philosophy and Polity*. Oxford: Clarendon, 1991.

———. *Subtle Is the Lord*. Oxford: Oxford University Press, 1982.

Pariente, Jean-Claude. "Problèmes logiques du *cogito*." In *Le discours et sa méthode*, ed. Nicolas Grimaldi and Jean-Luc Marion, pp. 229–69. Paris: Presses Universitaires de France, 1987.

Payot, Daniel. *Le philosophe et l'architecte: Sur quelques déterminations philosophiques de l'idée d'architecture*. Paris: Aubier, 1982.

Pérez-Gómez, Alberto. *Architecture and the Crisis of Modern Science*. Cambridge, Mass.: MIT Press, 1983 [trans. and rev. by the author of *La génesis y superación del funcionalismo en arquitectura*. Barcelona: Limusa, 1980].

Picon, Antoine. *Claude Perrault, 1613–1688, ou la curiosité d'un classique*. Paris: Picard, 1989.

Plotnitsky, Arkady. *Complementarity: Anti-Epistemology after Bohr, Bataille, and Derrida*. Durham, N.C.: Duke University Press, 1994.

———. *Reconfigurations: Critical Theory and General Economy*. Gainesville: University of Florida Press, 1993.

Prevant, L. "Esthétique et sagesse cartsienne." *Revue d'histoire de la philosophie et d'histoire générale de la civilisation*. Jan.–Mar. (1942): 3–13; Apr.–June (1942): 99–114.

Rée, Jonathan. *Descartes*. London: Allen Lane, 1974.

———. *Philosophical Tales*. London: Methuen, 1987.

Reiss, Timothy J. "Power, Poetry and the Resemblance of Nature." In *Mimesis: From Mirror to Method, Augustine to Descartes*, ed. John D. Lyons and Stephen G. Nichols, pp. 215–47. Hanover, N.H.: University Press of New England, 1982.

Robinet, André. *Le langage à l'âge classique*. Paris: Klincksieck, 1978.

Röd, Wolfgang. *Descartes: Die Genese des cartesianischen Rationalismus*. 2nd ed. rev. Munich: C. H. Beck'sche Verlagsbuchhandlung, 1982 [Munich: Reinhart, 1964].

Rodis-Lewis, Geneviève. *L'individualité chez Descartes*. Paris: Vrin, 1950.

Romanowski, Sylvie. *L'illusion chez Descartes*. Paris: Klincksieck, 1974.

Roth, Leon. *Descartes' Discourse on Method*. Oxford: Clarendon, 1937.

Rykwert, Joseph. *The First Moderns*. Cambridge: Cambridge University Press, 1980.

Schliefer, Ronald. "Analogy and Example: Heisenberg, Negation, and the Language of Quantum Physics." *Criticism* 33 (1991): 285–307.

———, Robert Con Davis and Nancy Mergler. *Culture and Cognition.* Ithaca, N.Y.: Cornell University Press, 1993.

Schouls, Peter A. *Descartes and the Enlightenment.* Kingston: McGill–Queen's University Press, 1989.

———. *The Imposition of Method: A Study of Descartes and Locke.* Oxford: Clarendon, 1980.

Shuster, John. "Mathesis universalis." In *Descartes: Philosophy, Mathematics and Physics,* ed. Stephen Gaukroger, pp. 41–96. Sussex: Harvester, 1992.

Spaemann, Robert. "Le *sum* dans le *cogito sum.*" In *Le discours et sa méthode,* ed. Nicolas Grimaldi and Jean-Luc Marion, pp. 271–83. Paris: Presses Universitaires de France, 1987.

Stout, A. K. "The Basis of Knowledge in Descartes." In *Descartes: A Collection of Critical Essays,* ed. Willis Doney, pp. 169–91. Notre Dame, Ind.: University of Notre Dame Press, 1968 [New York: Doubleday, 1967; reprinted from *Mind* 151 (1929): 330–42; 458–72].

Styazhkin, N. I. *History of Mathematical Logic from Leibniz to Peano.* Cambridge, Mass.: MIT Press, 1969 [Moscow, 1964].

Tafuri, Manfredo. " 'Architectura artificialis': Claude Perrault, Sir Christopher Wren e il dibattito sul linguaggio architectettonico." In *Barocco europeo, barocco italiano, barocco salentino: Papers from the Congresso Internazionale sul Barocco,* ed. Pier Fausto Palumbo, pp. 375–98. Lecce: Centri di Studi Salentini, 1970.

Teyssot, Georges. "Clasicismo, neoclasicismo y 'arquitectura revolucionaria.' " Introduction to *Trés arquitectos revolucionarios: Boullée, Ledoux y Lequeu,* by Emil Kaufmann. Barcelona: Edición Gustavo Gil, 1980. [Paris: S.A.O.G., 1978].

Valéry, Paul. *Les pages immortelles de Descartes.* Paris: Chastel, 1961.

van Leeuwen, Evert. "Method, Discourse, and the Act of Knowing." In *Essays on the Philosophy and Science of René Descartes,* ed. Stephen Voss, pp. 224–41. Oxford: Oxford University Press, 1993.

Vartanian, Aram. *Diderot and Descartes: A Study of Scientific Naturalism in the Enlightenment.* Princeton: Princeton University Press, 1953.

Vérin, Hélène. "Technology in the Park: Engineers and Gardeners in Seventeenth-Century France." In *The Architecture of Western Gardens,* ed. Monique Mosser and Georges Teyssot. Cambridge, Mass.: MIT Press, 1991 [Milan: Electa, 1990].

Vogt, Heinrich. "Zur Entdeckungsgeschichte des Irrationalen." *Biblioteca Matematica* 14 (1913): 9–29.

Vuillemin, Jules. *Mathématiques et métaphysique chez Descartes.* Paris: Presses Universitaires de France, 1960.

Weyl, Hermann. *Philosophy of Mathematics and Natural Science.* Princeton: Princeton University Press, 1949.

Wigley, Mark. *The Architecture of Deconstruction.* Cambridge, Mass.: MIT Press, 1993.

Williams, Bernard. "The Certainty of the *Cogito.*" In *Descartes: A Collection of Critical Essays,* ed. Willis Doney, pp. 88–107. Notre Dame, Ind.: University of Notre

Dame Press, 1968 [New York: Doubleday, 1967; reprinted from "La certitude du cognito," *Cahiers de Royaumont: La Philosophie Analytique,* pp. 40–64 (Paris: Minuit, 1962)].

Wilson, Margaret D. "Cartesian Dualism." In *Descartes: Critical and Interpretive Essays,* ed. Michael Hooker, pp. 197–211. Baltimore: Johns Hopkins University Press, 1978.

Wölfflin, Heinrich. *Renaissance und Barock: Eine Untersuchung über Wesen und Entstehung des Barockstils in Italien.* Munich: T. Ackermann, 1888.

———. *Kunstgeschichtliche Grundbegriffe: Das Problem der Stilentwicklung in der neueren Kunst.* Munich: Bruckmann, 1943 [orig. pub. 1915].

Zippin, Leo. *Uses of Infinity.* New York: Random House, 1962.

INDEX

About the Author. Claudia Brodsky Lacour is Professor
of Comparative Literature at Princeton University and
Directeur de Programme at the Collège International de
Philosophie, Paris. She is the author of *The Imposition of
Form: Studies in Narrative Representation and Knowledge.*

Library of Congress Cataloging-in-Publication Data
Brodsky Lacour, Claudia, 1955–
Lines of thought : discourse, architectonics, and the
origin of modern philosophy / Claudia Brodsky Lacour.
Includes bibliographical references and index.
ISBN 0-8223-1777-X (alk. paper). — ISBN 0-8223-1774-5
(pbk. : alk. paper)
1. Descartes, René, 1596–1650.   2. Architecture and
philosophy.   3. Representation.   4. Philosophy,
aesthetic theory, Modern — 17th century.   I. Title.
B1878.A73L33   1996
194 — dc20   95-40105   CIP